FANGIRLS

American Music Series
Jessica Hopper and Charles Hughes, Editors

HANNAH EWENS

FANGIRLS

SCENES FROM MODERN
MUSIC CULTURE

University of Texas Press   Austin

Requests for permission to reproduce material from this work should be sent to:
      Permissions
      University of Texas Press
      P.O. Box 7819
      Austin, TX 78713-7819
      utpress.utexas.edu/rp-form

♾ The paper used in this book meets the minimum requirements of ANSI/NISO
Z39.48-1992 (R1997) (Permanence of Paper).

      ISBN 978-1-4773-2209-3 (pbk)
      ISBN 978-1-4773-2210-9 (library ebook)
      ISBN 978-1-4773-2211-6 (nonlibrary ebook)
Library of Congress Control Number: 2020937035

doi:10.7560/322093

For every girl who has ever had an obsession

Suggestion: replace the word 'fan girl' with 'expert' and see what happens.
– Jessica Hopper, music critic and author

Look what I found! A conceptual space where women can come together and create – to investigate new forms for their art and for their living outside the restrictive boundaries men have placed on their public behaviour! Not a place or a time, but a state of being.
– Camille Bacon-Smith, fan scholar

CONTENTS

PREFACE

My parents weren't big fans of music. My dad loved football but I'd never enter the living room after a game was scheduled. The thunder hung around the ceiling and he'd be sitting straight-backed, stiffly sniffing and otherwise silent. Mealtimes following could be deeply unpleasant. He should just support a better team, I thought. On the odd occasion they won, glee would creep into every crease of his face. We'd know then to ask, 'Dad, how did they play?' and he'd fist the air suggestively.

I distinctly remember being cynical about fostering this sort of connection with something – with anything. What good was being a supporter if your very being was so precariously balanced on the shoulders of men you didn't know, creating enough resentment to permeate our whole house? I now know it took him away from us, from the house, to people who felt like friends, colleagues, to feeling a part of something bigger, when we lived, quite literally, on an island away from everything. That it was possible to transcend your surroundings.

The island I grew up on is small enough to walk across from one side to the other in a day, but big enough that you'd never bother to. Mobile reception is still intermittent, although not as unreliable as it was, and you could pick up radio stations just across the water from France (an otherworldly message, when transmitted into your car as you drove over the downs). It's a place where restaurant banners spell their own name wrong but don't bother to correct it and menus inside are yellowed; where the families that come each year for almost-warm weeks get fewer and fewer, and disappear, taking the need for jobs, and leaving empty wine bottles and summer crushes behind. It's somewhere with an ageing population, where you might hear a Beach Boys track in the biting cold of winter, but whose more appropriate soundtrack might be the eerie warble of a theremin. Somewhere beautiful and, to me, sad.

My feeling is that being deprived of real communication definitely contributed to my disposition. There was an aloneness that enhanced yearning of various kinds.

I wouldn't have guessed it but I would soon self-define in one way or another by being a fan. To my mind, life started at ten years old in the early noughties. I was taken under the wing of one girl, E—. With her coarse ginger hair and freckles so unruly in the summer they joined together to make a blob, she was considered almost as much of a weirdo as me, save only for the fact she'd been around longer. Her breath smelt of stale bubblegum; she seemed to always be chewing. She was very strange. I was strange. Soon we were inseparable, and the boys could only conclude: 'You lesbians are weird'.

Unlike mine, where other interests or worries commandeered the time, E's whole family lived through film, TV, art and, above all, music. I didn't have other friends or older siblings who had shown me culture before. And so long school holidays were spent at hers, as were weekends or evenings. I tried on everything she had: expressions, clothes, songs. Her mum, a photographer (which seemed impossibly cool), encouraged our interests by casually passing both of us banknotes through the driver's seat window on the way to the one nearby music retailer or even occasionally getting us tickets for gigs on the mainland.

E had many quirks. She could only fall asleep listening to quite loud music so we'd lie in darkness wearing her pyjamas listening to Marilyn Manson or Blink-182 or David Bowie. Despite trying to keep up conversation for as long as possible to avoid being left awake, I always was. Her Hi-Fi system worked like a record player and would restart an album once it was finished, leaving me in an endless loop of heavy metal through the night. Sometimes I'd creep out of bed and turn it off but it'd often wake her up, so mostly I'd lie there anxious, oscillating between frustration and appreciation for the time to learn the lyrics.

Much of the time we'd be creating on some minor scale: learning to play guitar, writing out songs or singing over instrumental tracks into webcams. But our greatest pleasure would be one of us exploding over a song that the other, coyly waiting for a reaction, had discovered. From this we picked a soundtrack beyond what we were fed. With this we could: pretend to inhale our first cigarettes; black our eyelids and dye our hair; get as drunk as our bodies would allow with scene kids from neighbouring schools on the outskirts of the woodland that faced the sea, watching boys on other worlds, having taken drugs we'd never heard of. In a way, it was like a secret club. Our personal fan club – one we weren't taught to have, but instinctively knew how to create together. Here we could avoid having combative dialogues about who was the best guitarist or which album in a band's discography was better with boys our own age. No response to music was off limits and I always felt validated. Nowhere else gave me the insight into personal politics that music did; I spent every evening on our first family computer researching riot grrrl and punk and feminism. Everything hideous that was happening to me as a teenage girl, either music or E had something to say about it.

Being a fan paradoxically gave me both the invisibility cloak I desperately wanted and a proud identity at an age when I felt smug about little else; it was the only identity that felt like it fitted comfortably.

The night I decided to put together this book, it was autumn and I was in a church. Ex-My Chemical Romance member and solo artist Frank Iero had just played an intimate show. I drifted about in front of the altar hoping to say goodbye to him. All I could see was his back, him sitting behind a table, and the faces of hundreds of fans feeling joy, agony, confusion, a mix of many *incongruent* things. I watched them move through: an emotional assembly line of girls, each mildly overbearing (apologising for their behaviour and existence; crying), asking very little (to be seen; their gifts taken; the 'thank you for saving me' heard), and, gathering around the door, they were transformed somehow.

I'd felt the same way too. I wanted to know why, at twenty-five, I was witnessing the same things I'd done a decade previous and I knew to have been done by fans before me, decades before. I tried to remember everything I'd learnt or read about music fan culture but recalled documentaries that showed fans merely as a footnote that highlighted the power of the musician, or articles by grown-up journalists remembering when they'd been a devoted fan (past tense). Work on this subject where young women are involved is frequently overtly celebratory or critically marginalising, neither of which are appropriate for the richness of their experience. I've often thought the people around the spectacle as curious as the spectacle itself – and as worthy of proper investigation. The question being not just what is captivating these people but who are those captivated?

I wanted to know more about what it meant to be a fan, to ask what they were doing, why they were doing it. I wanted to look (and with care) away from the stars themselves towards the people who gave them any luminescent quality. Those people are, so frequently, teenage girls.

'I don't see it as possible or desirable to understand fandom without gender being part of the mix, at least not until a time in the future where we are past gender,' communication and fan studies professor Nancy Baym wrote in 2017. 'But I suspect that rather than getting past it, we are more likely to keep delving deeper into not just how it colours so much of how we think, understand, evaluate and behave, but how many ways of being gendered there are, and how those genderings intersect with all the other social identities people claim or have forced on them.' Once you accept that, you see that there are infinite and nuanced ways in which to be a fan and that those suggesting that there is any correct way to 'do' it – which happens both externally, to fandoms, and internally, within them – are making subjective judgements.

This is a book about music fandom by music fans; previously untold or glossed-over scenes from modern pop and rock music history. To privilege a female experience I spoke to hundreds of women and girls, from the UK, Europe, North America and Japan, to illuminate themes for these chapters and gather stories to fill them. Since young fans are also increasingly exploring and embracing their gender-nonconformity or identifying as non-binary, it felt natural to reflect that in the research and interviews. My aim was to be as inclusive as possible whilst accurately representing fan bases. It would never be enough to write a singular 'fangirling' narrative because there simply isn't one, and we should not expect women fans, or any fans, to be conveniently categorised.

We're in a time now where, more than ever, girls and young queer people create modern mainstream music and fan cultures with their outlooks and actions. They're the ones at the helm of fan practices that the public have a vague awareness of: tweeting their favourite artist incessantly, writing fan fiction, religiously updating devoted social media profiles, buying 'meet-and-greet' tickets and following the band around to various show dates. This is slowly being acknowledged, in part for the money it generates for a changing music industry, and in part because of the 'women in music' literature that has been published in the 2010s. It has been heartening to read all of these books, to feel as though it does matter what women have to say about their relationship to music, even if it is only legacy musicians whose stories are heard (it's so rare that teenage-girl interests and lives are treated as though they're of consequence). Simultaneously, I've watched as fans of all genders have reclaimed the somewhat derogatory label of 'fangirl' online.

Of course, in its passionate exchange, fandom has never been inherently morally good – or bad. It deals in exchanges of money for goods, power struggles, privilege and intense interest or occasionally uncritical devotion towards another human being. To be a fan can be complicated, and I wanted to capture that with fairness.

E and I had an explosive argument in our teens, a fact confirmed by coldly cutting cords on social media and a one-way return of clothes and CDs. Like most immature friendship fallouts I can't remember the specific hurt, but the final straw would've been innocuous. Soon after, she left school and I've not seen or spoken to her since. I reflected on our time together a lot while writing this book – wondered about looking her up online and thought better of it – because there is so much to thank her for. She gave me something of a framework to understand my life, my career and my adult friendships.

About halfway through my research, I realised what it meant to be a fan. Fandom is a portmanteau of fan and kingdom – there is, as that would suggest, a king or queen regent but also a territory and community of followers. To be a fan is to scream alone together. To go on a collective journey of self-definition. It means pulling on threads of your own narrative and doing so with friends and strangers who feel like friends.

Being a fan is a serious business and this is what girls wanted to say about it.

1

AN ANIMAL WITHIN AN ANIMAL: A BRIEF FANGIRL HISTORY

You and me got a whole lot of history
We could be the greatest thing that the world has ever seen
You and me got a whole lot of history
So don't let it go, we can make some more, we can live forever
> – One Direction, 'Whole Lot of History'

Teenage-girl fans, they don't lie
> – Harry Styles

Imagine screaming so hard your lung collapses. You carry on cheering somehow, using your other lung, one that has not folded, because you're having a magical time and stubbornly choose to believe you're just out of breath. You go to the A&E afterwards when you realise something is seriously wrong. The examining doctor discovers you are not only breathing at an extraordinary rate per minute but with a tear in the lung that is causing air to escape between the lung and the chest wall, into the chest cavity and behind the throat. Imagine that when they press on certain parts of your body it makes a sound like Rice Krispies popping. The combination of the three symptoms is something the doctor has never seen before. They consult medical records and find what you have done to yourself to be so extremely rare to occur from screaming or singing that it's only been recorded twice in medical history: to a drill sergeant and an opera singer.

That is the story of an unnamed girl who went to a One Direction concert in 2013; her story wasn't published in a medical journal and publicised until late 2017. 'I never saw her again,' said Mack Slaughter, the doctor who treated the patient. 'I told her she'd be famous and get to go on the Jimmy Fallon show and meet One Direction but she was too embarrassed.'

That same year, 2013, a documentary about 1D fans aired on Channel 4 at 10pm. This was certainly not *for* fans, to hold a mirror up to their fun behaviour, but for parents and for viewers wanting more rowdy or licentious post-watershed material. The title sequence exploded with emotion. 'It's like a drug addiction,' says one girl. 'I've met them sixty-four times,' swears another. A voiceover dramatically declares, 'They'll stop at nothing to get close to the boys,' before cutting to a pink-haired nineteen-year-old from Northern England called Becky who points high up a building and says, 'I was sat outside your room when you was asleep, Zayn'. These girls are *Crazy About One Direction*.

Viewers are introduced to one group of friends outside Manchester Arena. As they crowd around the camera, it's evident from their colliding energies that they have a clear leader, fourteen-year-old leopard-print-clad Sandra. Each of them grasps at their face, clutching their phones to their aching chests as they share how much they love the boys, their words clambering over each other's. 'I go home and cry every, every night,' says Sandra, continuing after the others have stopped. *What will you do if you get to meet him today?* Suddenly they all scream and stamp their feet, Sandra convulsing, and one girl with dental braces almost out of shot says, 'Have an asthma attack. And cry. And die!'

Tickets for another round of 1D shows are set to go on sale. Sixteen-year-old Nadia from Dublin leans over the balcony of her block of flats, a plastic crucifix dangling. A true tableau of melancholy. 'It's just constant tears and frustration and you don't know what to do with your life.' In the queue for tickets, she sobs. Once she has the tickets, she sobs.

After waiting hours outside Wembley Stadium for the chance to meet the boys, older girls take the failure of their mission with self-deprecating laughs. This is the lifestyle they've chosen, for better or for worse. For younger ones, it's tantamount to heartbreak. The camera focuses on one girl of a group, her eyes filling with tears. A smudged 'I ♥ 1D' drawn on her sad face, and a faded red heart on each cheek, her lip wobbles. 'They could've come by now and they're clearly not coming.' She self-consciously scrapes her fringe behind her ears, a gesture of shame for the time and effort put into their mission and: nothing. We watch her but she can't meet the eye of the camera or filmmaker for more than a moment.

Yet those tears are a delicate side-serving to the rage featured. One tiny girl with wide kohled eyes says nonchalantly from behind her laptop, 'I'm part of a fandom that could kill you if they wanted'. A large portion of the documentary is given over to their jealousy of the boys' girlfriends, particularly pop superstar Taylor Swift, who at the time was romantically involved with Harry Styles. Sandra sent Swift death threats over Twitter which apparently led to Sandra's account being blocked. Leading her down a slippery slope, a voice asks what she'd do if she saw Swift now. Sitting in a full-leopard-print room, Sandra grits her teeth and uses her hands as claws, a gesture that is as comical as it is faintly disconcerting for its aggression. 'I'd stamp on her head, I'd rip all her hair out, I'd squeeze her eyeballs out, I'd step on her eyeballs.' She ends with an angelic smile. 'It'd just be like that.'

Plenty of the outpourings come from bedrooms, implying that whatever we hear are the girls' distilled thoughts, and any dramatic moments we see are relatively unprompted. One of these is 'the hunt', words that refer to the tracking down of One Direction, but it's uncertain if they are originally those of the subjects or the production team. In one sequence, girls pace around a hotel where the band are reportedly staying and find what they believe to be their room. In another, pink-haired Becky uses her phone to document the before and after of her crossing paths with Zayn. A large portion of the documentary is given to the often homoerotic sexual fan fiction and art that pairs Harry Styles and Louis Tomlinson as a bromance or couple – with no context or explanation that this happens across all types of media fandoms. 'Slash shipping' is the very commonplace fan practice of same-sex romantic or sexual pairing as imagined by fans, more or less done officially since the start of the term's use in the mid-seventies when the first slash ship – Kirk and Spock in *Star Trek* – became widely accepted. But of course the desire of fans to create relationships for characters, fictional or real, imagined straight or queer, predates the term. Ultimately, then, the tone of the entire hour could objectively be called 'hysterical'.

Hayley and her friends were filmed for the documentary but never made the final edit. She lives in Scotland and still calls herself a fangirl at twenty-two, five years on. Her social media profiles show reams of crying emojis at new songs she likes, happy birthday wishes sent to pop stars or countdowns for the days until she is seeing an artist. She recently shared a tweet with over 44,000 retweets that reads 'i'm sorry but girls who didn't have a one direction phase probably don't have a personality now'. When I ask why she thought she and her friends were not in the film, she says, 'We just weren't crazy enough'.

'We initially thought it'd been because there'd been too many girls but after watching it we realised we weren't outrageous. They asked us, "What's the most extreme thing you've done to see the boys?" and I talked about the boys' first tour and how I camped out for the tickets with my mum. They pushed, saying things like: "Is that it? What else?" It was like they were setting us up for failure. They were trying to hook, line and sinker. We knew that was the game so we just talked about real stuff. I was going through a hard time so I talked about how the boys helped me through difficult days because I'd put on their music. We talked about friendship. At eighteen we were saving every penny, birthday and Christmas money for this lifestyle. I'd not do anything because I needed the extra 20 quid in the bank account in case they did a tour or something, I was really prepared. But they wanted to know if we'd stopped over at their hotel or dragged them on Twitter. Just telling the good side of things didn't make the "cut".

After months of waiting excitedly for the final product, the documentary came out and Hayley was smouldering with shame. 'When the credits rolled we thought, "Is that honestly how people see fans of One Direction?" They wanted us to be crazy animals who are the reason the boys have security like they do. The girls in the documentary are supposed to look a danger to the boys when in reality they're just people who have a passion and, OK, sometimes they do take it far, but most of the time us fans are just here to have a good time and listen to music.'

Hayley's friend Lauren feels similarly about events. 'I remember being so angry because it portrayed all us fans to be something that we're not, if that makes sense,' she tells me. 'I remember when it came out people from my school were tweeting like, "Oh, I can't believe Lauren Hutcheon's not on this doc" because that's how weird they thought we were. I was angry that people at my school had seen it.'

At the time it was disappointing to see she'd been cut from something that seemed significant for the fandom, but Lauren was soon grateful for their removal. 'I said to Hayley, "it's a blessing in disguise". I don't think I'd have been able to cope if I'd been in it. People at my school were horrible to me about it afterwards and I wasn't even in the documentary so to think what would've happened to those girls...' They did recognise and recall some of the girls who featured in the film because they were there on the day, being filmed. They, to Lauren, seemed 'normal', all friends, like her and Hayley, through One Direction, and loved 1D and that was more or less it. 'I wonder whether they were made out to be weird when they were getting filmed.'

Bethany, who was also eighteen at the time of shooting, did make it into the film. She remembers how she was selected from millions of Directioners. 'They found most people at concerts and that as a fan is when you're at your crazier time. If they found people on the internet it would've been better because not everyone can afford to go to a big pop concert but everyone can afford the internet.'

To save money to get her own home, Bethany now stays with her dad in Nottinghamshire. She's a huge fan of Disney films now but continues to save up for the solo concerts of the 1D boys. I notice her email avatar is a 'KEEP CALM AND NEVER SAY NEVER' picture, referencing Justin Bieber's soaring R&B-inflected song. *There's just no turning back / When your heart's under attack.* Channel your truest version of self regardless of adversity, it said. Dig deep inside for bravery and strength because at one time or another you'll need it.

'They did pick out the worst moments and made us seem worse than what we were.' But after a pause she gives a laugh. 'Honestly? I'm crazy as it is so it didn't really make a difference to me.'

If you sit a black-and-white photograph of 'fangirls' from 1966 next to a high-definition image from the 2010s, the only element that's notably different is the fashion. Wet faces, eyes screwed up, fingers to hanging mouths or reaching outwards like straining talons: visual and audible signifiers of the female music fan. There's a futileness to this image. Scream as much as you'd like – you're unlikely to get closer to that someone, to touch them. You're one of many, after all. There's humour in it, humour directed at it, but also there's power in 'crazy'.

Hysteria – from the Greek word for uterus, *hystera*, ever the anatomical 'source' of problems – carries a lot of historical baggage. This womb-linked 'illness' manifests itself in a number of symptoms: anxiety, shortness of breath, irritability, nervousness, insomnia, fainting, as well as being promiscuous or desiring sex – that is: feeling things, strongly. Ancient Greek physician Aretaeus described the womb as 'an animal within an animal' and Hippocrates went even further to say that, especially in virgins, widows, single or sterile women, this 'bad' uterus also produces toxic fumes, which cause hysteria.

Among the limitless reasons a woman could be counted a witch in the Middle Ages were untoward sexual desire, poor mental health or any mental activity or behaviour that seemed to the average man unnatural, such as 'hysteria'. Nearly all Victorian physicians considered women to be more fragile and sensitive than men, prone to lapsing into a hysterical phase at any given time. Those who rebelled against Victorian society risked being put into an asylum. In the US it was a similar story. Taken from records belonging to West Virginia Hospital for the Insane, some factors that were considered to have contributed to inmates' 'illnesses' (alleged or otherwise) included: female disease (whatever that may mean), imaginary female trouble, fever and jealousy, greediness, disappointed affection or love, dissipation of nerves and mental excitement. Not only would I, along with my female friends, be 'suffering' from most of these symptoms, but these could all be categorised as classic stereotypical fangirling behaviours.

Where culture has been, so has hysteria. As it often does, fangirling began with a heartthrob. In 1812, poet Lord Byron was hot property, basically a tattooless Justin Bieber contained in a white shirt. 'The contemporary accounts of Byron's public appearances sound like something out of *Teen Beat*: crowds of admirers gathered outside his publisher's office on Albemarle Street in the hope of a momentary glimpse of Byron's trademark "sardonic smile" or a copy of his newest blockbuster publication,' writes Ghislaine McDayter in *Byromania and the Birth of Celebrity Culture*. Women fainted upon meeting him and fan letters piled in from all over the country. By this time, a woman's womb symbolised emptiness, which could be filled with maternity in a 'healthy' woman but, for the unhealthy, wombs were vacuums that demanded frequent sensual filling. The most dangerous women would simply become nymphomaniacs, seeking out metaphorical food to fill the void at their core (according to McDayter, the height of licentiousness in the 1800s: novels and spicy dishes).

Music fandom came along to help fill that void. In 1844, the word 'Lisztomania' was used by German poet and essayist Heinrich Heine to describe the 'true madness, unheard of in the annals of furore' that broke out at the concerts of pianist and composer Franz Liszt. A century later, Frank Sinatra tapped into a youth market that appealed desperately to teen girls. In *The New Yorker*, in 1946, E.J. Kahn Jr. wrote, 'Most of his fans are plain, lonely girls from lower-middle-class homes. They are dazzled by the life Sinatra leads and wish they could share in it.' Not long into Sinatra's reign it was realised that hysterical girls could move mountains (of money). In his prime Sinatra often released multiple albums a year, and quickly he became one of the best-selling artists of all-time.

Still, Sinatra's smooth, old-timey romance incited nothing like the frenzy caused by Elvis Presley and his swinging hips. He was equal parts enticing and alarming for what he represented. Everything, *everything* about him – his curled upper lip, his movements, his gruff moaning – screamed sex. This was highly controversial in the homes of 1950s North America that he thrust his way into through every TV set and radio in the country. To put his superstardom into perspective, when he made his first appearance on *The Ed Sullivan Show*, 60 million people tuned in to watch, which was eighty-two per cent of the North American viewing public. This record was only beaten later by The Beatles. The fact he was making girls in their masses scream, wilt, line up outside movie theatres to see his barely average films, on both sides of the Atlantic, terrified adults. By the time The Beatles began their career, the media's attention was no longer solely focused on the artists, but also on the female fans.

Suddenly fans weren't just part of something bigger than themselves, whatever that might mean, they were as important as the artists they loved. The word 'Beatlemania' was stamped on headlines, and if you were a part of this 'madness', if you followed them around, if you engaged in 'incessant screaming' (*New York Times Magazine*) the spotlight was on you. Contemporary fangirls became sassy and louder. When reporters asked why they liked The Beatles, they repeatedly offered 'Because they're sexy', which was an in-joke, a defiant personal victory, and a truth, at least to them.

After only their third album, Beatlemania caused so many difficulties that The Beatles had to quit touring. 'We were kids, we were all pretty scared,' Paul McCartney said of that period in more recent years. In the documentary *The Beatles: Eight Days a Week – The Touring Years* girls are seen having their cheeks tapped by policemen trying to bring them round from fainting. A criticism of the live shows of The Beatles, Frank Sinatra and Elvis was that you genuinely couldn't hear the artist themselves – the piercing howls en masse were so constant and deafening, it ruined the performances.

'Though not a clear-cut protest of any kind, Beatlemania was the first mass movement of the sixties to feature women,' wrote Barbara Ehrenreich, Elizabeth Hess and Gloria Jacobs in 'Beatlemania: Girls Just Want to Have Fun'. 'The screaming ten- to fourteen-year-old fans of 1964 did not riot for anything, except the chance to remain in the proximity of their idols and hence to remain screaming. But they did have plenty to riot against, or at least to overcome through the act of rioting. In a highly sexualised society (one sociologist found that the number of explicitly sexual references in the mass media had doubled between 1950 and 1960), teen and preteen girls were expected to be not only 'good' and 'pure' but to be the enforcers of purity within their teen society – drawing the line for overeager boys and ostracizing girls who failed in this responsibility... It was the first and most dramatic uprising of *women's* sexual revolution.'

Contemporary media believed the girls were a problem to be scientifically explained, either inadvertently using hysteria theory ('Beatles Reaction Puzzles Even Psychologists' was the headline of one science journal, and 'Why the Girls Scream, Weep, Flip' the *New York Times Magazine* promised to reveal) or lightly analysed in a snide, misogynistic and snobby way. In a legendary *New Statesman* essay by future *NS* editor Paul Johnson, he griped: 'Those who flock round The Beatles, who scream themselves into hysteria, whose vacant faces flicker over the TV screen, are the least fortunate of their generation, the dull, the idle, the failures'. Subsequently, to the confused parents following media reports, fangirling was viewed as an affliction.

Despite this (and, to some degree, to spite this), music fan culture became part and parcel of the average teenage experience. Pop and rock music broadened hugely with a multitude of options of diverse artists offering different fantasies through their worlds, the subcultures they were a part of, and offering alternative ways to explore your gender, sexuality and youth. Throughout the 1980s to 2000s, tried-and-tested models that catered to the boy-band fan – Duran Duran, Bay City Rollers, Boyz II Men, Bros, Backstreet Boys, Hanson, New Kids On The Block, Take That, *NSYNC, 5ive to name a few – never went away. There were just more people to fall in love with.

So although One Direction drew out the closest in fan response to The Beatles, the hype around them wasn't especially alien or unfamiliar to the public. At the same time that 1D were recording their debut album, in early 2011, a documentary came out on Justin Bieber, who had for years been making young girls wild for him, with his sweeping Lego-man hairdo (not unlike The Beatles' bowl cut) and pre-pubertal crooning. In *Justin Bieber: Never Say Never*, girls' displays of love and obsession are central to showing how beloved Bieber is. The *New York Times* review highlighted the 'crazy fans' whose senses are 'deranged', and suggested that as a viewer, one hopes security has the girls' 'picture on file'.

What made Beatles fans like none before was down to serendipity, sexy boys and television. For One Direction it was serendipity, sexy boys and social media.

If ungovernable emotional excess is the hallmark of a 'crazy' young woman, 1D fangirls fit the diagnosis. How fans have been framed in the 1D documentary is no coincidence. Hayley and Lauren weren't alone in probing the ethics of those making the Channel 4-acquired documentary. In 'A New Breed of Fan? Regimes of Truth, One Direction Fans, and Representations of Enfreakment', fan-studies lecturer Dr William Proctor questioned whether this show was even documentary, infotainment or reality TV. He wrote that the show 'cherry picks' a limited selection of fans and passes them off as homogeneous, something which fan studies has been challenging for over two decades.

Dr Proctor tells me about a fandom panel he and the documentary's creator Daisy Asquith attended. 'There were a number of One Direction fans in the audience who stood up and said "you made us out to be freaks". One girl said that documentary really hurt her and it was quite an emotional exchange.' He still contends that the documentary, by using footage of the fans portraying only extreme emotions, gives a snapshot of fandom that is, in his words, essentially untrue.

If he'd been in charge of a One Direction fan doc things would've been different. He'd have shown a spectrum of fans who were performing in different ways and ask fan scholars to be talking heads to explain the fan context and history of fans to give some sort of answer to the question: why do girls behave in this way? 'These fans in particular were looked at as being a "new breed of fan" as the voiceover says, but besides new technology, there's essentially nothing new here. They're no more dangerous, hyper-emotional, sexual or anything else than those who were part of Beatlemania or Frank Sinatra fandom or elsewhere.' Dr Proctor sighs. 'But once we start providing context, once we start showing an audience the history of fans, then I don't have a documentary anymore, or I have a documentary for Sky Arts rather than Channel 4.'

It'd be easy to let the director-producer who was approached to make a film on 1D fandom take the sole blame. You can never forget her presence, a voice faintly asking the girls questions throughout, but many people would've worked on the film. 'Unsurprisingly, there was some pressure from Channel 4 to include the most angry and hysterical fans, the crazy fans. I resisted this stereotype from the start, but I am also obliged to accept the commercial demands that ultimately fund my programs,' Daisy Asquith retrospectively defended herself in the essay 'Crazy About One Direction: Whose Shame Is It Anyway?' 'However, when it came to the title, it is significant that I was not allowed to keep my preferred choice: I Heart One Direction was changed by Channel 4 on the very last day of the edit to Crazy About One Direction.' She admits that the title, taken at face value, can stigmatise.

It has a vilifying effect: from the very beginning of the film emotions are pathologised. Any ounce of feeling an audience sees from the moment it decides to watch something called Crazy About One Direction is framed as unhinged, even if a girl screaming about tickets or trying to meet her idol is understandable. That is the bottom line: fans of a mainstream band must have their experiences limited and heightened in order to be at all worth documenting.

Loaded with subtext from the title onwards, the film was received critically in this negative light. Male reviewers didn't hold judgements back. In *The Guardian*, a writer jokes, 'One Direction's obsessed teenage girl fans are like Stan in the Eminem song' (a reference to a dangerously obsessed fan who kills himself and his pregnant girlfriend when his idol doesn't reply to him) while *The Independent* asks, 'are 1D and their overlord, Simon Cowell, fully aware of the twisted hold they have on these girls? It can't be healthy for anyone.'

I watched the film more than ten times, screams, tears, furious words and all, and don't see anything extraordinary or necessarily unhealthy in the girls' behaviour. When I put myself back in their position, before specific memories come into focus, I recall intense emotions sweeping through my chest. The feelings have violence to them. The adrenaline of your first shows is a drug and the next day there's excitement as your throat feels like it's been picked at with a penknife from calling out so hard, your lost voice a mark of pride like a love bite, a not-so-secret physical reminder of the night before. Your stomach rolls to music as you charge into your day. The reality of it is that far from emotions merely springing from finding something that significant to you, they're an acknowledgment of self – claiming a stake in who you are, who you want to be.

Emotions are performative by their very nature even when genuine. Emotions on film are doubly so, which anyone, if they've got a flair for dramatics and have had a camera put in front of them, will know. Ten years ago, MySpace pages were full of black-and-white pictures of girls looking sad with quotes from songs as captions. Now there are crying selfies on Instagram and other platforms. They say: look how emotional I have become, please witness my responses, my joy, sadness, loss, how much I can feel, and this is the way in which I have framed it. Rhiannon, a seventeen-year-old fan from Sussex, posts crying selfies, not only because she thinks they're hilarious, but with a competitive element, 'to show anyone who might see how much something means to me'. I look through Rhiannon's crying selfies, and all of them display her carefully painted-on make-up streaming down her cheeks and across her temples. Some of them are from her at the barrier of a gig, others are while watching a music video, some are while listening to an album. In the comments you can see her fan friends showing extra appreciation for these over other selfies, they carry value. Emotions declare: I was there, at this time, at this place, for this artist and I was involved. For that to be witnessed, it elevates all you've felt.

The girls in *Crazy About One Direction* perform up to the camera's anticipation and desires, as well as their own. Asquith noted this and wrote of them: 'The "becoming" they may have wished to solicit was the elevation of self into uniqueness, from "just another fan" into a significant fan, so significant in fact that the band were bound to notice them, and to see oneself projected onto the future, immortalized and made special, making the ordinary extraordinary'. Hayley, Lauren and Bethany all said that similar things prompted them to take part in the documentary. Emotions are the most immediate tool we have for expressing how much we care. And the hope is – isn't it always? – that someone else might care that we care.

The fan reaction to the 1D documentary was more fervent than the average observer or culture critic might've predicted. In fact, it was easily one of the largest, most far-reaching and dramatic responses to the media in fan history. British fans led the charge but overnight the documentary was ripped and put online for One Direction fans worldwide to see themselves in (one link Asquith found had over a quarter of a million views by the next day). On Twitter, furious hashtags began – #RIPLarryShippers, #ThisIsNotUs, #1DWereNotLikeTheseGirlsontheDocumentary, even a strong show of support from the rival fandom #BeliebersareHereforDirectioners – while death and bomb threats were sent to Asquith and Channel 4. Asquith was reported by the BBC as saying, 'Their response to the film is so much more extreme than anything I chose to include. It's really been quite shocking. I think the response itself is proof that we didn't just pick the most extreme fans there are.'

It's an exchange as old as time itself; impose qualities on someone and raise an eyebrow when they respond in anger or exhibit the characteristics you've endowed them with. Portray extremity and then be shocked when the response is extreme. Call girls crazy and feign surprise when they are emotional about it. No bomb threat should ever be treated as anything other than serious, but I don't think anyone for a moment believed a twelve-year-old Directioner would bomb the Channel 4 offices. For Directioners, saying you want to 'stab someone in the fucking face' online was little more than a passing comment during a minor disagreement. To declare that you want to die when hearing a pleasing new song was merely an overstatement. With the development of internet cultures, who really laughs out loud when they say 'LOL'?

This documentary didn't rise from nowhere and neither did its response. It came only a month after a significant incident with *GQ*. In a One Direction cover feature the male interviewer crudely described their (very young) female fans as 'a dark-pink oil slick that howls and moans and undulates'. When they responded in the same way as they did to the C4 doc – vulgarities and defensive attacks – *GQ* ran spin-off articles about the 'crazy' fans, embedding their tweets. Other sites ran news stories on it, branding them similarly 'downright insane' (*Complex*), 'crazy' (*Fact Mag*), 'psycho' and 'sweet little future serial killers' (*Spin*) and simply 'enraged little children' (*Huffington Post*). The individual responses broke through the oil slick: in becoming individuals they showed that they had more power and so the backlash to the backlash began.

Almost immediately, YouTube videos were uploaded to counter the documentary. Watching them in all their early webcam glory, the pixelated girls jerk about with feeling. Like the fans in the doc, they'd filmed in their bedrooms or homes. Most had only uploaded a single video – they had furiously created an account just to have a medium with which to upload their criticisms. I wanted to reach out and find out who they'd grown up to be, how they felt about it so long after the fact. But they lacked personal details and email addresses. They were just usernames with numbers and random words, the sort too cute to be set up in the late 2010s. Just tiny sad and angry footprints on the internet.

One white American girl in 'My rant about Channel 4's bullcrap documentary and suicide!' pretends it's a news bulletin. 'What's the daily news? Let's see. Oh, here we go: Channel 4 makes bullcrap documentary about Directioners,' she says, dramatically tossing a pile of papers behind her. Another Directioner in 'Crazy About One Direction Rant' lounges in her bedroom while music plays. 'I am sitting in my room laying down on my bed, making a YouTube video, I'm on Twitter and I've been listening to Pandora. Does this seem like some sort of villainous crime?' She starts singing along and laughing raucously. A third girl in 'Channel 4 Directioner Rant' spends most of the video swearing and stabbing her middle fingers up. 'Fuck fuck fuck fuck fuck you Channel 4 bleugh–,' making a sick noise, and ending on a final flourish of the finger.

Some friendship groups join forces. One group of teens sit in a back garden in front of 1D cardboard cutouts. Each introduces themselves with their own first name, second name belonging to one of the boys. They play on the American chat show format, discussion style. 'We have to eat, we have to get out our rooms to get sunlight, use the bathroom,' one says. 'No sleep though,' another adds in a self-deprecating tone. We're not all that crazy emotional, they insist, then say, sincerely, of the documentary: 'That was really emotional for us because we're so full of emotions'. Just like the doc they hated so much, they vox pop a girl they know, shoving the camera in her face. 'What do you think of this Channel 4 thing? Do you think it's stupid?' The girl says, reasonably, 'My friends are 90 per cent of that'. The camera cuts away – snaps off! – in disagreement.

Fury is directed evenly between Channel 4 and the girls who took part in the documentary. The former deliberately misrepresented the fandom – a fair comment – by leaving out the 'blogging and tweeting and fangirling with their Directioner family' and favouring those who had met the band or had the money to see them, and for giving over a large proportion of the doc to sexual fan fiction that shouldn't have been shared with people who wouldn't understand.

'You had to pick the hardcore fangirls, the three per cent fangirls. You should've looked on the ninety-five per cent.' The three per cent were too emotional, crazy, immature, aggressive. They needed to go to rehab, get help, have some self-respect. On both Twitter and in these videos, they're doing what fan studies professor Kristina Busse calls border policing, in which fans distance themselves from those not-enough or too invested.

Almost all the videos were made by American girls and, although it is never said implicitly, it seems as if a source of their frustration came from the fact that the documentary used British girls. Girls who were geographically and culturally – almost emotionally and spiritually, in some intangible way – closer to their idols than they were. The fan sitting in a converted country house in Upstate New York doesn't have the fan privilege of one who can kiss a bench in a One Direction member's hometown. The former might very possibly be envious. Jealous enough to say that kissing a bench that Harry Styles has sat on is dumb or deranged (and this was said).

There was one video I kept returning to. It was by a white British girl who actually used her real name. In the video, titled, as many were, 'My Channel 4 rant', Paige Parker's hair is scraped back in a bun and she sits on the floor of her bedroom against some wooden furniture. She opens her video with her hands up and swearing, apologising for not having make-up on, she's so angry, you see, that she hasn't had time for niceties. She's angry that a few girls in isolation have represented the entire group. 'I speak for the whole fandom,' she says without irony, putting her hand on her heart, 'when I say fuck you Channel 4. You have humiliated us, you have ashamed us, I don't even feel like I can go out in public anymore, I just can't, I want to stay in my room.'

Like many of the others, she's worried that the boys might've seen it and thought them 'psychos'. Her concern extended to the world at large. 'My mum, if she was watching that, she would've been like: you're not allowed to go on Twitter anymore, you're not allowed to like One Direction anymore, you're not allowed to fangirl over them anymore.'

By being 'too' emotional, fans could be stripped of the chance to be emotional at all. So, in these videos, they perform to the camera, for themselves and for the other fans. In some of them, the girls are half aware of what they look like, their eyes almost imperceptibly flitting between the camera and checking their own image. Sometimes they slow mid-sentence to adjust their angle or smooth down a stray hair. They know that this is their identity too, and their chance to take it back.

Paige feels so much and sees the possibility of that being taken away. A handful of fans can't represent a big fandom any more than a handful of girls can represent the universal experience of girlhood. But it's always the person with the most power who can define a narrative. In marking themselves out as 'not like the other girls' they show themselves to be more similar than they could know. Defensiveness and aggressiveness are learnt as necessary.

The morning after the documentary aired, one of the 1D members, Liam Payne, responded on Twitter saying, 'Just so all of you know we love you guys and we know how dedicated you are and tbh we can't believe it that you guys spend all your time on us / We couldn't give a fuck what any documentary says there (sic) dramatised for entertainment and full of bullshit anyway we all know…/… How hard you work for us and see it every day at our shows, Let's all take a step back and think about what we/you have all achieved…You should be proud.' Although he was trying to show gratitude and placate the mass of fans, he is, from a position of power, distancing 1D from the girls in the film and girls like them. He's unwittingly joining in with the border policing.

Scrolling back through one of the only remaining updated Twitter accounts of girls from the doc, I found Pip. She was one of the oldest and more mature of those featured, now in her mid-twenties. Her account is still filled with new tweets about the boys she loves, going to the band's solo shows. In 2014, a year after the documentary aired, she tweeted, 'I was on the 'Crazy about 1D' documentary. And when it aired Liam tweeted "I know you're all not like that" think about how that made me feel.' It made her feel it when he said it and she was still feeling a year later.

'The idea of a fan *is* someone that is emotionally connected,' William Proctor had told me. 'People perform their fandom in different ways, but it's usually girls rather than women who are enfreaked, who are shown to be extreme, overemotional, unruly, hyper-obsessive, hysterical. Whether we think that's extreme or not, that's a huge value judgement on our part, right? Why is it up to us to look at something like that and decide whether it's right or wrong? Whether it's the "extreme" emotions of these fans or the everyday ones, emotions are what elevate fandom into something more than an interest for many.'

Some 1D fans tell me that the emotions are the prize at the end, the aim, a reward for all your fannish activities. They're a glue that tacks fandoms together. Lauren finds it impossible to separate her 1D fandom from the pull of her emotions – not sure where one ends and the other begins. There's a knowingness about it. 'People think you are crying constantly. Girls *are* emotional. Once a year they come to your town and it's the *night of your year*. It's insane for teen girls to sit outside a hotel to see someone they like or cry at a concert but grown men go to sports matches and have season tickets and swear at each other, and we are ridiculed.'

'If I were upset I'd get the CDs out and cry to them,' remembers Bethany. 'I'd watch the boys in *The X Factor* video diaries too, so many times and be so happy I'd cry. I still get the same emotions, the rollercoaster, of wanting to get the tickets now for the solo tours and not being able to buy them; when their songs come on the radio I feel happy, or someone mentions something about them I get so angry and defensive. That's all the fun of it, I suppose, if fun's the right word.' She laughs as if trying to tally up how fun it could really be.

Among the thousands of angry post-documentary tweets there was a popular one that said: 'Why isn't it about our real fandom? Like the people who sit on their laptops all day&eat food&cry'. It was the closest description of the mundane everyday fangirling many fans had seen.

Lauren and I ended our conversation on the idea of a spectrum of fan emotions. 'It sounds silly but if the creators had explored all the feelings of One Direction fans then it probably would've been okay. It *was* totally heightened sometimes. Other times you'd just sit there and enjoy them, it wasn't always slobbering at the mouth over them. If they were going to look at emotions they could've focused on when girls were down and depressed they could turn to the music or they could go to Twitter where there was such a nice community of other fans that were feeling the same and you'd know they were there for you.'

Only a matter of months after the Channel 4 doc came out, another 1D documentary came out, created by Syco, Simon Cowell's entertainment company that the group were signed to. As with any management or artist-controlled documentary, it was made to be a marketing tool and to please the people who made his money-making pop group famous. It translates like a love letter to the fans. 'Literally from the second it finished,' talking head Cowell says of *The X Factor*, 'the fans made it their mission that One Direction were going to become the biggest band in the world.' Then Niall, sitting in an empty hotel room wearing a football shirt, says: 'This is why we have the best fans in the world'. He half-runs over to the window, opens it, and screams erupt. Endless happy wails. He postures, his back arched like Tarzan, pretending to scream back or scream as them, with them. 'Proof,' he says, at the hysteria outside. Throughout the hour and forty-six minutes there is no stop to the screams and tears. They are layered between scenes, piercing through like sirens. But they're anything but a danger signal. They're the rise and fall of the breath of the film, of the band.

And then there is the prominent scene that every fan remembers. 'These girls are crazy about One Direction and I have no idea why,' Cowell says, like a hopeless dad, rather than a shrewd businessman who has helped build a hugely lucrative product. Cut to neuroscientist Dr Stefan Koelsch dressed in a starched white lab coat – you know he's smart, a symbol of logic, the supposed opposite to emotion – surrounded by computers and holding a model brain in his hands. 'As soon as Directioners listen to music and find the music pleasurable,' he says, splitting the brain with his hands and pointing to all its cavities and pathways, 'what happens in the brain is that a neurochemical called dopamine is released and provides feelings of joy and happiness, shivers, goosebumps, strong pleasure.' Between this explanation, fans yawp with all their might, sprinting like hounds towards the camera. 'The girls are not crazy,' he says, turning Cowell's – and Channel 4's – word back on itself. 'The girls are just excited.'

'I were in the cinema in Glasgow with my friends,' remembers Hayley, 'and when that scene came on, the whole cinema of girls just burst into applause, screaming and cheering. Finally, an accurate representation of us; we were happy that someone had hit the nail on the head. My friend joked afterwards, "Well, at least we know why we cry when they walk onstage. Science."'

Beatles fan, Susan, 68, Melbourne, on feeling and memory

I wonder if the living individuals of The Beatles understand how important they were to us at that time. In my case, still important. Not just the screaming and the sexual side – that's very important too when you're a young girl – but it was more than that.

I had chores to do before school and I'd bounce around the house alone singing their first ever song and I never knew how it happened, but the radio station just *pumped it out.* They first came to Australia in 1964. It was overwhelming, with thousands of us outside the Southern Cross Hotel in Melbourne, waiting for The Beatles to arrive. Just a seething mass of people. Even though at fourteen I was with my big sister being chaperoned, I felt like a naughty girl. I was breaking out from being a normal daughter. It felt terribly, terribly exciting, and terribly unsafe. Looking back it wasn't, it was like a rally, we were all there for the same thing. A 'pro' rally; no one was 'against'. And the concerts – the energy release, you practically float out of the stadium when you're screaming for several hours. It's a shame you're not hearing the music, but you can hear that on the radio or wherever, and just to see them after fantasising for so long is enormous. That's what I say – let it go, enjoy it. It's good for you. Just do it. Because it's almost definite that you won't do that again. It's a healthy way of expressing yourselves, of expressing those emotions that scream in your body when you're a teenager. Press reports of Beatlemania said it was learned or learnt behaviour. It's not. My feelings are my own, I want to own those feelings. I behaved the way I did because I wanted to, I wasn't taught.

When we knew The Beatles were coming, the three of us – two girlfriends and myself – said wouldn't it be wonderful if one of us became ill and they had to come and see us. I will never forget that. Because one of us did. We were still fourteen when my friend was diagnosed with a life-threatening disease. You always feel when you're a young person you're omnipotent and that was a moment in time that informed the rest of my life. There was definitely guilt on my part. I thought I'd made that happen. I don't know if it was me who actually said those words – it could've been, I was pretty out there with my imagination, but they were said. She wasn't told but her parents, without asking our parents' permission, told us. At such a young age we sort of romanticised this, not realising the position having the knowledge put us in. We became her protectors. A terrible responsibility. That's stayed with me, and obviously it has.

There was special treatment: my sister worked for an agency that had connections and got my girlfriend personalised autographs and we got free tickets to a preview of *A Hard Day's Night*. I would go to hospital with her; that's when I saw a lot of treatment going on and the nurses being wonderful. That was part of my decision to become a nurse. And if I wasn't a nurse I wouldn't have met the man that I married and had two children with. It wasn't the best decision – I became divorced quite quickly after the children and changed my whole life around. I'm not abdicating the choices I made or the strength of my character but I'm saying The Beatles had a lot to do with a lot of my choices in one way or another. Even precariously, like then. My life with The Beatles just kept bouncing like a pebble on a flat river.

I loved my life, and it's a privilege to get older. But there's nothing like being a teenager; it's like Dickens said, the best of times, the worst of times. You're pretty fanciful. Everything is either tragic or brilliant. And they were there for it. They were there so we could deposit all our heightened emotions into their songs. When I hear The Beatles' music I'm back where I was. Dancing alone in my house, dah dah dah, meeting my husband, dah dah dah...every song tells me where I was, what I was doing, and what I was feeling.

2

THE WAITING GAME

No one expected me. Everything awaited me.
　　　– Patti Smith, *Just Kids*

Teenage girls are yelping. It's just after 4am and a huge rat – a heaving, greasy, small-dog-sized thing – is dragging its weight along the pavement next to us.

'Eurgh, fuck off!' yell fourteen- and fifteen-year-olds, one pulling the cord of the hood of her sleeping bag tight so only her eyes are looking out. 'You always see them this early, especially in London,' she says solemnly.

We're all sitting or lying outside London's Brixton Academy, one night in March 2017. Every ten minutes or so, girls arrive in darkness to wait for the pop-punk show happening the following night. Two friends, fifteen-year-old Lauren and fourteen-year-old Jess from across town in Bethnal Green, were already there at its steps when I shuffled over at 3am. They greeted me like I was another teen fan, not a writer in her mid-twenties. 'Come and sit down.' 'Are you excited?' Their immediate assumption was that I was there for the same reason. They'd had waffles and whipped cream one of their mums had made at about 1am and had been dropped off in her car. Both showed me their supplies for the night, day and evening. Out of duffels come blankets, a full-sized pillow, doughnuts, hair ties, make-up, portable chargers, money, exercise books, marker pens, t-shirts, CDs (very odd), phones, digital cameras, disposable cameras; enough for a camping trip. They are, I thought, camping, just with one of the ugliest backdrops I've ever seen. 'We're going to wait until security get here and set up the barriers and then we'll sleep,' Lauren says. Along the grimy beige pavement down the left of the building, multiple girls are already passed out in sleeping bags like a row of woodlice, some savvy enough to bring foam mats. 'Our mums didn't mind us being here because it's the last day of term.' She shrugs. 'We'll just say we're ill or something.'

A girl wanders over timidly. 'I was scared no one else would be here because I haven't got friends to come with,' she says. Lauren and Jess welcome nineteen-year-old Simran onto their perch. Soon they're chatting away about their favourite bands and talking the logistics of their joint mission. They're annoyed because they don't have signing tickets that allow you to meet the band. None could afford to be part of the exclusive paid-for fan club. 'If I asked my dad to pay for that every month he'd probably laugh in my face,' says Jess. Simran empties a bag of mobile phones onto the pavement. 'The things I do for bands,' she says.

'Get all these fucking phones for a start.' They're on various networks so she can get different priority tickets – the option to buy gig tickets a day or so before the rest of the general public. 'I come to shows early all the time. I've never come more than two days early, though – until they get portable showers at venues I don't know if I can do it.'

Over the next few hours, various groups play music off tinny speakers, knock back energy drinks and share origin stories, not of their own life but of becoming a fan. One girl with bright blue hair lying on her belly in a sleeping bag is eating baby food from a jar. ('Hey! It's only a fruit one, not weird, like a chicken one or anything!' she yells at me.) Quite a few need the toilet, including me, but the only nearby public ones are in McDonald's, which opens at 7am, so we collectively decide to stop talking about how much we could feasibly wet ourselves.

Through winter 2016 and early spring 2017 I've been waking up at 2 or 3am and taking the night bus across London from my Peckham flat to a music venue. I don't know who I'm going to find but since there's a pop or rock gig on the following night, the fans will be there, wanting to be first in. It doesn't feel especially exclusive to any type of music, as long as the fan base includes a lot of them. When I say 'them' I mean almost exclusively teen girls, since that is who I find every time.

The first time I did this, I arrived at a rock show a couple of hours early. Passing along the queue, I noticed a big group of laughing girls at the front of the queue chatting with a mum across a barrier. This would be the first of many times I met Bea and the others. This was a freezing cold night in February and Bea's mum had brought them all hot chocolates. They only knew each other because they lived across the south of England and had met queueing for nights and days pre-shows. They told me that they did this for every show they went to, and they went to as many as they possibly could, regardless of artist. Since most young music listeners now are less bound by genre, many of the same faces were at shows as disparate as hardcore punk and bubblegum mainstream pop.

Waiting outside venues has been an integral part of the fangirl experience and something of an embodiment of their lifestyle from the very beginning. Columbus Day, New York City, 1944, a Frank Sinatra show, and the New York photojournalist Weegee was there when the first of the pop stars as we know them was about to take to the stage. 'The line in front of the Paramount Theatre on Broadway starts forming at midnight,' he recalled. 'By four in the morning, there are over 500 girls… they wear bobby sox (of course), bow ties (the same as Frankie wears) and have photos of Sinatra pinned to their dresses.' The 3,000-seat house was quickly filled with girls waiting to see Sinatra for the first of his scheduled performances of that day. Apparently inside the theatre the ammoniac smell of pee was heavy in the air because girls refused to leave their seats for food, water, anything, unless they were physically moved by attendants. Over the duration of the day, a riot bubbled over outside where, according to records, police had to deal with 30,000 to 35,000 young female Sinatra fans, lining the streets around the theatre, calling out to be let in.

Across the world, the practice has spread in astonishing ways. In Helsinki, Finland, during David Bowie's 1976 tour, streams of girls who had been poised for hours outside Bowie's hotel propelled their arms through the open windows of his limo, hoping to get autographs as it passed by. London girls waited as his train pulled into Victoria Station ahead of his first shows in his home country in years, and some with multiple tickets stayed outside Wembley Stadium (then called the Empire Pool) overnight since he was playing a string of back-to-back dates. In Brighton, Bros fans – or Brosettes – in their bandanas and leather jackets and with packed lunches, sat from daybreak in the sea breeze before the Bros 1988 gig at the Brighton Centre. Decades later the same girls, who'd become women with families and careers, would wait in merchandise they had bought at those shows outside the O2 Arena for Bros's 2018 comeback gig. High school girls with 'Britney Spears Is God' badges pinned to their chests came from all over California to watch Britney perform a few songs at the Bill Graham Civic Auditorium for her 2011 appearance on *Good Morning America*. Queuing from the early hours of the morning for more hours than she played songs was normal for Britney performances. In North Dakota, in 2009, teen girls waited through the night and even from the previous day, sleeping in the parking lot of the Alerus Center. Nicole Robertson, nineteen, and Beth Dennison, twenty, cuddled together on the tarmac for warmth. When asked by local media – who were there for a charming human-interest story – how long they'd been fans of Britney, Robertson answered with a sarcastic 'Oh, please', and added that they'd been fans since the nineties. This? For Britney? This was no sacrifice, of time or of comfort.

Later some sort of record was set in Rio de Janeiro. Justin Bieber fans started queuing outside the Sambadrome a whole fifty days before his 3rd November 2013 show. They constructed tents and took it in turns to sleep in this Belieber camp overnight. Before the authorities stepped in and banned under-eighteens from staying overnight, they had a brilliantly executed rota of names and times, like an efficiently run restaurant floor. Fans returned regardless, and local businesses were letting them use their toilets and showering facilities for a small payment. This effort was only to be bettered when Bieber returned four years later for his *Purpose* world tour. Camp Bieber opened *five months* in advance of his March 2017 date this time. Again, the 130 or so fans took turns to guard the camp since they still had to pursue activities of a mundane nature, like going to school. One fan told the local paper, *O Globo*, 'We are here for our idol and our love for him made us do this madness'. Madness, to most, but you can't deny that commitment. It doesn't feel like acts of individual delirium either, when girls want to do this together.

When waiting is thrust upon you, minutes and hours become prison bars across your current reality. Why wait, if there's a choice, when our Western culture seems to be more and more about instant gratification, when a vegan tiramisu could be delivered to your door in the space of an hour or a taxi playing the music of your choice could meet you in five minutes? Both communication and validation are available in real time. Friends or lovers are even irritable if you haven't replied to a message within the afternoon. We're getting so bad at the skill of waiting that when we have to do so we find it utterly intolerable, anger inducing, sitting in it like it is a punishment. It doesn't come naturally at all. As such, the younger you are, the more alien the concept becomes, and Gen Z, current teens, the first real digital natives, are frequently depicted as impatient and demanding.

The white band around the 1920s-built dome of the Brixton Academy the night I'm there reads 'All Time Low', the name of the band, in blue lettering. One girl has already taken a picture to share on social media but curses because it's decidedly too dark. Lauren and Jess offer condolences. Era-defining and well-respected bands have played here before – The Rolling Stones, Nine Inch Nails, Alkaline Trio, The Clash, Blondie, Motörhead – making it one of London's iconic rock venues. Whether tonight's event will be written into the venue's legacy or completely lost to history, it'll have lasting meaning for everyone here.

Conversation turns to gossip about recent adventures in extreme queues. Fifteen-year-old pink-haired Nonny remembers her first. It was -3°C, snow and rain. They had to find somewhere warm or dry to sleep. She slept for a while under a bench, then was forced by security to move to a bus station, then a tube station, dragging around her little sleeping bag. There were fifteen of them and they lay across escalators to go to sleep, before being told to move. 'You've got to laugh at how bad your situation is. Scavenging for a toilet, security kicking you out of everywhere... We lost a girl at 4am or something. She just left. We were the first people there so we felt responsible. I'm like, "I'm fifteen! I have no idea what to do." I was so worried. We checked in the underground, all around the tube. In the end she was in the toilets.'

One recent legendary wait was in honour of Twenty One Pilots, a group whose music has pulled in a diehard fan base of young mainstream chart-pop fans. They played at Alexandra Palace on a Friday and Saturday in London, so hundreds of female fans camped all week. Notably mature eighteen-year-old Immy from Norwich was there that night. She sits slightly back from the others, smiling sagely, and speaks with confidence and clarity. She retells events: 'One girl there had frostbite on her thigh. It was really bad, where she'd been laid on the concrete for three days and nights. I think she got taken away by emergency services.' Apparently, security had to bring in special cattle-pen-type barriers that none of them had seen before.

Another girl pipes up from inside her sleeping bag: 'That was fun the first couple of nights but then when the younger kids got there it was so annoying. They brought ukuleles and kept playing Smash Mouth – 'All Star'. I personally find ukuleles so cringey.' Ironically, only five minutes previously Immy and the others had vented frustration at older fans finding them immature.

What they're describing, out of context, sounds like some sort of war zone. Being taken off to casualty, sleeping through turbulent weather conditions, minor altercations with security, rationing food. Once inside, it appears no better. A stampede, during which ankles are sprained and bodies fall down flights of steps.

You might wonder if there's an element of hyperbole in these tales, but the exaggeration simply lies in the melodrama of the girls' retelling, their grandiose gestures and the playing for laughs, as others shake their heads knowingly. Some of them offer queue stories that older teens once told them or that happened to their friends. What occurs when these girls wait passes into folklore; the only place these accounts are likely to be shared is on a pavement next to each other.

'On one of those nights, the amount of people who threw up in the crowd made me want to be sick,' says Lauren. I ask why and Immy says, 'You get young kids who don't understand that they need to hydrate and these are massive venues. It's intense standing up and it gets so hot in the middle. They've not been drinking or eating enough throughout the days and nights if they've been waiting outside. They don't think about it. Queuing people don't eat.' Jess pipes up: 'And the food inside is so expensive!'

There's community feeling here between strangers or those who've met once or twice. Phones are used to document their time, play music, or give them more to discuss, like photos of them with their favourite artists – Immy proudly scrolls, showing me pictures of her with members of All Time Low's support act – or videos of shows they were at. They're not crutches: signs of social inadequacy or awkwardness. These girls are not inside, hiding away on laptops. Some are on camping chairs like a red-faced dad at a music day festival.

In the age of the internet where so much is done online, these spaces are the (albeit unauthenticated and sprawling) IRL fan clubs that don't exist elsewhere. The waiting connects the public and private parts of fandom. Here the inner world of a person's fan feelings meets their outside world; it's both a personal and a group experience.

Eventually Bea arrives, to shrieks. Everyone knows Bea. She is a fifteen-year-old icon among fangirls of the south of England. She grins as she's prancing over, her blonde hair bouncing. I've seen her at multiple shows. Bea is *always* waiting.

Bea's mum will get up at any hour of the day or night to drive her the three hours to London to leave her in the queue. She'll entertain herself around town in the day, periodically coming back with anything Bea and the queue girls might need – blankets when it's cold, sun cream when it's hot. 'My mum is such a legend,' Bea told me the first time we met. 'Sometimes I'll have concerts Friday, Saturday and Sunday and she'll drive me to all of them.' I asked her mum how long she'd been supporting Bea's fan trips. 'Oh, she's been bossing me around since she was born. I have a half-term rule: no waiting before concerts in term time, but it never works.' Parents and mums in particular are crucial to the plans because without them – the consent, the transport, the money – it wouldn't happen.

In the hierarchy of fangirls, charismatic Bea sits at the top. She has tens of thousands of followers on social media through her frequent access to bands, shows and waiting to get to front row. This has come with its downsides – people pretending to be her friend for clout, people she doesn't know finding out her where her school is. Once someone sent a necklace to her home address in the post, and none of her friends knew who it could have been. Girls will approach her like she's a minor celebrity, having seen her at the front, tagged in barrier photos, or recognising her from posting prominent pictures on social media. She'll talk among fans about meet-and-greet tickets and back-to-back shows while others reply with barely concealed envy that they'd love to do it more but it's too expensive.

For a lot of fans camping out and going to shows exist more as a semi-regular treat than a central part of the music fan lifestyle. Eighteen-year-old Lucia shares her frustrations with me. After meeting girls waiting at shows she'll follow them on social media, and this is where comparisons are easily made. 'You see these fifteen-, sixteen-year-olds getting to go to London and spending all their time and money on shows. It's not their money, it's their parents' money. It's all right if you have parents who also let you do what you want with it.' She considers herself just as much a fan, but recognises that how she and many others are able to show that love and dedication is hugely dependent on wealth and social class.

I can sympathise. My significant teenage friendship allowed me to have experiences as a fan I'd never have been able to have otherwise. No boat to the mainland, no gig tickets. I wouldn't have been jealous of other fans, because I didn't know many. But I did know what I wanted to have. Any inequality in the fan experience has been slightly lessened since the internet; before, the only way to hear music by your favourite artists was to buy records or CDs, which cost money. Now, music is instantly accessible for free. Yet it's also thanks to the internet that fans like Lucia are hyper-aware of any differences in the fan experience, ones they'd have been mostly ignorant of before. Hierarchies exist in every teenage social group. The barely visible distinctions based on who your parents are, the school you go to, what you can and can't afford. Fandoms are no different, which is especially obvious when you start seeing the same faces at these gatherings. You realise who arrives at what time, who keeps appearing, whose voices are loudest.

'Oh *hi*, I haven't seen you since that concert last month,' Bea says, hugging every girl in turn. She speaks very quickly and with high energy, following every trail of thought. 'I need to sleep today. I went to a show last night and I haven't slept, I've just carried on going and at some point I'm going to get really tired.' She's arrived later than other girls but joins the biggest group right by the entrance to the venue. They've saved her a spot. When I catch up with Bea in a year's time she will have followed Fall Out Boy on tour to every date with her mum, and flown to America to see them.

Waiting is done first and foremost to get into the venue before others; this is the prize. When more than ten or so girls arrive, a queue forms by itself and through the girls' own organisation system. After the mass circle around the entrance they then snake all the way around the venue to the end of the building. Security won't turn up for hours but the girls have it under control without them. One of the first girls to arrive with a marker pen will always go around writing a number on the hand of everyone who gets there. Today it's more complicated. There are different types of wristband for the show depending on how much you could afford and each gives you varying degrees of priority entry.

'Either I'm that person who does numbering and I feel bad for myself or someone else does it and I feel sorry for them,' explains Bea as another girl gets branded on her hand. Everyone in our circle on the tarmac makes a tone of agreement. 'Security are completely useless if I'm honest. It's the fans who organise everything. Those lot barge over in the day when we've been there for *hours*, hours! "Guys, we're putting up barriers, move, move." And we're like: yes, we're in queues, we're ordered, we're organised.'

It's not that they have an actual problem with security. On the whole, security both humour and sympathise with the fans, but from the perspective of the girls, each party have a different task at hand and security wouldn't be able to understand the nuance of their mission. A group of adults on the clock are unlikely to keep as hawkish an eye on queue jumpers as someone who has been on tarmac in the spitting rain eating paprika crisps all night and day.

During one of these venue excursions, on this occasion at O2 Shepherd's Bush, I met a security guard called Toby. He was a ginger-haired man with spectacles, probably in his thirties but, out in all terrains, for long hours, looking nearer to fifty. He got into working music venues because of a lifelong love of music. Routinely when he arrives to do his job at 10am, the first thing he does is look over at the girls piled in their tents, smothered in duvets. 'A lot of the time artists come to London and play two shows at one venue so you have girls camping overnight, staying there all day, going to the first show, camping out afterwards and going to the second show,' he told me. 'It's wasteful but they buy the cheapest gear they can find then ditch them before the show. Sometimes they don't get cleared for days. It's a dump!'

He told me that the girls just seem to enjoy the waiting itself; that through the day, they are creative. They draw pictures of the bands, they make t-shirts and banners for the show. 'The other day, one brought gingerbread men and drew the band they were seeing on with edible ink, like icing. They drew parts on them and ate those parts... I'm not going to say which parts they were,' he said, looking down his glasses at me, bushy eyebrows raised.

His role in this strange dynamic is almost parental, like that of an uncle or aunt. When I point this out, he says, 'Well, you're responsible for them. If it's raining, you need to know they're warm. If they're not feeling well, you give them advice. Their parents aren't here and some are quite young, so you're acting as a guide and you've got to stick up for the girls.' Despite what the girls think, he sees himself as supporting their mission. 'You've also got to remember what order they're in. I'm very good at memorising the faces and making sure if there's one girl who's been at the front for two days then all of a sudden someone barges past before doors, they get stopped. I'm not saying there'd be a fight, but it could start to brew.' Most of the girls would laugh at his role being seen as vital, and they can certainly stick up for themselves, but it's nice to know they have allies. After a couple of trips to venues, even I started to worry about them being out all night in London under street lamps – not that I would've thought twice about doing something that brazen at their age.

Many of the older fans who arrive later, just before the main act – 'late-walkers' to security – hate the system that these girls have come up with. Bea tells me, 'At the show last night we had numbers and someone said, "If you do that stupid number thing I'll come and wash it all off with acid".' Another nods in agreement. 'People literally come up to us in the queue saying, "Fuck this system. We'll go wherever we want. I'm going to arrive at doors and just push through the crowd like a sensible person."'

These girls feel that older fans look down on them for what they're doing – just as they look down on the younger, more 'irritating' girls they were a few years ago. I feel that, for older girls, this arises from a mix of jealousy at not having the time to be able to wait in line for so long – now having jobs or college or university commitments – and a vague sadness that, truthfully, they probably couldn't be bothered anymore; the unvoiced suspicion that these younger girls might be bigger fans than they are. The waiting has an earnest optimism that is unsettling because it speaks to a jadedness that has crept in, something that younger fans haven't yet learnt. It cuts back to a past where they might have had the pure devotion to act similarly – maybe they didn't when they had the chance.

Later I looked online in forums for evidence of what people think of girls queuing and came across anger projected from men in particular.

One said: 'Any of these bands with the silly little fan girls are the same. The screaming little teeny boppers are all there early so they have a chance of catching a drop of sweat flung off the wrist of their pretty idols.' Another man spoke about how he and a friend turned up at different times for the same concert: 'He queued for 4 hours, I turned up as doors opened. He got front row, on the barrier, I was 3rd row. [The band] may have more queuers as they have mainly teenage fans, but it's an example of how futile queuing really is.' Others thought that the only reason girls wanted to be at the very front was to take a good photo or video – 'and aren't really there for the music'. But for these girls, three rows back is a poor outcome. Their efforts aren't futile: when they queue, they queue to be at the barrier, and they get it. Their waiting is about nothing as specific as taking a good photo or as sexualised as wanting to feel the sweat of their idols.

Girls talk a lot about memory. Being at the barrier means they remember the whole gig. When you don't have a fantastic view, if you're too far back from the performers to grasp it in focus – particularly if it's a stripped-back rock concert with zero pyrotechnics – then your recollection of the occasion becomes more blurred. You recall the people around you, the conversation you might have had with your friend. Individual shows merge with the other times you have seen that artist. When you're close, the experience is more visceral: you can see the expression of the singer's face, the texture of their outfit, smell the aircon, see the faces of the security looking through you all. You have no distractions other than what's in front of you – not the talking of someone else in the crowd who is less fascinated, or the moving of heads and bodies – everything is in high definition. You might take a photograph or video for yourself and as documentation for other fans, but ultimately it's a sacred opportunity.

'I just find,' sixteen-year-old Letitia tells me, after showing me a video from the barrier of another pop-punk show, 'that if I'm further back I just can't look back on it clearly and really remember. That's sad, don't you think? These are the best nights of my life.'

Stronger fans can barge through a crowd and get to a place they want; frequently, younger or female fans physically can't, or don't feel as comfortable with that possible confrontation or invasion of other people's space. When I ask Nonny why there never seem to be boys queuing, she explains it to me. 'It's simple really, mostly you'll see guys in the pit. Girls want barrier.' Anyone can participate in a mosh pit and girls often do. Yet it's not something that every fan wants to do; mosh pits are still a coded masculine space through the aggression of the participants and the ways in which space is taken up. If your prerogative is to mosh, you can easily reach the pit, a fair few rows from the barrier.

Fan-made time is an academic concept in fan theory, describing the way fans have created an entire method of enjoying something. It refers to the wait between the present and the anticipated event (an album release date, the night of a gig), which fans have made into a special experience that's as fun, often, as the thing itself. Owain Waine, a fandom academic, says actively using the wait is about 'more than the means to simply tolerate the wait, [it's] a way of taking back control of, and actively defying, the waiting period'. It's a 'block of time created by fans. It is, after all, fans that have chosen to wait for the release.'

The time these girls wait in the queue is time during which they get to possess the experience of the gig – the music, the crush of bodies, the thrill, the proximity to their idols. They're looking forward with all their hearts to something that might seem miserably brief – two or three hours at the most, for a show from support act to end of the main act – but by queuing, they're making the wait that might irritate or be ignored by you or me into a mini break from reality.

If it was boring they wouldn't do it, no matter how much they want barrier. It's so enjoyable, even to me, that by the time I leave them, I never notice the hours that've passed. 'You feel the adrenaline and the tension in the queue and feel everyone is getting really hyped as the night or day goes on,' says Lauren. 'Everyone's in the same boat as you because they're at the same concert. And if they're in the front they've got the same intentions as you. So you make loads of friends and you can talk about it, listen to music.'

Nonny says she's met all her close friends here, and many echo these sentiments. People at school don't like the same music as they do or they don't have anyone to come to the shows with. I wonder if it's competitive since they've mentioned tensions with other age groups of fans. Lauren thinks it's a 'tiny bit' competitive, but the fact that they're all together works to ameliorate those personal differences. 'Online you're waiting for something – the album, the show – and you don't see how it's affecting other people what you post, you're just blindly posting something. It doesn't feel like it's really you. But you can't be rude to them in person because you see them and understand them and why they're there. You're going to be queuing with them for sixteen, twenty-four or more hours so you've got to get on with it.' Most interactions happen semi-anonymously online day-to-day. This is a rare instance within fandoms in which accountability comes into play and the cycle of validation and rejection that feels intrinsic to being on social media is broken. Everyone can enjoy the format of what is expected of them, in an environment that they have created.

When it gets to the end of the final day, as night approaches, there's a protocol. 'Before the doors open you have to be ready. Around an hour before, you pack everything away, take turns to leave and pee and you have to defend your spot – it's important,' says Immy. She stops drinking properly four or five hours before to avoid needing the bathroom when they get in the crowd.

'If your friend goes after you, then, like, ditch them, as mean as it sounds,' says fourteen-year-old Tay matter-of-factly. 'Obviously you don't have to, but if it means going forward or getting barrier and not then they'll understand.' 'Yeah, I mean, we do understand,' agreed her mate, stony faced. Lauren and Jess jump in to say no way does anyone get left behind, looking at each other for reassurance.

There's an air of anxiety and tension. Girls continue to laugh and play music at an increased volume but late-walking groups and pairs come over, groups who look through and around the girls, surveying for an entry point. Most queue girls are acutely aware of this but won't want to say anything, whispering to a friend or elbowing a more vocal person in the group to point to the end of the line. Luckily, there is always a Bea figure to sort it out, if security doesn't. A lordly 'EXCUSE me, the line is back there!' will be delivered to the offending party, who will snigger or raise an eyebrow and slowly stalk back, looking for another entry point further down.

As soon as you get through bag search and your ticket check, you half-run, half-walk with everyone else laughing into a sprint towards the barrier. You grab onto the metal grating, squashing your whole body against it. It feels like victory. Watching from this very front spot, your chest crushed against the perforated metal, your t-shirt pressing through the holes, lungs taking shallow breaths, neck strained from grinning upward, your ribs hum with excitement and bass. You could get somewhere near to this spot without queuing – angering people around you, knocking over a drink, slithering your way through a crowd – but not *exactly here*. You're a part of something here, of a larger moment, but also made important in your own story. Finally, you're a star of the movie in your head, while being seen in other people's.

Why settle for less? You'll be older soon enough and somehow become satisfied with the peripheries, too anxious or irritable to forge through a crowd or bear being surrounded by kids.

'As security, you keep watching them throughout the day. For the day it's like a mini family and you're an extension of that, really,' Toby the security guard had told me. 'Everyone knows everyone and looks out for one another. Maybe they'll remember you the next time, which is nice. But every night, it's transitory.' After a moment of accidental poignancy he pulls his belt up again under his stomach and adds, 'Either way, girls are here *permanently*'. One shrieks past him and he shakes his head.

It's 8am and I have to leave to go to work. Brixton has come to life around us. The smells of bacon and jerk have hit the air, as parents and students pop to the corner shop to get bread and milk. Early commuters stand glazed over at the bus stop, free paper or coffee in hand. A few more of the girls have gone to sleep, the initial hype of the early hours having worn off. I'd bought a Fanta for a girl with blue hair, but by the time I'm back from the corner shop, she has her eyes closed. I place it down next to her head and wonder if someone else will take it. When I tell them all I'm leaving they're dismayed. 'God, you have work, ugh!' Jess says. 'Sounds boring.' 'But you're coming back later?' others ask. 'We can number you now and you can slip back in and we'll meet you?' When I next see Bea, she'll tell me there was a monumental argument with some girls staying in a hotel opposite. ('They said, "we got this hotel, we deserve

43

to be ahead of you." It's not the same! We were camping on the streets, there was a fox that could've killed us, the police came! But it was so fun.')

I wait for as long as possible on the pavement, scanning the faces of the commuters for a glimmer of surprise. No one starting their day bats an eyelid at the one hundred or more girls laughing, eating, crying, sharing and screaming on the street. It's like they don't exist. On any given gig night in the country, this is happening. And the rest of the sleeping world doesn't know about the party at the venue just down the road from them.

Shirley Manson, Garbage, on Siouxsie Sioux and Garbage fans

When we were growing up, because there was no internet, we discovered musicians primarily through either TV or just a glimpse in the *NME*. You'd see something that caught your attention, maybe fascinated you for their physicality or their style. And then you would just immortalise them in your mind, you know? They became sort of little fetishes.

I saw a picture of Siouxsie Sioux on the back of an album cover, *Kaleidoscope* maybe. But I was so obsessed with this image. I see her pop up in these music broadsheets. And then I see her on *Top of the Pops* and that just floored me. She had this extraordinary style that I didn't quite understand. I'd never seen anything like it. Here was this thing, this creature. I didn't know if it was a boy or a girl. I'd never seen women break out of the conventional representation of themselves. And she looked to me sort of like a First Nations warrior and I was literally spellbound. I fell in love with her music and I played it religiously. I got every single release I could get my hands on. I was getting bullied at the time and she was sort of the persona that I would escape into when I would sing along to her records. There was one particular track called 'Drop Dead/Celebration', which is a B-side to 'Happy House' and it's a song of unbelievable venom and fury. I would sing along to that and in that moment I would be powerful and I would be an avenging angel.

I think if you're a band who is lucky enough to last any amount of time you develop relationships with your fans. It's just impossible not to, you see them every night. Sometimes you see them in distress, sometimes you see them in moments of their life that clearly they're really happy. We've watched some of our fans change gender. It's an extraordinary moment, you feel like you've birthed a child almost. You go, 'Ah, here they are! Finally!' It'd give me the creeps a little when I was younger, I didn't really understand what the dynamic was. I used to be so uncomfortable and awkward around fans. And of course making our fans even more uncomfortable. It's an uncomfortable situation anyway for a fan to come up to someone they follow, and by you being a freak the whole experience for them becomes unpleasant. I don't want people to walk away feeling crushed by me, I'd rather they felt ignited, you know?

But then as I've gotten older I realised: I'm just in service of those who think like me or feel similar to me. Me and my band are able to provide them with connection, comfort, understanding, sympathy, joy and to me that's like, 'Wow! What a fucking privilege. How great is that.' And when they lower me into the Earth I can say 'I was in service to people'. I think that's clear to me now and it wasn't before.

Laura Jane Grace, Against Me!, on belonging and boundaries

The first word that comes to mind is obsessive. I was isolated from media until I was about thirteen. Growing up I lived overseas in southern Italy and there was only one American TV channel that certainly didn't play music videos. I would just go through real phases – that's definitely something that's continued on throughout my life where the way that I digest things is to get into something to death and understand it from every single angle and wear it out to where I'm sick of it and it's: OK, next. What's the next thing?

Sometimes it's about the identity of the artist, it draws you to them and I think a lot of that for me is trying to understand the music, trying to get to the source of it. It's 'what is this? Why am I drawn to this?' You can boil it down to really simple terms and just say: I did it because it made me happy. It made me really happy to be *in this thing*. When you're younger so much more of it is about wanting to belong somewhere. With punk rock, it was about wanting to belong to the genre. If I saw some kid walking down the street wearing an Operation Ivy shirt, I knew immediately that we would be friends, we would have similar politics, we would surely have other favourite bands that were similar, that we were part of a scene.

Punk rock taught me the breaking down of barriers, and that it's not about being a 'rock star', or isolating yourself; you need to throw yourself out there and be immediately approachable. Unfortunately sometimes it's impossible to have an actual conversation with fans and you're kind of just along for the ride. Half the time people are so worked up, so excited that this is their moment that they aren't paying attention because they're ready to say whatever they're saying. You just have to be a part of that moment with that person. I've really let people into my personal life by writing a book about it. In turn, after a show there'll be a group wanting pictures and someone will come up and tell you something heart-breaking. 'Hey, I tried to kill myself', or 'Hey, I went through cancer'. This heavy thing where you as a human being can't really process that. What do you say? You're in an informal setting and not an intimate conversation. I have empathy for people, and I don't want to just dismiss it. But then you have to go immediately to play a show.

It can be impossible to rebound from that.

Once at a book signing and gig in Brazil, 300 people turned up and wanted a kiss. Culturally that's how people greet each other in South America. So it was 300 people giving 300 kisses followed by 300 photos by 300 signed books and then 300 hugs at the end of the exchange. It was so much I had an anxiety attack, a breakdown afterwards. That was maybe twenty minutes before I had to play. Sometimes you feel like you can't express a boundary because people will think you're being an asshole. You have to create a barrier unfortunately because you can never live up to their expectation. That can be suffocating sometimes.

There are so many fans who are amazing. They don't want to cross over into friendship. There's Emily, who has come to about one hundred shows or something ridiculous, she's always so respectful and so nice. When I came out [as transgender], I was terrified of how I'd be treated, the things people would say, and instead it was so humbling. Fans were so kind, showing up just to say 'I'm not trying to be creepy, or take up too much of your time. I just wanted to say: *I support you.*' That's it.

3

I'M (NOT) OKAY: TO RETREAT AND RETURN

People cannot change music, it's music that changes people. It is bigger than you and me put together. It's a neutron bomb with the detonator set on 'kill' waiting for you to push the button.

     – Gerard Way

No one can remember how they found out. But they all agree it was arranged on the internet somewhere. Ultimately 'how' didn't matter; rather, it was why they were collectively so moved to action. For almost all the girls it was their first protest. For many, it would be the only time they'd be inspired to do so.

The attack on their deep connection to music began, as much dogmatism does, with the *Daily Mail*. In August 2006, the paper began its scare campaign against emo: journalist Sarah Sands wrote an article warning parents of a new 'cult of suicide' and suggested that the alternative rock group My Chemical Romance, among others, promoted self-harm. This was the trail of gunpowder to be ignited almost two years later. In May 2008, a My Chemical Romance fan from London, Hannah Bond, died by suicide. Her father said she had started self-harming and that she had told him the cutting was considered an emo 'initiation ceremony'. Reports blamed her death on dark lyrics that spoke about depression and self-harm and the *Daily Mail* swiftly followed its initial reporting with an inflammatory piece of commentary titled 'Why no child is safe from the sinister cult of emo'. It looked at the genuinely troubling rise in the number of girls admitted to hospital for self-harm and linked it – without evidence – to a clear-cut cause: music.

While MCR themselves might have rejected the label 'emo' to distance themselves from other bands popular in the mid-to-late noughties, it was clear: they were being targeted as a figurehead of a movement and were going to take the brunt of suspicion from conservative adults.

This was a mainstream matter, but an air of mistrust existed within rock too. A majority of fans – particularly the most vocal and visible – of that new, more commercial breed of emo music were girls. Old emo was born of eighties hardcore punk, especially popular in the Midwestern states of America, while the new wave was radio-friendly, more melodic and pop-punk influenced. It pushed the pre-existing expressive and empathetic elements to the extreme, and packed in dominant catchy hooks and anthemic riffing. Within that, My Chemical Romance were volatile misery; they were as much the aggression of Black Flag as they were the horror-rock of Misfits and, increasingly, the kitsch and pomp of Queen. Their third album, *The Black Parade*, released in 2006, the year of the *Daily Mail*'s first article on emo, lent into the camp and splendour of glam rock (think operatic soft rock and a polka featuring Liza Minnelli). With My Chemical Romance in particular, vulnerability and a 'hysterical' display of emotions, qualities traditionally viewed as feminine, were derided by some rock fans. Lyrically, these weren't especially new in emo, but combined with its sound and presentation – make-up, colour, enormous side-fringes and back-combed hair versus earlier acts who presented as regular dudes, jocks almost, in plain white t-shirts, sports jerseys and denim jackets – this was something very different. It was a scene that simply couldn't pass as conventionally masculine as the emo bands in the eighties and nineties had.

Paul Brannigan, editor of *Kerrang!* magazine between 2000 and 2009, saw the much-contested state of the ever-evolving genre as the result of gender and age prejudice of older male rock fans. 'Emo fans are the whipping [kids] of the moment,' he said at the time. 'There's a misogynistic air to it. A lot of the credible metal bands have got an older, very male following and they see teenage girls getting into bands like MCR and think they've not earned the respect to be called a rock fan.' It's not a coincidence that the belittling levelled at the genre overall was exactly the same belittling women received when trying to validate their feelings and symptoms.

These fans could no longer sit and wait for parents to read tabloid manipulation and ban or dissuade them from what, they felt, saved them: a protest was planned for Saturday 31st May 2008. Estimates from those present say between 150 and 200 were in attendance from all over the country and nearly all were teen girls. They would meet at Marble Arch in central London between 10 and 11am. The Marble Arch is a beautiful white structure with three arches which, for a long time, has sat isolated in its grandeur on a busy traffic island, where old and new incongruously coexist. Without the girls realising, it made sense as somewhere to meet, to rebel against accusations that felt current but were part of a historical bigotry and narrow-mindedness they'd barely yet had a chance to experience.

Thirteen-year-old Tabitha came to the protest from Brighton with four best friends and her sister, under the supervision of her mum. They got the train sitting opposite each other, sharing one pair of headphones and a little MP3 player between the two, and listened to MCR to stir themselves up. 'Once we heard about it we knew we were *definitely* going. It was just a matter of who could come, who was available. We all bought white shirts so we'd look like we were dressed in school uniform, like in their 'I'm Not Okay' video, but we drew positive lyrics of the band over them to make a point – and "Fuck the *Daily Mail*", obviously. There was something really righteous about it,' Tabitha said. They stayed the night before in London with Tabitha's gran, who was baffled by the whole thing, but supportive.

Jessica was fourteen at the time and lived nearby in Essex so didn't have far to come. 'This was seriously important to people,' she presses. 'Everyone was chatty and playing music. There was a big white flag with black writing on and everyone there took turns to sign it.' Some girls had identical sashes that said, in bold black stark opposition to the *Daily Mail*'s claims: MCR Saves Lives.

Kayleigh, then fifteen, travelled from Basingstoke with – her mother's one condition – an older friend. 'I remember when we got there, there were so many people and everyone was dressed the same and we all had our little banners. I was wearing black skinny jeans, obviously,' she laughs, 'and wore an MCR shirt and a pair of fingerless gloves. My friend had come over before the protest and we made signs with black paper that my mum had taken me out in the car to buy. I made one saying "I am not afraid to keep on living" and one that said "You'll never take me alive" in gold writing and the songs that those lyrics came from underneath.'

The protest had originally been intended as a march. The organisers planned to gather everyone at the Round Pond in Kensington Gardens and march to the *Daily Mail* offices off High Street Kensington, but the plan was derailed. Becki from Trowbridge, fourteen at the time, recalls how the trolling group Anonymous – a collective that, before being known for specialist, faceless hacktivism, was a group aimed at maximum offline and online disruption, often sharing right-wing, sexist, homophobic or racist content – found out about the march online and started advertising it as a mass suicide. 'About two weeks before it was due to happen Anonymous continually posted morbid videos online with words like, "This is the day it all ends". We were supposed to have over a thousand fans coming, so that affected us. When I saw them turn up on the day, they must've been in their twenties, thirties and we were in our teens. I thought: what are you doing?' Becki was lucky enough to have a mum who was genuinely as big a fan of MCR as she was and wasn't 'buying into what other mums were buying into.' They both knew it was just a place for fans to gather and celebrate the band.

As well as affecting their numbers and causing parents to change their minds about allowing their children to attend, the girls who organised the event reconsidered the method of protest, and police were stationed around the girls for its duration. Some groups went off to the *Daily Mail* offices to chant and sing while others stayed at Marble Arch. From the small amount of video footage of that day, the men who came in their masks to disturb the girls' mission don't look any older than thirty. Each wears the now infamous Anonymous Guy Fawkes mask with trilby hats or suits, hoodies, and random items of sportswear.

'At one point Anonymous took a load of *Daily Mail* papers and set them all on fire and encouraged us to start jumping around and burn them ourselves,' says Becki. 'They were trying to get us all riled up so they and the press could paint us in a bad way. A few girls did it but most of us just ignored them. That wouldn't have been the peaceful event we were there for.'

Much of the little coverage of the day has disappeared – relics of an era before new media. The BBC, *The Guardian* and *Kerrang!* were among the few media organisations who actively made efforts to understand the motives behind what the girls were doing. The bolder fans gave interviews. 'I shoved myself in front of any camera,' laughed Tabitha. 'I was excited and wanted to say something because I really was furious. I thought I had a message although what I delivered probably weren't the most articulate lines in the world.'

I found that what she had said to *The Guardian* wasn't so much inarticulate as passionate: 'I love MCR, it saves lives. The *Daily Mail* are liars and all they want to do is put the youth against the adults; they just hate us and it's really unnecessary, it's just wrong. I've read a couple of the *Mail* articles and they've actually misquoted lyrics and the research was so badly done, it was unbelievable. I actually thought [the story] was a hoax when I found it on the internet.'

The day showed that emo fans weren't all holed up in their rooms, self-harming and being anti-social, depressed to inertia, caring for nothing, ready to welcome death. They sang songs that captured happy thoughts; they picked up girls who came alone or in twos and banded together. 'We felt we'd actively defend that,' says Tabitha. 'We were young girls who'd made more effort than an adult would to protest. It's a big deal when you're that age to come to London and spend the night there. We were moved to activity and it showed that that stereotype was absolutely wrong.'

Jessica feels similarly today. 'I remember strongly feeling a part of something and like you belonged to this community of supportive people who cared. The community were out on a Saturday in London saying, "No, you're attacking this band and family and it's wrong and we're going to stand up for people in our culture and protest what we feel is injustice".'

From the other side of the Atlantic and all over the world fans were watching, in full support of their British counterparts. Superfan Cassie from Ohio, now twenty-seven, was waiting for news on message boards and social media during what felt like an international event. 'We might have not known what a shitrag the *Daily Mail* was at the time – for us it was just another newspaper – but we all felt the same way. That day I wrote "Fuck the *Daily Mail*" on my arm and it felt like even if you weren't there it was huge. The UK was on the frontline, there being the face of us, and the rest of the world supported, saying "this is not a fair representation of us or the band, this is bullshit". It felt like we'd all marched on Washington.'

As with the fans on the frontline, My Chemical Romance had in fact not driven Cassie to mental illness, but had been a unique balm for it. She was fourteen and an only child when she started exhibiting the first signs of her bipolar disorder: constantly crying, hurting herself. 'I was grappling with the beginnings of a serious mental health issue and I didn't know anyone else that felt that way. I remember the first time I tried to tell my mum I thought something was wrong with me, she said,

"You're just getting yourself wound up, you're fine." That shut me down too. I thought: I can't talk to people about this because they're gonna make me feel bad. So instead of talk I just hurt myself. I didn't know how to tell my friends, "I want to die". It was very lonely.'

Around the same time as her bipolar emerged, Cassie discovered My Chemical Romance. Their early tour documentary, *Life on the Murder Scene* – a fan classic and still a comfort to Cassie – opens with their mission statement. 'We're definitely a band that wants to save your life,' guitarist Frank Iero tells a third party interviewing him, sitting comfortably on a sofa. It cuts to Gerard Way, the frontman, at a gig asking someone in the crowd, 'What does your shirt say, dude?' The camera pans to a delighted fan wearing a white t-shirt with 'MCR saved my life' in black Sharpie over it. 'MCR saved my life,' reads Gerard to a crowd of adoring teenagers, adding: 'That's the whole point of all this.' Later in the documentary, after detailing his struggle with depression, suicidal ideation and addiction, Gerard says, 'We've always been pretty adamant or vocal about our message. It's just to know that it's OK to be messed up because we're five dudes that are just as messed up as you and we've overcome that in order to do what we do.' This was no underestimation: members were extraordinarily open about their mental health, at a time before musicians spoke about it much in the press, and certainly before the music industry's en masse co-option of mental illness as a selling point.

Tabitha says she, like 'almost all' MCR fans, went through periods of depression or emotional struggle. 'Being drawn towards a band like that, you're going to be. You'd see the band still going through it and being open and vulnerable and successful and that gives you hope. It makes you feel like one day, "I'll be an adult and would've got through it".'

To get people behind that message, MCR needed a hymn. Like Cassie, like so many teens at that time, I felt changed by My Chemical Romance's biggest hit to that date, 'I'm Not Okay (I Promise)'. The chugging into an exhilarating opening riff – it sounded like a heart breaking in excruciatingly slow motion. It was euphoric sadness. It embodied the performative drama of emotions and exhibiting symptoms of mental struggle. It was a cry for help and an admission of everything. Whether you had mental health problems or were just at the mercy of teenage hormones, we all knew why we liked the song. The concept of not being fine was a simple one but someone needed to say it. 'It was definitely an anthem,' Gerard once said. 'The straight-up lyric "I'm not okay" was a declaration from me, it was a declaration for kids who would become our fans, who would realize that: "You know what? Everything's not OK."'

What went along with listening to this music was a kind of retreat. The way girls talk about the private listening to this song, and others by MCR, is almost ritualistic: on beds, with headphones on because it's the suitable way to make Gerard's words scream into ears, eyes shut, tears pouring down cheeks to leave a halo on the pillow. What hearing their songs looks like, in that moment, is hiding from the world to try to heal.

'On a family holiday I'd withdraw into my cheap headphones and MP3 player and listen to them constantly,' said Tabitha. Jessica too pulled back internally and into the world of MCR. 'That's the relationship I had with them. I'd be in my room, miserable, listening,' she said. 'It was catharsis, which a lot of people find confusing: why would you listen to depressing lyrics to try and overcome that feeling? But it makes perfect sense. I don't think anyone cured mild depression listening to happy music. We've got to deal with those feelings rather than sleep on them and push them out.'

I relate to all of their stories and Cassie's in particular. I'm a similar age to her and started presenting symptoms in the mid-noughties. When I turned fifteen, I started seeing a child psychologist and miraculously – I have no idea how – managed to keep it from my parents for nearly a year. No one at that time spoke about mental health. Not your parents, not your teachers, not even your friends. The only references you had in order to piece together an understanding of what was going on were books, films and, primarily, music: part-fictionalised, part-autobiographical objects and the stories of the people who made them. On medication at that young age, I asked the same questions over and over again. Am I normal? What is normal? Am I damaged? First answer: seems not. Second answer: whatever isn't this. Third and final answer: refer to the previous two, and worry some more. If trite metaphors were all I had then something had broken inside my brain, and if I couldn't see it and I wasn't a doctor then how could I fix it? The *Daily Mail* and tabloids had antidepressants down as 'happy pills', people who were mentally ill were criminals and 'psychos'. They'd talk about cutting but divorced it from any broader issue of well-being or mental health. Self-harm and depression were trends to be reported on with bombast and fear, like the subculture many desperate girls had dived into.

Using music like this from across the rock subgenre, to hide away and process whatever was going on, helped. Even though half the time the melodramatic lyrics of bands like Hawthorne Heights, Dashboard Confessional or Bayside were about things like death and revenge and funerals and heartbreak, they still resonated. It doesn't especially matter if a line like 'So long and goodnight' is about loss of a loved one when it could be applied to any of your own losses. A lot of the time the lyrics were about depression or medication or mental suffering. Explicit themes of mental health had never before been delivered to young people, who were struggling without support, via mass-marketed rock. So when the adults writing the newspapers accused young people of almost abusing music in order to feel suicidal, of hiding away and perpetuating issues, there was a point missed. In terms of mental health and emo music this was, as Jessica says, 'a total reluctance to try and understand – "let's ignore it and blame it on the culture".'

This anger at the hypocrisy and lack of willingness to connect the dots was exactly how the girls felt at the time. Tabitha, like others I spoke to, said, 'The *Daily Mail* profited off Hannah's death when actually MCR probably made her feel better than most things in her life, it probably gave her escape. We know that's the way music makes you feel. It doesn't glorify anything, it doesn't make you want to kill yourself. The opposite, if anything. I still stand by that now.' She pauses. 'I felt like the band and the music would've held her hand. That's how I felt at the time and I do now.'

Cassie still has thick black hair, a cloud of it. In the way that cartoon characters never age, she looks almost identical to how she did ten or so years ago, and is no less of a hardcore fan at twenty-seven. She paints her lips black, has little chokers with gothic pendants and almost a dozen Wednesday Addams dresses. What has changed is the grasp she now has on her mental health condition.

'Obviously to me I understood that the music was therapeutic and never the reason I would hurt myself or was sad, it was what would pull me out of those moments. At the time I remember being so confused about the perception of adults and the *Daily Mail* and other teenagers even. If your kid is hurting themselves you should take them to a professional because something is really going on there. The idea that mental health was treated as a trend and still is is so upsetting. I'm on medication to stay alive and it's not the result of music. The music was always something I could listen to that would make me feel better. It's always been hard to reconcile that stigma being related to something that has helped me so much.'

It's absurd to think that music can ever be viewed as the cause of danger to fans, but moral panics around music, particularly rock, have been long standing. Associated with the first wave of rock 'n' roll in the mid-to-late fifties was the racist fear of whites and African-Americans mixing – that young black and white kids would bond over the genre that came from black music, find common ground over its 'primitive' and sensual beat. The sexual nature of the music, to adults, meant their daughters would become hungry for more stimulation, growing depraved and spoiled. In the 1980s, conservative America saw heavy metal as inspiring Satanism, sexual activity, aggression and anger, and linked it to suicides and deaths. This overlooked the simple facts that the music offered an escapist outlet, was enjoyable as an art form, and very often was simply employed to annoy blue-collar parents in run-down towns.

The moral panic surrounding metal famously erupted again in the nineties after the mass shooting at Columbine High School. The earliest reports of the tragedy falsely claimed that the two student shooters were fans of anti-Christian rock star Marilyn Manson and pointed out that they dressed in trench coats, as Manson sometimes did. This turned into early headlines that read 'Killers Worshipped Rock Freak Manson' and 'Devil-Worshipping Maniac Told Kids to Kill'. When asked by Michael Moore in his documentary *Bowling for Columbine* what he would say to the kids affected by Columbine, Manson said, 'I wouldn't say a single word to them, I would listen to what they have to say, and that's what no one did.' Later, a father from North Dakota would claim in court that his child, who loved Manson's *Antichrist Superstar,* had died by suicide as a direct result of listening to the music.

Sociological studies using the term 'moral panic' arose in the sixties – the moral part is the social condemnation, and the panic being the shades of alarm and overreaction. In 1972, the sociologist Stanley Cohen argued that mass media is the key transmitter of moral panics: the media either initiates the moral panic or uses it as a tool to carry the message of other groups. Crucially, moral panics about music do not look to uncover fans' desires to escape from hopelessness or marginalization and to seek out others and form protective bonds through their music choices. The media does not ask adequate questions about why children feel this way. It reaches for superficial blame. In this context, My Chemical Romance provided a perfect storm: young female fans, dramatic music and mental health.

Music scholar Rosemary Hill told me that, from an academic point of view, the discourse on moral panics is self-perpetuating and, through a heated lens, offers little insight. 'Things are written and said about fans and music – we've got academics who have to respond to that, and psychologists trying to do experiments to find out if listening to metal makes you want to go out and kill people, and on the cultural studies side of it people wanting to defend it [metal] saying of course it doesn't; so there's no room for middle ground in that conversation to say: well, actually, maybe it's quite complicated and maybe we don't know what's going on here.'

Hill was the only music or fandom scholar who represented that middle ground quite well. In a paper called '"Emo Saved My Life": Challenging the mainstream discourse of mental health around My Chemical Romance', Hill argues that MCR fans' 'willingness to discuss depression has been misinterpreted by their detractors' and instead offers a positive story about the benefits of emo music. She saw nothing more than a vague correlation between being an emo listener and depression, and even suggests to me that emo would've helped some fans. In 2017 I became unwell again – this time in a state of such high anxiety and deep, soul-aching depression I wouldn't have believed, before it happened, that the two states could exist alongside each other with such intensity. I sat in my therapist's office and while she spoke to me in the manner of an owner to a scared pet, I dissociated from my body completely, as if I were looking on myself from up high. She brought me back down again like someone lassoing the moon. Her orders: stop working immediately, rest. My reaction: to take a long-haul flight. On the day of returning from that trip, within a few hours of landing, I became immobile: my body and brain conspired without my knowledge and completely rejected continuing with whatever had been going on, as if with a resounding 'no'.

I had to retreat. I threw completely miscellaneous items into a suitcase to go back to my mum's house. The sea was grey, the ferry terminal grey, the sky and the island approaching looked like mould on a single tile. For much of that period I was dissociated, locked out, waiting for body and mind to stubbornly make up. My hair was like wet sand to pull fingers through. I couldn't write, I couldn't read, but I could listen to music. I wanted familiar aids. One of the only jokes I could muster was putting on 'I'm Not Okay'. Hearing it as an adult, aware that I was trying to trigger myself, to be mildly ridiculous, I did have a hearty cry. I wondered whether I'd have the same emotional response to it hearing it the first time as an adult. Possibly it wasn't the same, but it did remind me of a previous time. There, in my body, were memories of a healing process.

Inside those songs, and likely the songs of many artists prior and since, girls found asylum. Music can be a place you go in a compromised state of being, where entering has the embrace of a cocoon. It's isolation that feels necessary on every possible level – physically, mentally, emotionally and spiritually. A position from which you can look out at where you're from and where you've been, but for whatever period of time you can allow, you are shored up securely.

Day to day we blunt feelings, consciously or unconsciously, sometimes to self-protect, but with music we have the possibility of opening up to feel deeply and to become aware of all that comes with that. To actively dip into miserable music at a time of pain can be to refuse to gloss over and say 'I'm fine'. With our societal refusal to deal deeply in feelings, there's a fear of retreating. Loneliness is, they say, an epidemic. Aloneness – being alone, rather than feeling lonely – has, by virtue of this, been tarnished, tarred with a shade of danger and immorality; it is something to be concerned about. To retreat literally means 'the act of moving back or withdrawing'. In other words, to not be continually, relentlessly forging ahead, prioritising productivity. It is to process and to reconnect. It's about indulging yourself, existing in the private spaces out of reach.

While I was in bed, the whole package of retreating into fandom felt like no-cost self-care. I revisited old filmed interviews, and listened to the same melodramatic albums over and over. The meaning was there – pain and drama – when I couldn't verbalise anything. I thought to myself: anytime you need to come back here, you can.

MCR SAVES LIVES. It sounds tedious and altogether false. The sort of platitude used by both music writers and industry heads providing a product. In the case of MCR, it was truer than that. Cassie agrees wholeheartedly. 'Back in the day it was such a cliché to say MCR saved my life, or rather it became one, but for many it was absolutely true. It wasn't even just the music, it was the whole world they created.' A weird world admittedly, but one in which there was a place, however temporary, to feel.

It's okay not to be okay – as long as it's a temporary state. You can retreat as long as a return is a part of your near future. As dangerous as a 'hysterical' fan is, a lonely one is far worse. True fandom obsession can very occasionally become troublingly all-consuming. This is the 'unhealthy fandom' reported on in tabloids to shock and disgust the curious reader. It's the fan who underwent multiple plastic surgeries to look like Justin Bieber or those who go bankrupt following the purchase of every single ticket and piece of merchandise; this is the rare incidence of embracing extreme fandom to the detriment of one's life.

Therapist and self-professed fangirl Kathleen Smith literally wrote the book on how to be a healthy fan (*The Fangirl Life: A Guide to All the Feels and Learning How to Deal*). She is passionately against seeing fangirling as a symptom; it is something to attribute neither positive nor negative values to. 'You can approach being a fan very thoughtfully and it can inform how you live your life and what meaning you want to draw from it or it can just be a distraction,' she tells me. 'You don't have to necessarily tie greater importance to it. For some people it is a way of engaging with and thinking about their mental health and for some people it's not and they have other ways of doing that.'

According to her, there are two ways to deal with mental illness or difficult life circumstances: to engage or to distract. Neither, she says, is correct or inherently good, but both are necessary for ideal mental health. 'As humans our brains are built to distract,' she explains to me. 'There's a lot of research into how to grieve for someone who's died. You might laugh at something or take a break or not think about it for a while. Our minds are programmed to do that, so distracting yourself from other things going on in your life with fandom or being a fan, there's nothing wrong with that.'

'I always remind myself and tell my clients that the people who do the best with their mental health have a buffet of distractions, and ways of engaging with it. If anything becomes your only way of managing your anxiety you're going to be in trouble.' She mentions her clients who are involved in fandoms and that they have ways of distracting and managing their issue, other than simply their fandom. 'I'd say the same to anyone who uses a relationship, or exercising, or things we think of as being really healthy, right? I think of it as spokes on a wheel, you need more support than just one spoke.'

Times change – you can open any tabloid Sunday supplement and see a celebrity talking about mental health, or self-diagnose on Google quicker than making a doctor's appointment – but disappearing into fandoms still happens. The MCR fan base has huge numbers of young fans joining all the time, despite the band itself having long disbanded. It's remarkable, really, that teen-girl My Chemical Romance fans exist in a world where connectivity and information and understanding of mental health and well-being have never been so high – yet they still talk about My Chemical Romance in a similar way. The frontman is still inadvertently singer, leader, therapist and self-help teacher, as well as someone they're in awe of. 'I'm Not Okay (I Promise)' hit over 100 million streams on Spotify in January 2019. An anthem lives on, and methods of self-soothing remain.

Aubree is eighteen and lives in the Central Valley in California, a world away from drizzly Marble Arch or even New Jersey, the birthplace of her favourite band. She's lived there her whole life. Her dad walked out on her and her mother when she was a two-year-old baby. She doesn't go into too much detail about her mum and subsequent step-dad, hesitating when saying, 'things weren't great between them, shall we say'.

'My mom always tried her hardest to make sure my life was happy and she did so much, and I felt like I had to be her outlet for emotions when she was really sad and needed someone to talk to. I was the strong one,' she says. As a teen she was bullied relentlessly, receiving death threats. 'They'd tell me to kill myself, it was violent bullying, they'd pick on me and I wasn't ever really doing anything, just sitting there. They nit-picked at every flaw I had.' She was suffering from depression and was suicidal throughout that period. 'My Chemical Romance – I'd listen to them and they saved me from doing something regrettable.' Despite the strength of her emotions, she never let them show. 'As a little kid of course there'd be times that I cried but somehow that got blocked along the way. I think that's where the depression came from.'

Aubree describes a haven she can go to where feelings could and can finally come out, the only place she felt was an option for her. Other fans give similar accounts. For seventeen-year-old Samantha from Pennsylvania, MCR are both an expression of her feelings and an outlet for them. 'They gave and give me a place where I feel safe.' Eighteen-year-old Berliner Anna had a 'private relationship' with the band. 'I just had a really shit time at school, didn't have any friends, didn't know what to do with my life, or if I even wanted to go on. I had to always listen to the music and it definitely became my way of coping. It was the one thing that kept me from doing something stupid. If I was feeling really bad I'd turn on the music and it'd help and I'd be able to face the world again.' Of the near-dozen girls I spoke to, all but one said that when they picture themselves listening to the band, they're on their beds and alone.

Cassie once spent endless hours on her own bed, with the music. 'My Chemical Romance was this huge movement but it always felt like this movement was inside of me. Maybe inside of all of us in different ways; no two fans' experience with the music will be the same, but I always feel like My Chemical Romance are *My* Chemical Romance, you know?' Cassie laughs, and remembers the live shows. 'It's personal to the point of still being personal in a room surrounded by thousands of people.'

Sometimes leaving the personal space the band had created for them, Cassie and the others had the impetus to create and participate in online spaces. On the band-related message boards they would have discussions about mental health and how they were suffering and finding coping mechanisms. The things said were what they wished they could say to friends and parents but couldn't. Reactions to others' problems would be similarly personal and unfiltered. 'My Chemical Romance created this space where they said it's okay not to be okay. They're all a bunch of fucked-up people and it's alright if you're a little fucked up. We had that space and we had each other and it wasn't the music that was the conduit for that, it was what helped me through it. It was internally relating to a lyric and finding solace in that or actually talking to a fan who was going through the same thing,' Cassie says. Everyone was feeling comparable internal pain, together.

At the end of our conversation, Kathleen shared a metaphor that could summarise fan retreating and returning cycles. 'I think of it as like superhero movies. Superheroes go away for a while and train. I think of that as returning to a band that motivated me and gave me a kick in the butt before and it helps a whole lot.' This is something she does and something that I recognise in myself and other girls I spoke to as well. 'I like to think of my superhero being off screen for a while, thinking and hibernating before I'm ready to get out there again and go.'

To see fandom as a straightforward escape from it all is too simplistic. I enquired after the well-being of the girls from the march – they all had their mental health under control, or were going through patches of ill health but keeping generally positive. Returning from a bout of poor mental health can be disorientating. But we work towards return and we want to.

Tabitha was happy after the 2008 protest. She thought it'd done its job, bringing fans together, making their voices heard and getting media coverage to combat what had been so damning. 'It was the same week that you weren't allowed to drink alcohol on the tube anymore,' she says to me, while her mum potters around in the kitchen just in ear-shot. 'In protest, adults got on tube carriages and got drunk on there. There was press that said on the same week people were behaving so badly, acting like children, the actual children – girls – are having a protest about My Chemical Romance and behaving well and getting their point across. We all read it together in the paper on the way back home. I've never felt so validated.'

This happened years before the mental health conversation essentially began in 2015, a conversation that happened in the public eye partially via music. Suddenly, record labels were using mental health as a selling point, musicians would 'open up' about depression or anxiety, and stigma was, according to music, a problem to be tackled and soon to be of the past. There can be no doubt that emo fans to some degree helped to prompt this drive by talking about it all, in an unfiltered way.

Cassie might have spent most of her time as a teen buried away talking to other My Chemical Romance fans on MySpace and forums, but the other fans, the culture, the feelings and lyrics helped her return to her days, slowly, surely and with more defiance than she'd otherwise have been able to muster. She was in college in southern Ohio when the band's final album, *Danger Days*, was about to be released. Cryptic clues were left on the internet that signalled a total change from the gothic glamour of older albums: ray-guns, drones, the band's rebrand as the rebellious 'Killjoys'. Everything was primary colours, bold, an explosion of treacherous pop with clean punk guitars. After pulling themselves through *The Black Parade*, an album created during a period of extremely poor mental health for the band, prompting a total change in the way they worked, they wanted fun. Instead of burrowing away in a house, deliberately trying, mentally and emotionally, to access darkness in order to channel for an overall concept, they went into a studio and wrote quickly. They wanted to party. This album was set in a futuristic 2019 during 'The Helium Wars', where California is a barren wasteland, and a corporation called Better Living Industries control everything and try to wipe out all colour and erase every last emotion.

Ahead of that album, Cassie hadn't wanted to leave her dorm room. Every night she was struggling to sleep, tossing and turning, distressed. Her anxiety, caught in a perpetuating cycle, made her feel she couldn't leave. She couldn't step outside her door. Her room became a cage.

We came to party, kill the party tonight.

'So, I created a Killjoy character. I'd put on my red fake leather jacket and paint my whole face like Gerard did and it would give me the armour I needed to make me want to step outside. It was protective when I was feeling alone because I was absolutely alone in college until my junior year. You know that one picture of Gerard where he's got the make-up on that looks like scratches on his face?' she asks me. I say yes, from the *Three Cheers for Sweet Revenge* album. In the photo, Way is almost zombie-like, a creature either dead post-scrap or injured but fiercely hanging on.

For every time that they want to count you out / Use your voice every single time you open up your mouth.

'One day I did that and came back to my dorm room and one of the girls on my floor said, 'Who did this to you, Cassie?' She was so mad and ready to beat someone's ass because she thought I was getting bullied. I was like, "It's make-up!"' Cassie kept going outside whenever she could and continued through her college course.

I can't slow down / I won't be waiting for you / I can't stop now / Because I'm dancing.

When My Chemical Romance broke up in 2013 Cassie wrote an Instagram caption to accompany photos of her meeting the band over the years. It read: 'Thank you, #MCR. Thank you for grabbing me by the shoulders when I was fourteen and convincing me not to throw my life away. For allowing me to be a part of something larger than myself and larger than most people will ever understand. For giving me something to believe in so violently that sometimes it hurt, but most often it lit fire inside of me to want to change the world with you. For a place to find comfort when nothing felt like home.'

Interviews with girls after the signing bench at Slam Dunk Festival, Leeds, 2018

Lizzie, 18

My heart was racing, I was trying to think of things to say to them that they hadn't heard before. If I met them I'd like to be remembered rather than just another one of them fans that says, 'I love you, you're my favourite'. So I complimented them, tried to…I don't know! When you meet them your mind goes blank and you just forget everything that you wanted to say so mostly I was trying to tell myself to remember things. I don't have any words for it: I feel like I could die happy.

Megan, 18

I'm shaking! I feel like it wasn't real. It'll cement itself in ten minutes time. They were very, very polite – I didn't know how I expected them to be. If they were rude, it'd crush ya! For old times' sake. They were your life, so to have that ruined… They weren't like that though. They made you feel like they had time for you, even though they've got people for miles.

Hannah, 18

They're obviously a massive band now so you understand they've got to go through protocols and stuff – it felt a bit impersonal... But I love them, I love all of them. I'm so excited, I'm so excited, I'm so excited! The singer's been my lock screen since I was twelve. I've seen them in concert but it's not the same as seeing them in person, you know what I mean? They're real people! They're real. It grounds you. But he was on his phone while he was talking to you; he's so rude. He didn't look interested at all, which was very sad. [screams] He's a diva! But I've got his autograph so it's fine. I'm gonna frame it! On my wall!

Penny, 18

When you've seen them behind a screen for so long it's nice to know that they're actually real. It's nice to solidify that. It brings you back down to earth in a weird way. They look exactly how I thought they would. But I felt like I shouldn't have been talking to him when he's on his phone? I guess you can't expect it to be personal when there's so many people – look how long that queue is, how long that'd take. Management have probably told them to do it.

Daniela, 17

I really wanted them to compliment my hair – and they did. I was trying to think of what to say that'd make them say something nice back to me.

Kirsty, 20

I need a beer! I was nervous because some bands are a bit dickish. It's always when you look up to people, you don't want them to be dicks so that's great. We just talked about random shit. I'm gonna go get a pint, and I'm gonna never wash this tie, ever! Signed it. I'm never undoing that.

Devon, 18

[sobbing] I did expect to cry, I'm a very emotional person. I just wanted to say thank you and just…just…know that they appreciate me being a fan. I started crying as soon as I saw them, I didn't even have the chance to get any words out. They were asking me if I was OK because I was crying and they were telling me not to cry, which was just really nice. You weren't allowed to take selfies, which is really upsetting because I really wanted to get a photo with them. I got something signed by them so I have something of theirs to keep. It's because it takes too long or something but I am really, really upset because I wanted to get a picture with them.

Claudia, 18

I got my arms signed, Justin got a whole arm to himself. I was bossing them, telling them, 'you sign that arm, *you* sign that arm'. God, I feel great.

Rosie, 16

It's like someone took a picture of them and copied and pasted it into real life. It was just how you expected them to be. I am the shyest person ever and I'm so proud.

Hannah, 14

They said that 'it means a lot that you've actually come'. That's the most important part of being a fan to be honest. Knowing that they really care about your welfare – not just 'oh you're just another fan, goodbye, I don't care about you'. Knowing that they're actually there and they'll listen to you.

4

LADY GAGA WILL SEE YOU NOW

For aura is tied to his presence; there can be no replica of it.
    – Walter Benjamin, *The Work of Art in an Age of Mechanical Reproduction*

We have this umbilical cord that I don't want to cut, ever. I don't feel that they suck me dry... They are part of my person, they are so much of my person.
    – Lady Gaga on her fans, *Rolling Stone*, 2011

If eyes are the window to the soul, is to stare into those of a famous musician, from six inches away, to experience their pure essence? Say that musician is one of the most beloved in the world; one of the most recognisable faces on the planet. Say it's Lady Gaga. Have you felt Stefani Joanne Angelina Germanotta, the person, unfiltered and uncensored, a beyond-3D experience? Have you witnessed her spirit? More so than the vast majority of pop stars, Gaga's connection with her followers inspires them to meet her in person.

Many fans notice the eyes when meeting her. 'You can't look her in her eyes for more than two seconds because if you do it, you will die,' says Sara. The Italian fan met Gaga as an eighteenth birthday present a few years ago; the meet-and-greet ticket was bought by her parents. She can't forget those eyes and talks about them with a hushed and gushing tone, her breath so urgent I can hear a fog of sorts around her phone mouthpiece. 'Her gaze, it's crazy. She's like a goddess, a doll.' These two descriptors are different to the point of contradiction – one full of life, the other powerless, either an almighty angel or a walking-talking marionette or figurine. Whether celestial or manufactured, it is clear. Lady Gaga does not possess an ordinary body.

Sara continues: 'It happened in the moment after I took the picture; we both looked at each other. Deep *into* the eyes. She wore sunglasses but I could see her eyes underneath and they stunned me…so beautiful.' How she saw Gaga's eyes clearly enough to be stunned through dark lenses is questionable, but testament to her belief in their power over her.

There's heated discussion within the 'Little Monsters' – the name Gaga gave her fandom in 2010 – over what colour they are. Some who have met her say hazel, others green-blue, some more grey, bright and flashing like the Greek goddess Athena, while some insist they're gold. Like an engine oil spill or an opal, the pigment looks different in every photograph of her. The colour disappears – it eludes capture. But can you even trust a reproduction anyway, particularly for the mass media and possibly heavily retouched? All fans can do is speculate. Most of them will never know the real colour of Lady Gaga's eyes because they'll never look keenly into them up close.

Sara tried to locate their exact hue when she had her photo taken with

Gaga but the glasses were too dark. In the picture, they are wrapped around each other: Gaga sitting on a leather couch with Sara on its right arm, Gaga seemingly allowing Sara to sweep her up and pull her left leg into them both. In her bizarre glasses and black and nude catsuit, with long, light brown waved hair, Gaga looks like halfway between some sort of crazed bug and a sixties cult leader. Sara chose to wear a long loose white blouse that day and, with the sweeping white curtain behind them, it looks as though Sara has entered a sect. During the Q&A session with Gaga, which was included as part of the experience, Sara had better luck: the sunglasses were removed. 'They were deep green,' Sara says, sure.

What's enchanting is that if Gaga's eyes do change with the light and the specific day, fans will see differently. They'll never agree. An incomplete list of what struck fans when considering the question 'What was the first thing you noticed about Gaga when you met her up close?': *How soft her skin looked; how drunk she was (after a show); how huge her hair was; how good she smelled – even though she was sweaty as fuck!; how fragile her little body actually is under all that art; when we were face to face I noticed all her veins showing on her chest; how soft her lips were, because she kissed me and hugged me too; her smell and actually seeing her peace tattoo on her, I was like, oh my life, this is actually her; how she smelt, like a sweet smell between perfume and hairspray.*

What they can't believe is that Lady Gaga's body exists in their world. Ordinarily of course their two worlds are separate, and will rarely collide except in the case of a chance or organised meeting. They are overwhelmed by her physical form, the fleshy reality of her. It's the one part they haven't had access to yet, because Gaga puts so much else out there for her fans. Everything a fan knows of a musician's image until they meet is two-dimensional – endless photos, music videos, GIFs, interviews. The closest they usually get to experiencing her body is at the front of a show, and that's often from far away – too far to notice textures or pores or wrinkles or to smell a trace of her favourite Thierry Mugler Womanity perfume. A star of Gaga's stature predominantly plays stadium gigs – if you're watching her at an arena, you're probably seeing the show on a big screen. Yes, it's the action as it happens, but the sweat on her brow is just a Tetris block of digital pixels. There's nothing to be gleaned that isn't already known.

As one Gaga fan found, there's the full realisation (which could be applied to any fan talking about meeting their idol): 'She's not a poster, she's a person'. It's a paradox that we know a person exists away from their photograph, or an interview, or a documentary about them, but we don't *know* it without seeing them in the flesh. 'I just wanted to know that she's *real*,' Kirsty, nineteen, from London, told me. 'You know she's real already, in a way. But I need to know that for myself, having followed her over the years, by seeing her in person.'

Musicians do let us know, in hints. Any closenesses they give us is a performance of intimacy – the sighs on their records, their whispers into microphones, their confessional tweets. Britney does a video tour of her house as her children mess about, Adele posts screen-grabs of her text conversations with her best friends, Gerard Way shares photos of him and his wife on their anniversary. It's the same way we use the internet but with an added awareness that their audience is larger and what they say will be screen-grabbed and saved and reposted; their emotions will live forever.

Being subject to that isn't special. Traces of corporeality are what make real intimacy. After a break-up you draw your ex's jumper to you, and smell sandalwood and what you came to know as their family smell, and it makes your own body react. Someone with the same cologne as someone you loved passes on a tube stairway. It shocks you, your gut pangs, pain bleeds from your throat involuntarily making a noise. It's the tiny parts of someone's body that you find curious and eventually endearing – a little scar under someone's lip, the curvature of their ear.

So it makes sense that people – young women, certainly – have wanted to interact with the bodies of their favourite artists since the beginning of pop and rock history. In 1956, fifteen-year-old Kathy Campbell was taken backstage at the Florida Theater in Jacksonville after an Elvis show she'd been to with three of her female friends. She got to see his swinging hips up close and when she pulled near to him for a photograph, he lightly kissed her on the cheek. 'You can tell from the picture that he was more concerned about being photographed than kissing me. But I didn't wash my cheek for over a week,' Kathy told the Official Elvis Presley Fan Club. In 2000, at the peak of *NSYNC's fame, Justin Timberlake had breakfast at a New York radio station. The hosts put his half-eaten French toast on sale online and a fan, Kathy Summers, bought it for $1,025. 'I'll probably freeze-dry it, then seal it…then put it on my dresser,' she told *Entertainment Weekly*. In 2004, an online auction for some chewing gum apparently masticated in the mouth of gum-lover Britney Spears reached $14,000. In any given fan group on Facebook you'll see people who worship the items they've gathered from their favourite musician – Shakira, the Spice Girls, Courtney Love – and will often proudly say they haven't washed the stuff, not just because of the smell, but due to the closeness to the traces of corporeality. It reminds me of the way people have historically revered the Shroud of Turin, a cloth supposedly bearing the negative image of Jesus. Even Gaga herself, at the time a huge Michael Jackson fan, said in 2016 that she had 400 pieces of his wardrobe, promising to archive and care for them in a temperature-controlled room, to preserve them for future generations.

Clearly then, Gaga understands the importance of the artist's body to a fan. The Gaga body has always been central to Gaga, the concept: she's a living, breathing performance-art piece of wonder and revulsion. Her costumes – the meat dress, the white yeti outfit, the spiky inflatable dress, emerging from a giant egg at the 2011 Grammys or arriving on a unicorn at the American Music Awards – have been part of her statement on celebrity culture (that pop culture is hilarious and theatrical but also traps stars – by dressing absurdly, she felt she had power over her image). In the memorable video for 'Paparazzi', she's thrown off a balcony by her lover. In a wheelchair and wearing a red jewelled neck brace, she is handed two walking sticks that attach to her metallic body. Media observers and the public alike questioned her gender near the beginning of her career, imagining which body parts she possessed (the 'Telephone' video addressed the latter of those queries, featuring an imprisoned Gaga stripped naked as guards say, "I told you she didn't have a dick"). And she is one of the greatest living pop performers, singing and dancing to a tremendously impressive level live. Of course fans would especially want to witness the body in action; more so when she encourages it by letting them engage with it through her performance art.

When Gaga met her fans early in her career, she'd let them grab her boobs or she'd sit on their heads. In 2010, she nominated these fans to *V*

Magazine, as embodying the 'new fan', and thousands sent in photos of themselves dressed as her in response to a call-out the magazine posted; the most physically grotesque or beautiful were picked to be featured in the magazine. In Tokyo in 2013 she wore a dress that was made from fan gifts. She has a Little Monsters tattoo on her skin in homage to them, just as they have Gaga tattoos on their skin. Even when she discovered thirty-five fans camped out in her garage via her security camera, she shared the rest of her Thanksgiving feast with them. She even tweeted that she found it funny and that she loved them (also tweeting that she had been creeping around naked eating leftovers when she found them). By her embracing her fans in real life, and inviting them to experience the bodily alongside her, her own body becomes even more prized because the possibility of intimacy is there.

Fan scholar Allyson Gross has written about how we construct ideas of musicians based on our understanding of their personality, likes, dislikes and what we know for a fact they are doing. 'All of those pieces of information collapse into the body,' she tells me. So much of our relationship with a musician is imagined. We imagine what they might say to *this sort of comment*, or *in this situation*. We do this to match the real Gaga up with the Gaga we have in our heads. 'Often fans think that when the artist is *there*, that is the most *them* they can be. No matter what I imagine them to be, no matter what I project upon them and however I envision them in my mind, that stems from this body, this source, this person. Meeting them can feel like magic.' If fandom is about piecing together parts to make meaning, then meeting the source of those parts makes the most sense. Of all artforms, it makes sense that it's with music we most want the person. Music is personality-driven, artist-made and is delivered emotionally with the musician's own body.

It's one thing to witness the body of Gaga in performance. But fans want to know how she is reacting in real time to stimuli, particularly when that stimulus is the fans. What's paradoxical about this is that the Gaga fans I spoke to want to prove she's 'just normal, down to earth' but also say she's otherworldly, extraordinary – more than normal. Fans kept repeating the word 'aura' but were unable to elaborate much further. This aura couldn't possibly be captured in GIFs of Gaga or anywhere online, through a screen. An aura only emerges when someone is there to adore it and properly witness it. It is the ultimate prize for people who have followed their 'Mother Monster' and have pledged allegiance to her. To see her in reality is to see the true and full manifestation of the Mother, to see the goddess in all her cyborg strangeness and splendour, to bask in her aura.

After a few years of loving Gaga, it was time for Laura, twenty-two, to meet her. A lesbian from Amsterdam, with a trumpet tattoo inked onto her arm, identical to Gaga's, she has a calm and warm demeanour about her. Laura's story of meeting Gaga is magical, with a sense of the fate that can come from the crazy journeys fans take to try to meet their idols. She and her friend saw Lady Starlight, one of Gaga's best friends and collaborators, in the street. 'She said to us, "I've been completely lost for three hours in Amsterdam, my phone is not working, I have no money, I can't find my hotel." The whole crew were so worried about her.' So they hired her a cab and helped her across the city. There was a slippage in reality, it seemed. They were in Gaga's world, given a special look into it. She gave Laura and her friend a tip-off: that Lady Gaga would be out of a specific hotel at a certain time, after the Haus of Gaga (Gaga's creative team and close points of contact) left, to throw off some of the fans. Laura stood under the stars for hours outside that hotel sipping the hot chocolate that Gaga had the hotel staff bring out. All of a sudden, with no warning, Gaga emerged through the hotel doors. Laura knew right then that Starlight had told Gaga about her because when Gaga came out she went straight to Laura's yellow hat, the same hat she had been wearing for the duration of this secret mission. It was *meant to be*. 'She walked out and she looked straight at me and I could feel that and I was just…done,' says Laura.

'I didn't say a word to her, not anything. But I felt like my life changed at that moment. It was like she inspired me. It made me see in that moment who the Real Me was, the Real Me that I'd lost. I could feel it. I realised that I wasn't close to who I really am, but saw suddenly who that person is. Now I'm getting closer to who that is, I know that's the goal. It's very spiritual, I think.'

Sara had a similar experience. 'Just with a look, she told me everything. It said: I know how you feel. It's her vibes. It was almost religious.'

If Gaga is one of those artists who has built a career of saying 'I accept you and encourage you to be everything you're scared to be but know you are,' meeting her, for fans, can feel like returning to their maker.

Whatever Laura saw in Gaga's eyes as they looked into hers, in that moment it triggered something inside her.

On this occasion, paparazzi were there as well as other fans, and Gaga danced around like a wild thing, playing to everyone, moving her body to please the camera. On the internet for all to see is a picture of Laura's grinning head right by Gaga's perky latexed behind. How many fans can say they've got a photo of their religious experience (Gaga's butt)?

The Langham hotel in London is a place of total exclusivity. A single night with your head on one of their silk pillows can cost almost as much as the average person's monthly rent in the capital. Renowned as Europe's 'first grand hotel', its stately exterior of seven floors of yellow brick delighted Victorian high society and later Winston Churchill and Princess Diana. Its magnificent entrance is held up by tall pillars, and those who parade out do so with an enormous chandelier overhead – flags and slim trees standing to attention – and down four steps to an open area of paved street, with London ready to welcome them. Ever-present male hotel concierge staff in grey suits and black top hats lend an official mood to it all.

When in London, Gaga will always stay at The Langham. This is common knowledge within the fandom. The cordoned-off pavement area for her to perform as she wants becomes a sanctioned space, and fans line along it and prepare to potentially see her leave. All it takes to witness this is making the effort to do so – and a bit of luck.

Olivia goes to wait outside The Langham every time Gaga is in the country and has done for years. She talks about Gaga nourishing the fans' bodies as they wait for her, always sending down food when they stand outside. 'One time years ago she literally sent out a candy cart,' she says. 'The last time, she didn't come down because she was in so much pain, about to cancel the tour, but sent us all down little cups of hot chocolate that had the hotel name on. She doesn't have to do that. It's our choice to stand there. She doesn't owe us anything. And I think that's really, really sweet of her.' The fans see this as Gaga acknowledging them and showing she's grateful for them even on days she is too busy to come down and interact.

The street is ordinarily just a London pathway but Gaga turns up and, as with all things that come into contact with her, it becomes something meaningful to them. There's an unspoken contract between Gaga and her Little Monsters – that she will always acknowledge them wherever she goes, making a space like this, and it happens in hotels all across the world. Gaga is unusual: many A-list artists don't want this to happen, and will go to great lengths to hide where they are.

There are differences, even in Gaga fandom, around how much contact fans want. They're embodied in Laura and her other Gaga fan friend, Ofry. The twenty-six-year-old from Israel is the polar opposite to her Amsterdam-based friend, despite their both having a love for the singer. Ofry is older than Laura. She is intense and to the point. She lives her life dedicated to Gaga in every sense of the word. Being a live-at-home student and working multiple jobs means every penny she makes goes to getting physically closer to Gaga.

For Laura, meeting Gaga once was enough, while for Ofry there is no 'enough'. She went all the way to America for the VMAs when Gaga was nominated for an award but Gaga wasn't there to receive it; she was away working on tour. 'I was like, "fuck you", I went all this way and paid for flights and hotels,' she laughs bitterly.

Laura wouldn't pay for a meet and greet – the price of one or two months' living costs – but Ofry doesn't mind. Anything, in her book, is worth it to meet Gaga. There are marginally more fans in agreement with Laura than with Ofry. 'If you try to stop her in public I feel like that's going to be a bit more special because she actually chose to stop and go over, and if that's outside a hotel that's you out of a hundred or so people,' says Millie, twenty-one, from Liverpool. Nineteen-year-old Kirsty from London, who met Gaga outside The Langham, agrees: 'I wouldn't do a meet and greet because it's a lot of money and it's a group picture which is...*fine*...but I feel like it was a lot more organic the way I met her'. It's not uncommon to have a mixture of Little Monsters and elite members of the public at meet and greets, much to the disdain of the real fans. Olivia says, 'There was a couple in my meet and greet who were stuck up and middle-aged, dressed fancy. They're flashing the cash, asking silly questions, not really invested.'

That said, most fans who have had both an 'organic' meet and a paid-for one would choose a paid-for one if money was no object. Despite all her transformative experiences at The Langham, Olivia preferred her paid meet and greet. In an arrangement like this, even the set-up itself can feel holy. 'For every respectful, chilled-out fan outside a hotel, there are people screaming, pushing, not acting humane and just being completely weird about it,' she says. 'As sad as it is to say, money can buy an experience that is better than that. My meet and greet was the most calm and lovely environment; she was sat on a stool and had a candle lit next to her, everyone was quiet, everyone was calm, we took it in turns to speak, it was civilised.'

Jennifer Walker, a music journalist for *Kerrang!*, has run the rock magazine's signing tent at festivals for years and has observed that many of the more timid girl rock fans prefer the controlled nature of an official signing. 'If you see someone in a band in the street it can be quite scary to approach them and hold a conversation, whereas here you know all you've got to do is stand in this line, go up and worst comes to worst you can walk along and they can sign something for you. There's no pressure. Going up in public or waiting around with only a couple of girls after a show, that would take an element of confidence.' It's at these controlled signings that you really see the full spectrum of fans' personalities and responses to seeing a favourite musician: tears, overbearing forwardness, hugs, awkward handshakes, the lot. You can watch the people go before you; you know what to expect, and how long the interaction will go on for.

Laura edited Ofry's Gaga picture taken in 2018, during the *Joanne* tour, so that instead of the group shot that was actually taken by an official photographer, it looks like the pair of them, side by side, touching. It's only when you zoom in you can see where their two bodies have been cut-and-pasted together. It looks legitimate, but it doesn't have true intimacy; it's make-believe, pretend, as big a leap as someone thinking because they met their idol once, they're practically joined. It's the closest thing to a friendly photo that someone who's paid to meet another human being can get.

Because intimacy is such a desired goal, competition between fans who want to meet an artist is high. It is perhaps the most contentious and touchy area of debate. Paid meet and greets mean those who can afford it get to meet their idol more often. You also become a much more visible fan within the fandom if you've met your star – meeting them is the nearest thing you can do to being a main or super fan. The frequency with which you get access can, very rarely, even mean they'll know you. Ofry speaks of her rivalry, rolling her large eyes. 'I have a guy from here, in Israel, who always competes with me. He was supposed to go to nine shows of the *Joanne* tour and he also got a meet and greet two days before me just so he could meet her before me. It's annoying as fuck. Now I bought a ticket for the Vegas show and he bought four! Just to get closer than me. Dude!'

However, it doesn't matter if you're sipping a hot chocolate in the dark outside The Langham or next to a posh couple out for an amusing evening (because why not?), you can't ever predict what happens in those minutes or seconds. You can't guarantee you'll be pleased with what happens. You don't know exactly how she'll act or the quality of the interaction. You know absolutely nothing. For once in your fan life, you have lost control entirely of the outcome. It's partly why fans freak out when they're confronted with the idol. At least Gaga, unlike so many other artists, is known to appreciate the lack of control and make up for it by constantly projecting her aura, a presence, into the moment, always performing up to the fans' expectations.

Allyson Gross got to meet her favourite musician completely by chance, seeing him walk across the street when she was sitting in a café. 'I felt like my organs were shutting down,' she tells me, grinning. 'It's like running into a fictional character in the street – one that you wrote! I know on the outside I looked fine, but I was writing something and I lost motor function because it was such a strange occurrence. I was glad I had a photo because otherwise I absolutely would've thought I'd hallucinated.' Even Sara, who knew she was going to meet Gaga, lost everything she had planned to say in her head: 'We could ask her anything we wanted to. And I didn't ask her anything... I was crying too much, really too much, I couldn't even talk. When we took the photo the only thing I could say was "I love you, you're my hero, thank you." That was the only thing I said to her. She looked at me in the eyes and said, "Thank you, I love you too," and goodbye. So that's it.'

Everyone has different reasons for wanting to meet their idol and many can't articulate them succinctly. Sometimes these impulses are unconscious, sometimes the fan is simply following what everyone else wants to do. Many describe meeting them as the logical next step having followed the artist and having spent increasing amounts of time and money on them, going to shows and buying merchandise.

For Olivia, when she was thirteen she was 'immature' and mostly wanted a selfie with Gaga, but by seventeen it was paramount to her that they have a conversation. That was always the aim of meeting her, which she did frequently, both at meet and greets and at The Langham. Continually fans want to thank her in person for the music, but also to thank her for saving their life – or something equally dramatic. 'Thank you for saving me' is repeated again and again by girls in interviews I conduct. Girls who had eating disorders, were depressed or had family who were sick or had died, or are lesbian, bi, queer or trans, all say she gave them strength, often the confidence to come out.

Standing in front of Gaga, they find a maternal safe space. People have always stood in front of a sacred person who is considered to have curative powers, and to some extent that 'healing touch' is found in Gaga. They leave feeling that what happened was a serious breakthrough or cathartic moment in their own personal healing narrative.

These aren't stories of the imagination anymore. Not daydreams about what Gaga would do if you met, how she would laugh at your joke or stroke your hair and thank you for being a fan. These are tales made from glances, skin, sweat and bone.

Only fans 'knew' this but Lady Gaga was not content. She smiled in pictures. She tweeted things about loving her Little Monsters. And still – this was not the *real* Gaga anymore, not at the end of 2017 into 2018, according to her fans. She was not 'being herself'. The fans know the real Gaga because they've met her multiple times and have processed all the pieces of information from others that have met her. She was not matching up to the 'truth' of her that they'd created. Something had changed in the way she carried her body, they said; it was just something they *felt* from her, something non-verbal they couldn't express. Perhaps she was depressed, being controlled, something more than just 'a bad day' or week or month; they had tens, hundreds of in-person accounts to verify this, to the point it became common fan knowledge, practically canon. Journalists, the general public and casual fans would never have known this because they saw her output: a polished exterior. All of the fans I speak to, however, say, with a weary sigh or expression, that she was not happy.

Ofry said it'd gone as far as Gaga no longer enjoying the process of taking pictures with Little Monsters outside hotels, even 'running away from fans'. 'I think there are people in her life that are making her like this, [her ex-boyfriend] Taylor and her father treated her so bad, and I think she needs to rest and pull herself back together to what she was. Ever since Taylor broke her heart, she doesn't trust in people anymore. I think she lost faith in people, even her fans. The fans have seen she doesn't feel the same love that she used to. That's really sad. And I wish I could talk to her about this but I can't.'

Laura added, 'She is not true to herself at this current moment. After Taylor, she got back to family. And her family is not very healthy so when she starts listening to them, she gets depressed because she's not being herself. What's happening at the moment made her illness worse. Her dad hates a lot of things about her being famous so he would say that he doesn't want her to be hugged or anything, he's a big influence on her at the moment.'

Then, the *Joanne* tour meet and greets in 2018 were different. The first thing fans noticed was her pain. The body, which was so conditioned, firm, lustrous – bona fide celebrity skin – was not as it should have been. Millie from Liverpool said, 'Her eyes looked vacant, it was strange. I don't know if it was because she wasn't feeling well but she kept looking like she was about to burst out crying.'

All the fans clocked it, and any who didn't were prepared for it after others had flagged it in the fan groups. 'Everyone said the same thing,' said Millie. 'At first we all thought she was stoned or something because her eyes were heavy. She looked cold and tired. We knew she probably wasn't feeling well so we all felt bad.' Bad for demanding her time, her engagement with them, and uncomfortably bad to see their poor Gaga's body not as it should be.

Olivia was there at the very last show before the rest of the *Joanne* run was cancelled. 'I'm even more humbled and grateful because our meet and greet was the last one of this tour and when I was in there, when she was talking, I had a suspicion that she was high. She was listening intently, she was answering everyone, she was talking, putting her full effort into it, she was herself. But I could tell looking at her and listening to her – because I *know* her – that she was high and what made me sad was because I was like, OK, if she's high what does that mean: she's in pain, and then what happens? The whole fucking tour gets cancelled. And it was like, I *knew* it was coming.'

And it was. On Twitter, Gaga wrote, 'I'm so devastated I don't know how to describe it. All I know is that if I don't do this, I am not standing by the words or meaning of my music. My medical team is supporting the decision for me to recover at home. We're cancelling the last 10 shows of my *Joanne* World Tour...'

The documentary *Lady Gaga: Five Foot Two* follows Gaga around the recording of and promotion for *Joanne*, and centres around the shocking strength and fragility of her body, even when it's perhaps not meaning to. It opens with the body being lifted, slowly by a crane, like an angel to be put on the top of an invisible tree. Her frame is capable of incredible acts – dancing for hours, physical acting, messing around in the studio while rehearsing vocals. At one point, forty-one minutes in, Gaga's lying down and weeping into a white towel. The right side of her body is in spasm and she has an ice pack on her neck; her face, she says, even hurts. 'I don't even know what childbirth will be like. If I can. I know I think I can get pregnant, I just don't know what my hips are going to do? I don't fucking know,' she says, distraught, as a masseuse kneads her face. The next scene moves on to her working out, her body so present, small and compact. And yet multiple times her body becomes seriously inflamed or a symptom flares as a result of her illness: fibromyalgia. Her body is, at times and aggressively when it comes, aflame. This hurts the fans too: emotionally, even physically, when it makes them cry, or even feel her pain.

Gaga's pain was severe during the *Joanne* tour, and the fans were heartbroken, first at knowing this, secondly and twice as violently when she cancelled the rest of the tour. Ofry didn't leave her Gaga-themed bedroom for a week. She stayed in there and sulked. 'I had worked so hard and waited so long for this, and now she's just cancelled it? Just like this? I'm so done, I'm so done.' When I suggested that fans had received refunds she replied, annoyed at how blatantly obvious it was, 'Money? It's not about the money!'

Meet and greets are lifeblood to Gaga fans, and Gaga had been doing them in some capacity since the beginning, so the thought of her stopping this seemed unreasonable to many. They had become an essential, irreplaceable part of being a Gaga fan. Even if you didn't go, you knew one day you could. You knew that other people in the fandom were going to them, which is a comfort in itself, because it means *someone* is there with her, and it means the collection of more knowledge. Even if it's just what Gaga is wearing that day, the intelligence keeps expanding. But at this point there was a real question to be asked – will meet and greets continue? She is, after all, a performer, a musician. It's not a necessity to meet your fans.

'You see a lot of people saying, don't be sad about this show being cancelled, there will be other tours, but I'm at a point where I'm like, will there?' says Olivia. 'It's on Gaga's track record that she's so intense with touring she completely shuts off in terms of taking care of herself. I feel like this is the point she's thinking that, and being like, "shit, I really need to take care of myself".' For all her frustration, Ofry wouldn't be put off by a lack of meet and greets: she'll find her in real life. 'I'll just go all the way to the States and wait outside her house and try, just try. Over and over again.' Something that Ofry had wanted but not received from Gaga was a hug. The physical interaction would never happen, not when her body was in the state it was.

This frailty serves as a reminder that these people that fans love so much are human beings, who get ill, hurt, are in pain, cry, and eventually will die just like the rest of us. Justin Bieber famously cancelled all future meet and greets in 2016 for the *Purpose* tour after admitting to fans that he finds them 'draining'. He said, 'I end up…filled with so much of other people's spiritual energy…I always leave feeling mentally and emotionally exhausted to the point of depression.' If your artist stops doing meet and greets when they previously did, you weigh up in your mind if you find this acceptable. Some were furious at Bieber for cancelling, despite loving him.

Laura, with her holistic view of fandom, understands why Bieber stopped. 'Everyone was really pissed. I thought it was logical because, first of all, girls try and touch and kiss him and that's not OK and, second of all, lots of people have just come straight off a plane, haven't showered for days, are in really gross clothes, and then try to hug you – I get it, at some point, you'd just be like, "I'm done".' Some fans don't admit that their energy can be a drain on the physical, emotional and mental health of an artist. Some clearly do; there's an inherent respect for Gaga's body from her fans, a need to protect the aura and her health. 'I understand because I am hyper-sensitive. If those people also feel like they *need* you that is a big pressure. A lot of people come to you and say "you saved my life" and that would be a heavy thing I think.' Despite this being said, Laura goes on to say that 'all' she wants from Gaga is to feel her soul.

'I think a lot of other people don't love themselves, and they want confirmation from Gaga that they are good enough and Gaga is probably the only one in their lives that really voices that,' says Laura. 'So I think that's what a lot of people are really looking for: that she looks into your eyes and says "You're good enough". That's what has always been Gaga's message, right? I always got your back; if nobody believes in you I will. I think Gaga fans are always looking for who they really are, that's what I'm seeing from everybody.' She references the people in the fan Facebook group she's in: 'All those forty-year-old women, they're still married with kids but they're still looking for and struggling with who they really are'. Laura is only young, but she's learning, and getting very wise.

Now feels like a time when we desire, more strongly, unmediated experiences with other human beings, real connection. For many fans, Gaga's illness didn't signal a natural end to that connection – the ultimate conclusion of being a fan – they wanted more closeness. Because what happens once you've had everything you wanted: you've seen the aura, and it was glistening, and you already know the colour of Gaga's eyes – what then?

Fans would still want to be a special fan, to be recognised. Once upon a time, Ofry threw a Mother Monster necklace onstage and Gaga took it away with her. When she met her much later, she got Gaga to sign her arm – which she would turn into a tattoo immediately after the meet and greet, to have a piece of Gaga on her forever – and she asked Gaga: do you still have the necklace? Gaga was shocked and said that she certainly did and that she genuinely loved it and thanks again for making it for her. Ofry was delighted but cynical ('I was like, "yah, right!"'). Then in 2018 she was captured wearing it. Ofry watched the video over and over. There it was: really, her necklace, around Gaga's neck, sitting there, warm on her skin. She'd taken a piece of Ofry away with her and it was on her body. Who – who else – could say this?

A few days later Ofry and Laura would be in Venice with other Gaga fans for the premiere of *A Star Is Born*, her new film in which she plays a talented but unknown young musician who becomes a megastar. Ofry didn't get to look her in the eyes this time, but she did get to the front of the red carpet to take photographs of Gaga from very close up, just behind. Gaga was in a feathery baby-pink dress, with her blonde hair piled up on her head and greased back – you can see the texture of her hair in the photos, Ofry was that close, and the skin of her neck looks almost powdered in her picture. It is bare and glowing. In the breeze some of the pink feathers are flying back and grazing her softly.

'I wish I could see her more,' Ofry mused, from her bedroom, floor to ceiling in Gaga posters and merchandise. 'Do you want to be friends with her?' I asked. 'Absolutely. If I was part of the Haus of Gaga I wouldn't let anyone hurt her.' But even the love of a fan can't stop Gaga's body from burning.

Melissa Auf der Maur, Hole and The Smashing Pumpkins bassist, and solo artist, on women idols

I was the shyest person you'd ever meet until I found rock music. I could not speak publicly; in class I was the unbearably shy red-head blushing. It started with Cyndi Lauper. There was a lookalike competition in a mall in Montreal when I was twelve years old. The cool thing is I got my mother to write me a letter – I still have it in one of my old diaries – *Dear whoever my math teacher was, please excuse Melissa out of school after lunch, we're participating in this Cyndi Lauper lookalike contest at the mall.* So she gave me the note but the fact is I went there all by myself. There was just this tiny little girl dressed up as Cyndi who brought herself out of school without her parents, and got on stage and lip-synced. I don't know why I thought that possible, when I couldn't speak in class.

Most of my idols were women, I realised, when I was a kid. Cyndi evolved to Debbie Harry. I've never been boy crazy.

My mother had her own radio show and she was the first female rock disk jockey on the airwaves in Montreal and she raised me on that music. I think I was probably pretty shocked that there were no women. I don't remember that intellectually but the fact that by the time I was going to the record shop at twelve and I could buy a crazy red-headed woman's record called *She's So Unusual* was like nothing I saw in any of my mother's records.

By the time I entered the doom and gloom of my teenage years and realised you're alone it was The Smiths and The Cure and that was all I listened to for a long time. I had a very odd and brief love affair with Rick Astley, and I developed a crush on him and had a poster of him on my wall. I realised it's probably because he looked exactly like me. I had short, cropped new-wave hair, no make-up; most people thought I was a boy.

I was always the biggest fan – every step of my life has been because I was a fan. So I've always been nice to anyone who was a fan of anything I've been a part of. I wrote a PO box to Billy Corgan of Smashing Pumpkins and I ended up joining Hole and the Pumpkins because of it. I have always had no ego, never trying to be cool, I've always said what I love. I love it, I love it, I love it, I love it, I go go go go. And I do it. And it has always resulted in beautiful, great things. So many people who either try to be cool and not say what they love or worse yet don't give the love back to people who love their work, that's not in my make-up. I could never in a million years.

Viv Albertine, The Slits guitarist, solo artist, and writer, on Marc Bolan and David Bowie

Male fans were always about: 'We understand music, it's about the technicality of the music.' They are the status quo. They've made that more important than how you feel about it. It's not about how fast you can play a guitar solo or weird time signatures. They've made it like a bus timetable. They're little anoraks, trainspotters about music. It's trivialised, the way women feel about music.

It was very unusual that I was a mad music fan. I looked my whole life for a girl to follow and couldn't find one. There's probably lots of girls now. Now that women have bisexual or lesbian musicians they can follow, I wonder how that's changed for girls and how they are fans. But I found ones as close as I could get: it was a wake-up to my sexuality to explore it following people like Marc Bolan and David Bowie. I almost felt I could be them. You get it all a bit confused. I fancied Bolan but I think at that age, you don't really realise the difference between fancying and projecting. I could fantasise about meeting Marc Bolan in the street, or Scott Walker, and it wasn't a threatening or frightening fantasy. They were such feminine men, they wore girl's clothes, I could copy it. I could wear Marc Bolan's girls' shoes.

Being a fan was a way of leaving a world which was so dull back then. The only way to have an interesting life then was through a man; marry someone interesting or go out with someone interesting. No girls played in bands, no girls went to rehearsals. None of that happened. We still are quite hobbled in life, so it is a way to transcend the everyday through the musician, which we did to the nth degree when I was young because we didn't have very good lives.

5

SEX & IPHONES & ROCK & ROLL

(I) 'FUCK ME DADDY' (OR, SCREAMING OBSCENITIES AT OBJECTS OF DESIRE)

To assert an active, powerful sexuality by the tens of thousands and to do so in a way calculated to attract maximum attention was more than rebellious. It was, in its own unformulated, dizzy way, revolutionary.
> – Ehrenreich, Hess and Jacobs, 'Beatlemania: Girls Just Want to Have Fun'

Imagine being a celeb & writing a tweet and within 0.5 seconds someone replies with 'CHOKE ME DADDY' no matter what the context of the tweet.
> – Twitter user @lolzdons

In the back of a 20,000-capacity venue that smells like Pepsi and body spray, young girls are shouting PG-13 smut. Fan's faces are as visible five or six people away from you as those you're rubbing shoulders with. The lights from the stage shine on every forehead, cheeks and grin with the same luminosity. It's hard to tell the age of the pair of girls standing next to me. If I were still a teenager I'd know the year group instinctively but once you're into adulthood everyone younger than you becomes about the same age. It's the last day of March 2018, during a Fall Out Boy show at the London O2 Arena, and as if everyone's breaking through into a 'first days of spring' mood – everything's heating up. One of them howls 'Fuck me, Pete!' The other girl laughs and does it too. None of the girls around them notice or at least seem to care.

At the end of the show, I walk out and see these two girls bound over to their mums, who have been watching safely at the back of the show. 'Did you enjoy that, darling?' says one mum, placing a hand on her daughter's bouncing shoulder. 'Weren't they good!' adds the other mum. 'He's so hot,' one girl responds. The mum, clearly used to her nonsense, ignores this.

Pete Wentz of Fall Out Boy is an objectively attractive man. He's also the bassist who outshone the frontman – unheard of – to the point that, as one Fall Out Boy fan tells me, her friends who don't know much about the band think he's the singer. I've interacted with him a few times and seen him up very close, once, our faces not much more than thirty centimetres away from each other, when interviewing him in broad summer daylight. His smile crinkles, his eyes glint hazel and you can almost hear a dozen girls' hearts throbbing, reverberating on the wind. His painfully white teeth are distracting but the real distraction is his face. Unprofessional to say, but to deny it would be absurd. When I was thirteen and obsessed with the band, he was one of my many husbands. I am now in my mid-twenties and he has three children and a current wife and ex-wife, neither of whom are me. Testament to the band's career and Wentz's longevity – ageing like a fine wine, one fan told me – he has continued to be a heartthrob for a new generation of teenage girls.

Conveniently for these new fans, Pete enjoys taking photos of himself and he posts a lot of them on social media; sometimes close-up videos of his face with eyebrow raised or curling a lip to show teeth. Often they're topless shots, showing off the tattoos on his chest. Written underneath his selfies are comments by dozens of his other 'children', chirping like little hens. Calling people 'daddy' or its variant 'zaddy' is an internet joke that got out of hand and became part of popular culture by 2016 – now no longer a reference to your literal sugar daddy or your other half in a sexual real-life relationship, but a meme, a pet name to jokingly refer to older attractive masculine people, especially celebrities. And so, these comments to Pete: 'Dad' 'daddy' 'Shaddy' 'Zaddy' 'father pete' 'still daddy material' 'I AM CRYING THE DADDYCATION IS STRONG TODAY'. Funnier still: 'woah there cowboy', **heavy breathing** w r o w', 'cause of my death: Peter Lewis Kingston Wentz II', 'look at this four course meal', 'SNACKKK', 'I'M PREGNANT'.

The commenters are near-exclusively in their teens, mostly early teens, twelve to fifteen. One sixteen-year-old girl is a daddy commenter. She says most of the time they mean it in a sexual way, but there are also people who post it for 'jokes and trolls' meaning 'sometimes it's hard to tell'. In the way that teens do when a month goes by and they feel full of wisdom and weathered by the world, another lifetime of experience under their belt, she grew out of this endeavour 'ages ago'. She pre-empts the paranoia around the sexualisation of young girls by telling me: 'Adults think it's inappropriate and crazy what kids are saying these days. But honestly it seems like a phase every teen goes through but they grow out of some time or another. Plus, I don't think teens understand it sometimes – I only figured it out a while ago.' Which is to say, they don't necessarily understand the sub/dom context of the word 'daddy', or even really want the sexualised experience. They are not imagining it, or meaning it with any more depth than that of just being attracted to a man.

I started messaging more of the teens who had posted some of these things under Pete's photos. 'No I'd never sexualise Pete, that's not fair,' writes one young girl bluntly. 'It's kind of awkward to just randomly comment things the boys won't ever read…?!' writes a different fan. Another girl tells me, 'I think that it is OK for people to comment on how attractive a "famous" person is, but there is a line with that kind of stuff that has been crossed many times'. I asked her what that line is. 'Just downright saying that they want to have sex with them. When I leave a comment it is usually just a quick "hey, I love you, you're awesome". On one particularly cute selfie of Pete, she had commented 'STRANGLE ME WITH YOUR PHONE CHARGER'.

None of this means that these girls are being overtly sneaky or outright lying. On an individual level they don't want to reveal themselves as a fan who would 'cross the line', but as a part of a stream of comments they've all made together it's clearly acceptable. Each comment is sexual – there's no denying that none of these girls would want their parents, or even me, seeing them and attributing any to them under their real identities – but taken as a mass, the sexual braying feels benign. The conflict within the girls arises from sexualising artists and being personally seen doing so, particularly on an internet where a new generation of teens can protect their privacy with usernames, fan and private accounts. Even at the Fall Out Boy show in London, out in public, mooching around the O2 arena, small groups of girls outside condemned saying similar things or sexualising the artists. But inside some did, and god, is it funny.

Sexuality and music fandom have always been tightly linked, to the point of being inseparable. The same girls who screamed at The Beatles and Elvis, responsible for their rise, could be typing obscenities out to rock bands today. If you were a girl, Beatles fandom meant you were extra stirred up, that your energy was quite particular. Critics and journalists Barbara Ehrenreich, Elizabeth Hess and Gloria Jacobs noted in an essay that while mainstream culture, led by America, became sexualised in the 1960s – counterculture proclaimed that it was socially acceptable to have sex outside marriage, the use of the contraceptive pill became more widespread – teenage girls were still expected to be perfectly pure. 'To abandon control – to scream, faint, dash about in mobs – was, in form if not in conscious intent, to protest the sexual repressiveness, the rigid double standard of female teen culture,' they wrote. In every moment that girls fetishised the bodies of boy bands, they said, girls were one step closer to sexual freedoms – they could vocalise any sexual desire they had in ways they never could before. It just took a crowd of them to feel normal.

The lineage is clear. The Beatles fans mobbed their idols – love, love me do – and newer fans can mob online – fuck me, please – in an update on sexual pack behaviour. Decades ago feminist scholars decided that the teen girl's part in the sexual revolution was buoyed along by boy-band fantasies and fetishising men's bodies. Similar fantasies and fetishisations now happen in a hypersexualised society, where a girl's role is (mercifully) less clear, less defined. It's not a reach to wonder if, in the current climate, fans being openly crude about musicians is, in part, them grappling with freedoms too. Sex talk – from all ages and genders – has become more delicious and aggressive and frequent on the internet but not always meaningful, sometimes utterly meaningless. What does throwing a 'fuck me' at a picture mean, when 300 fans did it first? Fuck who?

Yet female music lovers frequently deny their sexual attraction to musicians. In the past, I was invested, in public at least, in the idea that I was a 'real' fan. Desire was non-existent, or at least unacknowledged until in private or among trusted confidants. With friends, I'd gossip about tabloid shots of Pete Wentz and his new girlfriend nestling into each other on a shopping trip or fan-shot footage of emo band members in homoerotic moments pecking or pawing at each other. Bedroom walls were mosaics of posters cut carefully from magazines – the sort you wouldn't likely find on a straight male's wall. Fewer serious band shots, more solo shots, usually, of lead singers, unbuttoned. These were some of the most intimate and replayable crushes I'll ever have. The most secret. This side of enjoyment was sealed away from older groups of boys who liked the same music, especially from first boyfriends, who would always be music fans too, someone to measure up against. In my internal world, I felt that appreciating the music and appreciating the fantasy of the musician could sit comfortably beside each other, but I knew that one was seen to nullify the other outside of it.

Interviewees were found to repress their sexual enjoyment of music in the research stages of Rosemary Hill's new book. In *Gender, Metal and Sexuality*, Hill argues that while everyone has the ability to enjoy music for music itself, in a similar if not identical way, our subjectivity also affects our enjoyment. As Simone De Beauvoir said of girlhood in *The Second Sex*: 'In a more or less disguised way, her youth is consumed by waiting. She is waiting for Man.' If through girlhood and adolescence we're conditioned to think about securing a man, and if the norms of heterosexuality determine our early lives and relationships, it isn't a surprise that our thoughts and impulses towards musicians, whose music we genuinely love of its own merit, may become affected by those ideas. But to enjoy music in a sexualised way is deemed societally unacceptable, illegitimate – or not serious. 'Why is that to be derided is the important question in my mind. It's treated as if it's second-class fandom and not worth thinking about,' Hill tells me. 'To deny women sexuality as a music lover is problematic and actually quite sexist.'

The debates around whether it's 'problematic' or childish to sexualise a musician only seem to apply to young women whose agency is denied. If neither enjoying the sexual side of music nor simply enjoying the music itself is acknowledged for these fans, what aspect of their fandom is ratified?

Musicians have been marketed as sex symbols for decades: they're hot and they've been sold to us as hot. With the birth of the modern teenager in the sixties came the establishment of teen magazines and music magazines, the former of which, in particular, linked up channels for selling. They featured soft-pornographic centrefolds of musicians and some of the first and most vibrant and considered insights into pop groups. One of the popular titles was literally called *Boyfriend* magazine.

The boy-band format has always insisted that there be something for every girl – each member had their own appeal, rather than just being monolithic entities. Each boy had a distinctive personality, a slightly different haircut, little quirks detailed by the magazines in a gossipy tone. Subsequently there have been The Osmonds, New Kids On The Block, Wham!, Boyz II Men, *NSYNC, Backstreet Boys, Take That, Westlife, Hanson, Jonas Brothers and more. The attraction and marketing of these bands has extended outward from bubblegum pop and been reproduced, directly or sometimes inadvertently or accidentally, in rock and alternative music too: Panic! at the Disco, 5 Seconds of Summer, All Time Low, Black Veil Brides, Sleeping With Sirens, Pierce The Veil. The list is endless. The mechanics are similar in the East Asian music industry, with the global rise of the new boy bands filling the hole that

One Direction left, such as BTS and GOT7, bands where each member is a product in themselves. Tactics to heighten the value of a boy to young amorous girls are employed, from publicly unveiling members, thus increasing excitement and tension, to being able to vote members in or out, instilling a loyalty to a beautiful boy. There is a machine manufacturing desire and doing an excellent job of it. If you look at any of the successful male artists or groups that have thousands, millions of dedicated female followers, not far behind is the suspicion that the pretty looks are a substitution for quality music (not always untrue) and that the only reason women like them is because they're good looking.

Teen mags are one thing. In music magazines, it is rarely openly acknowledged that sexuality could be a legitimate part of any of woman's fan experience. Historically, music mags have been run by mostly male in-house staff understanding music and fandom through their own lens; this has often resulted in a focus on groupies and sex, and a sexualisation of female artists, and even fans. The consequence then is that murmurs of sexuality have been included sparingly and rarely in the work of female music journalists, or the work of female academics. Instances to the contrary are rare. Patti Smith's music writing, for example, often included her sexual response to music. Journalist Ann Powers more recently gave voice to the power of fan sexuality while writing on abuses within the industry. It's significant that now both Hill and another academic, Nancy Baym, in her book on technology and music fandom, choose to acknowledge and commit their own sexual urges within fandom to print. 'It's a risky career move,' Baym told me, 'and I don't know that I would've written this book, using my own fandom experiences with my crushes at the centre of it, if I had not been in the professional situation that I'm in now in my career, where I know that I can give younger, less senior people permission. My choice to do it is an explicit choice to change that conversation. With music journalism it's even riskier because you need access to the musicians so to brand yourself as someone who has crushes on them, that really complicates the professional dynamics.' This is certainly true even if the crushes are in the past. Hill was more personally conflicted when it came to the decision. 'If you say you fancy them you think it undermines you being taken seriously,' she said. 'If you admit it you have to go on and say, "If you think that's not the right way to be a fan you're being sexist".'

I flip through old copies of *M Magazine* on my adult bed to find a quiz. The pages are filled with pictures and posters of musicians, the sort I obviously don't have on my walls anymore, but I did and I had plenty. Some are Valentine's specials that involve talking to rock stars about who they fancy, what their relationships are like, whether they'd have intimate relationships with fans. For tweens, it's a little more tame. 'Who'll make your heart sing this spring?' one quiz reads. The sub-heading: 'Find the guy you're totally in tune with'. Get it? I answer with the band 'Plain White T's' to the question 'You wish your crush would make you a mix CD with songs by…'. The next question is 'Your crush says YOU should pick where to go on your date: You choose…' and I pick 'A rockin' concert'. Next: 'Your crush totally has a cute style. You love that his clothes are so…' and I choose 'Edgy but fun'. Down at the bottom of the quiz my four potential suitors are there, each a pop or rock star. I got 'A hot rocker' and there he is, grinning underneath a heavy side fringe with his beautiful teeth. 'You're a fab fem who loves to have a good time letting loose! A rock star like Pete Wentz will totally complement your wild child ways.'

Rule 34 of the internet: if it exists, there is porn of it. This is a popular saying of questionable origin repeated by non-citable members of message-board communities and commonly associated with grim corners of the internet 4chan members frequent, but nevertheless accurate. Like the internet, fringes of large fandoms will always provide. For any specialist or random interest, there is another fan to link with. For any kink, a family.

While scrolling fan social media feeds and obscure hashtags to glean something different about Fall Out Boy fans, I came to the edge of a fringe. There were profile names – most of private accounts – that seemed peculiar. The same letters 'rp' appeared in hashtags.

On one account, Alice posts a deliberately blurred picture of herself holding her phone from below by her waist. She's half looking down at it through thick-rimmed glasses in a library, all the used books behind her peeling their plastic skins. 'I'm gonna cry I hate school' is overlaid in text.

She has very short hair and tells me she has been toying with different images. She identifies as female but has been questioning that recently, along with most aspects of her world. Mostly she dresses in hoodies to cover up, stay safe. People at her school are 'judgemental assholes' so we don't speak on the phone; she's not used to that. She plays Fall Out Boy and her other favourite bands on loop through her headphones (music isn't allowed in class but she slyly listens since she's sat at a computer all day) and all the while she pretends to be Pete Wentz.

'Pete Wentz' and her closest friends, a mix of real-life mates and internet friends, role-play or 'rp' together. Each acts, via a social media account, as someone from the band's world. Imagine a live-action rock-star movie with two teens typing the script in real time. 'There's usually a quick talk about the basic plot, setting and characters, and then either person can start,' she tells me. The story or conversation 'starts out awkward and dumb, but then both people start to get better and you both accept that it's a pretty dweeby thing to do.'

Her handle has 'daddy' in it because she thought it was funny, obviously. Sometimes other teens will reach out to her – usually through rp accounts or through normal fan Instagram accounts – and they'll get to know each other, ask each other their pronouns, 'so I can get to know them better and not insult them'. 'Pete' asks what format to use, what ships [sexual pairings] they like, and whether they want to enact smut (sexual and romantic stories) or angst (self-harm, depression, abusive parents and so on). Often it's a crossover of the two, which makes sense to me and it does to 'Pete' too. 'For most people, the teen years are just horniness and depression,' she says.

It may seem extreme but it's a variation on fan fiction: writing your own versions of stories, pre-existing characters and people across all forms of media and, if you so desire, self-publishing them. It's been practised almost completely by female, non-binary and queer fans since at least the sixties. Some fics are totally PG involving imagined adventures, some insert the reader as an 'I' into the text, some are romantic and some are very, very sexual. As with crossovers in fan fiction, teens will often do inter-fandom roleplay where members of Panic! at the Disco, My Chemical Romance, Paramore, Twenty One Pilots, and other emo or alternative groups hook up. Role-playing is by no means just a music fandom exercise – 'Pete's' friends who are into anime shows like Pokémon or Dragon Ball Z, for example, do it on Google Docs, so they can play comfortably sitting at a computer rather than taking part on a phone app. Over the weeks I spent looking into rp-ing, it was unusual to find someone over sixteen doing this. There are plenty of multi-role-play accounts run by teens who pretend to be more than one band member, to appeal to the widest common denominator, and accounts that will role-play the band member's real-life partner.

When writing, some fans will put the actions in asterisks and others will do 'third person literate' – write in full paragraphs. Another thirteen-year-old girl, who got her whole friend group into rp, sent me part of the latest one she's working on sporadically throughout the day – her as Gerard Way and someone else playing another My Chemical Romance member. It involved a lot of awkward flirting, a kiss and little else but bumbling about. What happened after this scene? I asked. 'Shit happened.'

The role-playing is happening totally in private. It's far more hidden than even fan fiction, and fans who engage in this sort of fantasy play are strict about keeping it insular. Although many fan fiction stories are held publicly on websites, it's against fan rules to draw outside attention to them. Harper, thirteen, from Illinois, writes Peterick (a portmanteau of Pete Wentz and the Fall Out Boy lead singer, Patrick Stump) slash fan fiction. She gets mad if someone, fan or not, tweets Fall Out Boy members about slash. 'It's like, no, he's got a wife, he's happy with his family, just leave him alone. If you want to do something like this you can do it on your own turf or terms but don't drag him into it because he might not be comfortable with it.' Occasionally she has moral concerns about her writing because Pete and Patrick are such close friends or because they're dating people in real life. 'It's like you wanna write about it but you don't want them to feel uncomfortable about what you're writing about, because you still look up to them and you still want to respect them.'

When 'Pete' talks about her favourite times role-playing, she uses 'emotional' interchangeably with 'favourite'. To raise the stakes of the fantasy to meet the overwhelming feelings inside her seems to be the aim. 'The most emotional moments I've had are at the height of my angst. Like, once there was something I related to where my character bullied his crush because he didn't want to be judged for how he really felt, and he was cutting and smoking a blunt to forget his problems in the bathroom. His crush caught him and tried to convince him that it's okay.' Did she relate to that, I asked? 'No, not relate, it's from my life. I have a habit of being mean 'cause I'm scared of judgement then cutting to forget about it.'

There is a lot of shame around role-playing. This feels oppressive the more 'Pete' does it but there's so much comfort competing with that guilt. 'Oh trust me, rp-ing makes me understand how much of a lonely loser I am and I don't want anyone really to know about it.' These teens know they're not necessarily doing something that's acceptable in the fandom or in the wider world, generally.

Still, is it a mark of anything but curiosity to observe artists' close relationships and wonder what if there was more there? 'Romance elements? I believe they have them,' Carrie says of Fall Out Boy. Ultimately it's 'because they have such good chemistry I'd write things about them'. Is it that fantastical of them? Sammy, who started writing Peterick slash when she was seventeen, thinks not, saying 'I think the bands initiate it a lot of the time, always super close on stage, hinting things in interviews'. This bandom slash fan fiction was at a peak around ten to fifteen years ago when I was a teenager. The three core bands that people wrote sexual fiction about on both sides of the Atlantic were Panic! at the Disco, My Chemical Romance and Fall Out Boy. Fanfiction.net banned this sort of real-person fiction in 2002, so fans often took to message boards, archives and LiveJournal. With hindsight, it's unsurprising that fans explored this route. Members of emo bands like this were known, as the girls suggested, for kissing each other onstage and talking about kissing men – not queer, but messing around, bending heterosexual norms with their appearances and relationships.

Really, it's a creative extension of what any fan does when they fantasise about a musician. Above all, the rp-ers and fan fiction writers I spoke to have a huge amount of respect for the musicians as people and as artists and for their work. The reason fans write them into a second existence is that they know them and can do something with that. They're using the musician as a blueprint for a character that is an extension of themselves. They need something to start with to explore themselves, so Pete might be the person that they end up calling a 'character'. It might as easily be any other musician.

Having almost outgrown writing Peterick slash and starting to have her own sexual experiences, Sammy has some analysis of it. She splits fans into various factions who all express themselves in different ways. 'Younger kids tend to write more things like fanfic, most younger kids, because they're still under their mom and dad's roof and they don't really have another way, while adults or older teens, seventeen and up I guess, might have their own freedom where they can explore things that help them express themselves.' Older teens can engage in more public modes of expression and fandom, like going to gigs. That's when they start to reflect and laugh and move on, because they get perspective, their fandom evolves. 'I think that a lot of teenagers don't really realise that they're writing about a real person because they're so out of reach for them. When I saw the bands I wrote about in person I was like, "wow, you wrote really weird stuff," and it kind of creeped me out to be honest.'

It's an established and private way to enjoy a band together, but it's ephemeral. Many people delete their stories as they move on. Much fanfic history gets lost as archives get deleted, sites close, and communities migrate to other spaces. What could get lost quicker than conversations had in direct messages by teens making short-lived rp accounts? No sooner had I spoken to one girl than the account had vanished.

On Twitter – public accounts, that is – people feel more accountability. It's unlikely you'll find girls displaying their sexuality in the same way there. Jess, a nineteen-year-old girl from Southampton, tweeted things like 'Daddy, it's cold outside, let us in' on a pic of Pete and Patrick and 'can't wait to see my daddies [tongue out emoji]' and 'Pete Wentz is bloody gorgeous [tongue out emoji, heart emoji]'. The night before we spoke she'd laughed at a snap Pete had put up of himself in glasses: 'Proper feeling himself, very "I look good, yeah!" He definitely loves himself,' she tells me.

'He's very good looking,' Jess says of teen girls commenting on his appearance. 'I think it's just because he's hot and people just say it when he's hot.' It's as simple as that. When I ask her to be more specific about why she does it she just laughs again. 'Because I knew that not that many people would see it. I look up to him but, also, I thought – he's hot, why not just say it? Get it out there.'

After a long discussion trying to distil the urge, we haven't got much further. 'People say, "why would you say that?" And when you're asking me now: it's difficult to explain to people. Because I love them and I wanted to.' Desire is infinitely complex. Sexuality is confusing, especially when you're younger, and the lines of external crushes are so blurred with your developing identity and understanding of your own gender. Music is a whole package that can cater to that; it's an artist, the way they look at you, their image, perhaps a stage, the whole world they've built and invite you into.

Pete Wentz wasn't just a dreamboat because he had perfectly straightened hair and effortlessly smudged eyeliner. I could plausibly believe he was a beautiful human being with an inner life, not like the moronic boys I knew who were more two-dimensional than my crumpled band posters. Musicians had empathy, emotional intelligence (I thought). They were talented, hardworking and creative. They – crucially – didn't know me, so couldn't appear to ruin my mythology of them, disrespect me or worse, reject me. I knew they understood everything I faced (see: their lyrics) and spoke to me – through my earbuds, inside me, moaning about how much they loved me, how much they wanted to be loved and how those other girls had destroyed them. It had to be this way. In reality these men weren't the embodiment of their songs, they were flawed men like anyone else, but together their song lyrics and smiles – neither of which were for me specifically – became the blueprint I needed for drama, beauty, romance of cinematic proportions.

Other musicians can colour your more complex desires. In my preteens and early teens, Marilyn Manson's music was a world I wasn't old enough for, a world that terrified and excited me. You may centre your feelings on the musician but it's not just about the person. It's the whole package, the music, the aesthetics, where your mind takes you. For me, it turned out that fear and sexuality were separated by only a thin line. In 'The Beautiful People', he was a terrifying doctor, twelve foot tall, a true picture of horror. In 'This Is the New Shit' he's dead-eyed and pale as ever, licking the legs and feet of a woman touching his chest under a thin Lycra vest. *I stick it you know where / you know why, you don't care.* If I, as an adult, could put words into my thirteen-year-old mouth I'd have said I wanted to be consumed by him. Ripped apart somehow. To be his half-human girlfriend or wife. I also wanted to party, to rage, spit, to fuck, to punch my fist in the air and drain a drink, anything he sang about explicitly or through suggestion. Some warm creeping feeling in my abdomen said it was all coming to me. I wanted his power and freedom, I wanted to be him and I wanted to be bad. To be tall, and spindly and powerful and confident enough to crush everyone. I wanted to possess his foreign power, to scream and have people listen and love and fear me too. I wanted to be him, the object of sexual attention and I wanted to be – or rather, was – the girls squirming over him. He felt like danger, everything that sex was, and I couldn't wait.

What else could you realistically expect to get from Marilyn Manson? 'I am the God of fuck' are the words he chose to introduce himself to the rock scene. His videos feature (simulated, sometimes) sex acts. Who he's shared a bed with and how has frequently appeared in his interviews. And there's the PVC. Seeing female desire from the outside, men have smugly perceived that they know it. They think they know what girls want: an inverse of their own hungers. They want him, the star. Romance and, perhaps, sex. How flat. It takes arrogance to assume knowledge of the amphitheatre in teenage girls' minds. Would anyone have known that I – and countless others – contained the multiplicities to both act out preparation for my inevitable future happiness by googling 'How To Deal With Long-Distance Relationships With Musicians', listening, glass-eyed, to a sad man in skinny jeans sing about being dumped, and also contemplate a horrid and delightful existence being a sexually deviant, translucent freak.

The crush tells you more about the girl crushing than the object. It's no coincidence that I'd grow up intensely interested in sex and power as subjects, want to be a writer, like him, want to make things that allow others to feel. Some of my other fan friends grew up to work in the music industry or start their own bands. It's all about so much more than a musician. It's a new landscape, their freedoms. It's about us.

To avoid puritanical values in fandom, which lurk everywhere, would be to acknowledge that it is plausible to be sexually attracted to musicians, that music itself can be sexual, and that it is also possible for sexuality to not come into your enjoyment of an artist and their work whatsoever. There is room for different ways of enjoying an artist or a piece of music and none has more value or weight than another. Where would you want to draw artificial boundaries around music and sexuality? To neuter music, to try to rip the two apart, as if to pull anger from metal or polish from pop. To deny that when you're stood watching a band perform, mixed up in the powerful euphoria, there can often be quite erotic sensations. Sex courses through it all.

'One of the things we don't understand is the multiplicity of our musical experiences,' Hill said on the phone. This will come from allowing different people – people of all genders, sexualities, ethnicities – to dig into why they feel certain ways about different musicians and what it is they love about music. If anyone recognises a misunderstanding, it's teens. There will always be another fan within the fandom calling you inappropriate for tweeting smutty things about an artist, or people on the internet writing think-pieces about fans going too far, or musicians calling their fans perverted for making fan fiction, or their own internalised shame bearing over them. With age, you can appreciate how, for all your own romantic and sexual experiences, music is one of the greatest sexual forces imaginable. Music is built, in whatever way, to date you, arouse you, pull you in close.

While interviewing the daddy commenters, one girl says, when I'm pursuing the question of why she comments these things: 'Honestly dude, it's not that deep'. Sometimes you just want to call a spade a spade and type into the void or scream into the dark that a rock star is a motherfucking snack.

5

SEX & IPHONES & ROCK & ROLL

(II) QUEERING WITH *STRANGERS*

'Don't tell your mom' or 'We shouldn't do this' or 'This feels so wrong but it's so right'. That narrative is so fucking damaging to bisexuality and its place in society. That's something I've had to fight my whole life and something I still fight.

　　　　　– Halsey, *Paper Magazine*, 2017

Halsey made a habit of kissing fans. Cupping their faces, her lips would butterfly onto someone's mouth or land on a cheek. Sometimes she'd have kisses hover just away and flutter in the air. It happened in the street – a fan would run up to her, explain their allegiance and ask: can I kiss you? Before she'd even put out a debut album, queer teenagers searching for meaning on the internet knew her. She was a bisexual teen, a singer-slash-social media 'famous' person. 'One hundred girls asked me to be their first kiss,' she said in one of her first blog interviews, 'so I said "OK".' Fans recall that the whole game started after an individual plucked up the courage to ask for one, and once news of it spread, any queer or questioning fan wanted to receive that prize.

Kaylee was one of those fans. A then-teen from Tennessee with long bottle-blonde hair and a stencil of roses, identical to the one Halsey has, tattooed on her right shoulder, Kaylee is neither straight nor bisexual. Like many of her generation, she doesn't identify with any label strongly enough to use it. When she discovered Halsey's social media accounts in 2014, Kaylee was drawn in by her blue hair. Once she heard Halsey's songs online – the small amount of music she'd put out herself at that point – Kaylee knew she wanted to kiss her.

She watched countless Halsey-fan-kissing videos or recordings of fans outlining for other fans how they asked her for a kiss. Her first chance came at a bar in Nashville in 2015. Kaylee was waiting outside with other fans to make sure she got to the front of the stage, given it was a small venue and would fill quickly, when Halsey walked along. She greeted them all with hot chocolates from Dunkin' Donuts. In the weeks following Kaylee thought back to that night, frustrated that she'd had the opportunity to ask for a kiss but was too scared to do so. Another chance came a matter of months later, when she had VIP tickets that granted her a meet-and-greet arrangement. Instead of taking a kiss, Kaylee gave Halsey a Hello Kitty goodie bag she'd put together because she knew Halsey liked the cartoon cat. It didn't feel like the right time. That year in October, she went to see Halsey at her *Badlands* tour, and camped out for over twenty-four hours to get to the front and centre of the stage. She got very close. Halsey came right up and stood on top of the barricade, her tiny frame perched directly above Kaylee. Kaylee held Halsey's hand and used the connection to push up and hold her steady. Still, she had not achieved her 'goal'.

Two years to the month later it happened. By now Kaylee was on the edge of turning twenty. For the Atlanta show of the *hopeless fountain kingdom* tour in 2017, she had meet-and-greet tickets, and knew she had to make it happen. Halsey was in a purple hoodie with her hair dip-dyed to match when they met. The singer explained they would have four photos taken together, the implication being, as it often is with those paid-for fan scenarios, that Kaylee could more or less dictate poses.

'We weren't supposed to just go up and kiss her or anything so I didn't want it to seem like I was breaking the rules. I was super nervous, I would never in a million years want to make her uncomfortable, so when I asked her I said "I would love to have a kissing picture with you but I want you to do whatever makes you feel comfortable" and she said "no, that's fine", and… we had the kissing picture,' she laughed. In the picture, Halsey holds Kaylee's face in her hands and both girls lean in equally to kiss full on the mouth. It was uploaded onto Instagram with the hashtag #spiritday, an annual LGBTQ awareness day for people to show visible support against queer bullying. Was it everything that she'd hoped? I asked. 'Oh, it definitely was,' she confirmed in a Southern drawl. 'It took me a long time to process that it actually happened.'

To do so, a few days later Kaylee uploaded a YouTube video called 'I KISSED HALSEY' in all capital letters. Wearing her *hopeless fountain kingdom* tour shirt and standing in her house with her device recording on a counter, she flicks her hair and grins with the thrill of a crush, using her manicured hands to emphasise each part of the story. The video opens to a slideshow of the photos Kaylee took with Halsey, hugging, posing and kissing. 'Ahhhh! Oh my god, oh my god!' Kaylee's voice screams over the pictures.

The video was made so she could share the experience, to bask in the achievement. There was another motivation: she knew fans would be angry because Halsey didn't kiss them anymore, which meant they'd be more jealous than they'd already be. This refusal on Halsey's part was established after an incident in 2015: Halsey kissed a girl during a gig, and it turned out the girl was underage, which was met with heavy criticism from the fandom and adjacent ones, policed mainly by other teenage girls. Mere weeks after Kaylee posted about her kiss, Halsey tweeted that she felt increasingly uncomfortable being asked by fans to kiss and in a DM sent to a fan, she highlighted that at meet and greets fans were always told repeatedly not to kiss her.

Out of her teenage years and signed to a major label, becoming a more legitimate pop star week by week and with fan numbers growing, Halsey's kissing gimmick couldn't be maintained, nor would it be desirable for her career to maintain it (where exactly would kissing your fans fit post the #MeToo movement, when fan-performer power imbalances are finally and justifiably being probed and questioned?). She was getting older but attracting younger and underage fans. And so, the kisses became folklore. A 'you had to be there from the start' situation. But even looking back, they meant something real to the individual: you and Halsey are the same. They signalled a safe crush, for the time being – saying you wanted to kiss an artist was different from wanting to kiss a girl in your friendship group, right? The photos and videos of kisses were often used and posted online to make a coming-out statement. This is why fans believe that Halsey kissed: to help them. The kisses suggested something pivotal: there is a queer club, one you hoped existed, and you had been initiated into it.

Performative kissing aside, bisexual and bi-curious fans remember knowing that Halsey was one of them from the first time they came across her social media profiles. Her changing hair, the way she presented, and particularly her posts about LGBTQ or women's issues on Tumblr – the platform best known for housing queer and fandom communities and, far from coincidentally, the platform Halsey organically shot to fame on. 'I never came out as a musician because I was already out when I started making music. I was out in high school! I was in high school with people walking past me in the hallway calling me "Dyke", you know what I mean?' she would tell *Paper Magazine* in 2017. She didn't do what most artists do, often out of a need for safety: hide her sexuality until achieving a certain amount of success.

Over the course of a few years, more than any other modern artist, Halsey pushed a conversation around bisexuality forward. A huge music fan herself, she claimed the label, assured her audience it was a reality for her and others, and teen girls picked this up and ran with it. She literally said 'this exists', defended it in interviews and girls started to realise it did for them, too, and they joined her. When Halsey said 'I am bisexual enough', fans quote tweeted their own variant on that. When Halsey said: 'So if I date a guy I'm straight, and if I date a woman, I'm a lesbian. The only way to be a #True bisexual is to date 2 people at once', bisexuals from all across the globe elaborated on the nuance of that observation with their own experiences, and the conversation as a whole made headlines. When Halsey fought against certain LGBTQ publications that questioned her validity as a bisexual, fans stood alongside her, giving anyone who came into contact with their social media accounts a lesson in biphobia.

This was the first half of the 2010s. Bisexuality was only a nebulous presence in existing music culture and scarcely better-defined in wider pop culture. David Bowie paved the way for bisexuality in pop, adopting different labels at various points in his career, one of them being bisexual. Brian Molko, the Placebo singer, spoke about his bisexuality in the nineties, while Green Day's Billie Joe Armstrong came out in 1995 but didn't speak much about it again. In the noughties Lady Gaga became the most obvious bisexual figure in music (she'd later seemingly retract her position on this somewhat, telling contestants in an episode of RuPaul's *Untucked* that she was 'not necessarily part of' the LGBTQ community in a way that she 'can understand what you all go through') and Black Eyed Peas singer Fergie came out in 2009. Sleater-Kinney's Carrie Brownstein stated she was bisexual in 2010, having never publicly defined her sexuality in the press before. Pop star Kesha said she was not gay or straight but admitted to 'liking people' in 2010, and two years later Frank Ocean started a conversation about sexual fluidity by outlining his love for a man in a Tumblr post in 2012, though never adopting the labels 'gay', 'bi', 'pansexual' or 'queer'. In 2014, Debbie Harry came out as 'bisexual', then only a few years later put any sexual feelings she'd had towards women in her early life down to 'hormones', much to my disappointment. That same year Christine and the Queens came out as pansexual, however she has a very specific audience; older, educated and into indie music. In 2015, Miley Cyrus came out as pansexual, but although extremely famous, she was undergoing a radical image change – wild, weed-smoking, partying – and the public tended to see her claiming her sexuality as part and parcel of a borderline mental breakdown-cum-rebellion, typical after being a childhood Disney star. None of these figures seemed to represent current teens.

The difference with Halsey was that she held the label close, made it part of her personal brand and showed that she was comfortable being a spokesperson for that sexual identity. She stepped into an ambiguous space, where bisexuality was sparsely referenced and few, during that time, were really speaking about it as a possibility. She was part of a generation who were ready to tackle sexual fluidity, where gender and sexuality were ideas to deconstruct. It was this unusual and fierce position that made bisexual female and non-binary fans gravitate to her immediately.

Bisexual culture suffers from invisibility. There's almost no language for how it exists because it's almost erased by the mainstream, by both heterosexual people and the rest of the LGT community. In a relationship, bisexual identity dissolves into nothingness for everyone but the individual. Bisexuals are constantly being read as either gay/ lesbian or heterosexual, depending on their partner at that time, as Halsey stated. It is a strange and lonely way to move through the world when you're first grappling with it, but can be so freeing and fluid once you're more comfortable. Anything is possible. Once the expectation of choosing a gender to love has gone, what else can you lose?

'The older generations refuse to admit that bisexuality exists, whereas we're all more open about the idea,' Ali, a Halsey fan aged seventeen told me. 'Teenagers are the ones that made it acceptable, we're the ones that are talking about it, we know it's real and we know that people need to accept that it's real. I really think Halsey and the teens who love her made the bisexuality convo happen and I don't know where it'd be without us. You have bi characters on TV but that conversation is specific to TV people, whereas music is for everyone.' As with many things, Gen Z teens are more welcoming to bisexuals than any other generation – and far more likely to claim an identity under the bisexuality umbrella. It's in fandom spaces where this is miraculously happening.

Resisting a life in which only one gender is seen as a potential sexual or romantic partner often makes both heterosexual and homosexual people feel very uncomfortable. The persistent belief is that bisexuality is unstable, fake, predatory, dangerous, perverse – which is a simple step away from admitting that people think bisexuals are slutty, unfaithful, confused, inauthentic and actually gay, lesbian or straight. This leads to people not knowing they are bisexual, for a long time, and even denying their bisexuality. In those early years of Halsey's career so many girls shared online photos they had taken with Halsey saying, 'Thank you for making me feel safe' or 'the place I feel safest'. Something impossible for most people to conceptualise exists because Halsey says it does. And then it exists because the fans make it so.

It's the day after Valentine's Day 2018 and two months prior to a secret Halsey event. This is not the precious universe of Halsey's personal space – this is the real world. Rach has her arms around her noodle bowl in a bow to show me a photo of the blue-haired singer, the same girl that Kaylee and countless others fell for, on her phone. We're eating food on the top of an enclosed roof in Shoreditch; she is across from me in a pair of black-framed glasses.

'I fell in head first, *deep*,' she says. 'These were all the photos I first saw, and I was like, "wow, OK" and started developing a big fat crush on her. All these photos from this tour but mainly this one made me fall for her. For me it was her hair.' It changed with every whim: aquamarine, purple, pink, deepest blue.

This was one of a series of events that confirmed that Rach was attracted to women. At that time she was listening almost exclusively to Halsey and other queer female pop and alternative artists. It makes sense to her that it was music, rather than anything else, that helped her understand those parts of her identity. 'I look to music more than anything else, so anything music related is going to teach me most.' It was with music that she eventually realised she identified more closely as being a lesbian than a bisexual.

I've seen Rach at a few gigs and signings, and we've spoken a few times on the phone. She seems more mature than eighteen. There's something understated and trustworthy about her. When she speaks it's necessary, her chin sticking out slightly. She exudes, too, the confidence young born-and-bred Londoners have, and even though it's winter, and we're only half-inside on a rooftop, she's wearing a t-shirt.

'Pop culture is really sexualised. For better, for worse, with positives and potentially negatives,' she says. The sexualisation does have positives for queer communities. This is not often acknowledged, but it can crack open possibilities for teens.

Although music videos until recently catered almost exclusively to a heterosexual, usually male gaze, they were where I started exploring my sexuality. Strangely, my response to them was more of an indication of my feelings than any attraction to real flesh and bone. If, that is, I'd been monitoring closely. One summer I spent every hot day inside slumped on our cracked leather sofa, legs like hams stuck with sweat, watching the one free music channel we had at home. It was 2002 and 'All the Things She Said' by t.A.T.u. was looping multiple times a day. The song is now a tongue-in-cheek queer anthem, despite the fact it was sung by a couple of girls only one of whom later came out as bisexual, put together with a kissing performance designed to take an already electrifying, dramatic pop song to the top of the UK charts for four consecutive weeks. In the video there were bottle-green pouring skies, and two girls in tiny school uniforms soaking wet, kissing, running up and down a fence, seemingly to escape. Disapproving adults shake their heads. I was obsessed with it, and got a lump in my throat each time it came on. Then there was 'Dirrty' by a Christina Aguilera dripping with sweat in a boxing ring, wearing assless chaps or a skirt like a belt, dozens, hundreds of bronzed wet bodies dancing with her – I stared at them too. There was the chemistry that Eve, with her simmering attitude and paw prints chest tattoo, had with Gwen Stefani, someone I desperately wanted to look like ('Let Me Blow Ya Mind'). There were Britney's sad almond eyes and oiled washboard stomach and a phallic snake ('I'm a Slave 4 U').

Significant musical moments like those were sexually seismic, for myself and I'm sure for many others my age. But there were two options at hand: gay and straight. I knew I wasn't the former because of an attraction to real-life boys and male musicians, so that was that. A twofold process began of not understanding urges and repressing them, only to have them resurface and cause problems in my twenties. I hid compulsions from loved ones and wounded other people, letting the poison of my confused state seep through into longer relationships and the briefest ones. It sounds absurd that I knew bi or pan-sexuality existed but it never occurred to me as a valid option. All the while these videos followed me, as a music fan and culture writer, images teasing their way into my real experiences, cropping up when the songs came on in a club on a night out or when the artists were referenced in an article I read. I remember being stuck to that sofa, sipping squash and, if I could go back with age and self-awareness, I would realise the lack of clarity on who or what I was, or would become.

Rach eats slowly and in a considered way as we talk about Halsey, stopping to prod at her food with a fork, or put it down if she's getting to an important part of the story. Something that drew Rach to Halsey is that her story doesn't look too different from Rach's own. Like many Halsey fans, she's a white-passing femme person of colour; like Halsey, she has a black dad and a white mum.

She uses her utensils to show how long it takes her to get to her girlfriend's house. 'So long, it's *so* long. I try to get her down to London, it's easier for both of us here.' She doesn't get on with her girlfriend's dad ('I don't get on with dads') or sister, who is conservative. There can be some hints of racism ('I'm white passing and I don't say anything'). Crucially, her girlfriend isn't out to her mum yet. But there are places they can be together openly.

A couple of months later, on April 5th, comes the dampest of days in the city. Rainbow flags flip heavy and bright for anyone prepared to raise their eyeline. Down a dark street are a pair of wooden doors – something straight from a Disney film that might open to reveal a princess inside – almost concealed by scaffolding and a tight and oppressive tunnel of walls. London's Soho has historically been a space for all activities considered seedy to occur, for outsiders and maligned characters to congregate, which was why, at one time or another, it became home to queer communities. Despite moneyed regeneration and gentrification it still houses a number of gay bars and clubs, where it doesn't matter whose mouth is closed over your own.

Outside the doors, eighteen-year-old Dee lugs her suitcase around. 'Hell yeah, they must really like Halsey for them to let her rent it out for this. I don't feel like they would normally for any other artist.' Willow had been to the highly exclusive club inside once previously and her openly gay and transgender friends love it ('I just felt so at home here. It's one of the few clubs that my friends love – *if* they get in.'). I ask Dee about her huge suitcase and she tells me she was en route to Amsterdam on holiday from London before finding out she'd won tickets to the event. 'Look, I've stanned this girl since 2013. I can book another flight.'

Queer teens have gathered in this paradise to see something special. Originally, the theatre housed the first club in England where naked girls performed. Under various owners and in different incarnations, girl-on-girl acts were displayed for crowds desiring titillation and merriment. Now it's simply – or crudely – called The Box. Tables usually cost, on the average night, thousands of pounds and, for discretion, photography and social media are banned. Once through the doors, the girls hand over their phones willingly but with suspicion. Rach is one of them, reluctantly letting it go, and wondering how she's going to capture whatever happens inside.

The club's interior is all intricate wood and tactile textures, something of a Sleeping Beauty cottage-cum-brothel. The walls don't need to speak: debauchery is in the air, musty with the powder of drag queens and perfumes overzealously applied to wealthy busts. But instead of sex and grandeur, strips of flesh and flashes of sequins, in every booth dozens of girls and femme people are sitting around politely, sipping water rather than champagne. Only the most tenacious and hardcore of fans managed to get here to this small event. The vast majority identify as bisexual.

Nineteen-year-old Shauna is here from Northampton with her bisexual Londoner friend, Jasmine, twenty, whom she met at a Halsey concert. At Halsey gigs or fan meet-ups they'll often end up sharing stories of coming out. They'll also talk about how many parents actually guessed or had inklings of their child's sexuality by their being Halsey fans – knowing about Halsey or hearing songs and watching the videos through their children.

'Coming out is always a process, you're always coming out to people because they always assume you're straight,' says Shauna. 'When I came out to my mum, having people in the media like Halsey, who are openly bisexual and you can look up to, always helps. Everyone says the internet is so bad but it helped me understand who I am, my attraction to girls and my attraction to guys and how I can have both.'

In many cases, Halsey is used explicitly in coming out. This was so for Tina, a nineteen-year-old woman of colour from London. 'This is a new sexuality for a lot of people, but everyone is starting to know about bisexuality, so I feel more hopeful people will know what I mean. Now I feel comfortable saying I like all genders, and she's a great example because she's someone quite a few people know about, you're using her as a reference, which works. I like doing it like that. "*I'm bi, you know, just like Halsey.*"

When Halsey steps out onto the stage at The Box you can imagine the thick red velvet curtains drawing themselves back in respect and modesty. She glows. A shining neon crucifix on either side of her frames her glamour. 'I've had a *very* good time here,' she tells her fans, laughing. She says she picked the location in Soho for them to gather because the Baz Luhrmann-like aesthetic matched that of her album, but what she didn't explicitly say was that it could be an appropriately safe space for them.

She was there to promote a new song from her upcoming album *hopeless fountain kingdom,* a work designed to give her fans representation, even if in a superficial way. In the world of the album, the main character is called Luna and has a male love interest called Solis, but female love interests exist in the songs 'Bad at Love' and 'Strangers'. Halsey picked featured artist Lauren Jauregui, a member of pop group Fifth Harmony, for the latter track because of her sexuality, to create a staged romance that could be real.

As a bisexual woman of colour, Dee had gravitated towards Halsey and her music immediately. 'I feel like gay culture is represented well in music but bisexuality isn't. She's a really important artist in terms of identifying her sexuality in songs that talk about hers and hims. I personally don't like songs that are he, he, he. I'd want songs that say her as well, as a bisexual. Halsey gets that.' It is important for bisexual fans to have their own representation in music. As Professors Marion Wasserbauer and Alexander Dhoest wrote in one of their queer fandom studies, 'Music fandom is closely linked to notions of the self and expressing one's identity, as is music more generally. Involvement with music is also connected to sexual and gender identities, which are indispensable and crucial (if not always the most central) aspects in the lives of LGBTQs.' Each part of the LGBTQ community craves their own music to speak to them in different ways, rather than all identities being lumped together under some broad category.

This desire is felt far from where Halsey is in real life. Just as fans write fan fiction about Pete Wentz and cute boys in hot bands, these fans write sexy and romantic material about non-male musicians.

As I'm scrolling through one of the sites teens use for distributing these stories, it's clear most of the people doing this are girls, some genderqueer and in their early teens. The perspective of these works is clear: queer girls creating porn for other queer girls. In self-insert fic – where the person reading immediately becomes the 'I' – fictional Halsey can sleep with any of us, regardless of gender identity.

Tali from Tennessee is sixteen, nearly seventeen. Her high school is populated by Trump supporters, so many it makes her feel uncomfortable. She only knows straight Halsey fans, and plenty of those. They're all around her in the hallways, in the locker rooms, in gym class. Perhaps some are queer, but haven't come out either. Halsey has never come anywhere near Tali – the closest was a show she played in Nashville, but that's three hours' drive from her, out in the suburbs.

'Are we ever going to get married?' I asked, finally looking into her eyes. 'I don't know, I hope,' she responded, pulling off my shorts. 'When?' 'I'm ready whenever you are,' she smiled.

Alongside her stories, readers have placed notes of encouragement 'GO ON' and 'yes girl' but also suggestions, making each work a conversation. Some fans request non-sexual work, and in those cases, Tali sends them, personally, chapters without sex in them. There's everything here from soft romance to hardcore kink, as imagined by girls who haven't yet ventured out into those experiences. 'I feel like you miss every shot you don't take,' she tells me. 'Writing made me more confident. And I thought: if I express my feelings to people I'll get what I write in return.'

'I love you, morgan,' ashley interrupts, sitting up on her heels. 'and I'm sorry I didn't say it back to you this morning. But I truly do love you, and I –'

Separated by a state from Tali, Nia is similarly alone. Every day in Texas feels the same to her. As is often the case with diligent book-smart girls, her dreamy interior life is something only she's aware of. 'Nothing is exciting or entertaining here and the people can be judgemental. People take religion very seriously. My parents weren't born here either, they come from a culturally traditional home and even though they're divorced, the house is still very much the same when it comes to opinions on how we should live.' Coming out was a move intended to bring her and her mother closer but it in fact made the distance palpable. She wants to escape and is preparing applications to college. California is the dream – somewhere out queer women of colour will be. Nia likes to use women of colour as Halsey's other half. 'Whenever you think of a woman who likes another woman you don't really picture a WOC in your head, or at least, that's not your first thought.'

Your eyes began to fall, sleep was taking over once again. You waited for Ashley to try and wake you up, but she never did. She moved closer to you, putting her lips against your neck and began to kiss your soft skin.

It's not just isolated queer fans who create this sort of soft smutty material. Luna, sixteen, lives in Copenhagen and is openly bisexual. She writes requests from other queer women and non-binary or genderqueer people (her profile statistics show only one per cent of readers identify as men). Most of her reads are from Australia, but many are from India and Africa, or other faraway places she wouldn't have thought of. She likes that she feels helpful, exploring her reader's sexuality with them. It's not about Halsey, the specific person, Luna highlights, rather the ease of having a real-life prompt whom you already have a crush on. 'If Halsey said she didn't like it I would still write fanfics, just not about Halsey. It's all about respect, especially the kind of stuff I write. I would totally be cool if she shut it down.' But Halsey is a child of the internet and a fan of artists herself – she would almost certainly know all this smut exists, even if she hadn't read it. 'Exactly.'

At the end of the Halsey fan event, Dee, Shauna and the others are granted a treat. Halsey tells them they can each get a photo with her. A few collapse onto their seats or the floor. Later they share them on social media, and all of them retweet and repost the others' photos too. It wasn't 'I met Halsey', it was 'We met Halsey'. All of them had been there, and all of them had existed.

If there is ever a time when bisexuality, the concept, could be made tangible, it would be on Bi Visibility Day. In 2018, it falls on September 23rd, the second of the back-to-back dates Halsey is playing at Hammersmith Apollo – but there are not only bisexual fans here, unlike the earlier fan event. Halsey no longer belongs to queer fans. Her second album now out, the one whose material she teased at the start of the year, was built for mainstream radio and there'd been a consolidation of attention she'd garnered for her worldwide hit with 'The Chainsmokers'. In short: mums know who Halsey is. Simultaneously, the popular music landscape had been queered. That year, Janelle Monáe came out as pansexual in a *Rolling Stone* feature after much fan speculation during the course of her career. Her album *Dirty Computer* was 'a homage to women and the spectrum of sexual identities' and after her *Rolling Stone* interview, the Merriam-Webster dictionary website reported an 11,000 per cent increase in people looking up 'pansexual'. Brendon Urie of Panic! at the Disco came out as pansexual in *Paper* magazine and singer Kehlani came out as queer on Twitter. Rita Ora's name appeared in seemingly endless tabloid headlines with the words 'comes out as bisexual' after defending her bisexual anthem 'Girls' inspired by Katy Perry's 'I Kissed a Girl', and pop star Rina Sawayama came out as pan. Halsey doesn't have to be a sole source of comfort or a figurehead in music anymore, because something is happening to the space she helped open.

Angel has postbox-red hair in pigtails and is alternating putting a fag to her mouth and the straw of a large McDonald's fizzy drink cup which, she tells me, has Diet Coke and vodka in it. The nineteen-year-old from Croydon didn't have a friend to come with but is hoping to find a bisexual person to connect with here. She attempts to show me the other people she thinks could match that requirement. A thorny task in itself – anyone, of course, can be queer – which she recognises, but her point is that there are plenty of straight people here. 'You'll probably find it's more of the edgier fans that've followed her since the beginning, they are likely queer.' She rattles the ice at the bottom of the cup with her straw, vodka running dry. 'It's easier maybe to tell online; bi fans will stand out more.'

Online it's easier to see similarities between the activity of lesbian and bisexual fans than straight and bisexual fans. From the conversations had with girls outside the venue, it's clear both lesbian and bi fans will make it their priority to defend Halsey against trolls and publications who attack or question the validity of her sexuality, and push forward the discourse around bisexuality. They'll prioritise the online sharing of music news in which Halsey talks about her sexuality. These fans will keep 'going on' about the gay or queer songs – for Halsey that's 'Strangers', 'Ghosts' and 'Bad At Love' – with hopes that they'll sail up the charts, settling some scores. They'll repost pictures of Halsey with hearts and pervy little messages. As one fan grins at me: 'Queer fans will speak about Halsey in a certain type of way. I feel like we go straight for the compliments, whereas other fans will say, "Yeah your music's cool", we'll be like "You're really fit! You have good music too! But you're really fit!"' Like a secret language, it's a public but coded way to find each other. There is a divide, however amicable, between straight fans and bisexual or queer-identifying fans.

Angel gives up pointing out fans with brightly coloured hair. One has long blue shiny hair – a wig? – like Halsey's old look, which seemed promising. 'God, it's so hard to find bisexual people in real life. But I can be a weirdo here, still. There's plenty to bond over here, besides being bi and loving Halsey.'

Sat around chatting, everyone gels. The girls with the bisexual flag painted on their cheeks and eyelids and the straight girls here with their boyfriends or other straight friends. Rach is here, of course, and has a scientific eye for the configuration of a fandom. 'I'd say it's seventy-five per cent queer or bisexual fans and twenty-five per cent straight,' she says of tonight, without too much thought. Which, she notes, isn't exactly an LGBTQ-specific space but vastly different from anything in the outside world.

With this influx of straight fans, there's a danger of losing a queer space but it wasn't a strict club: there were no LGBTQ-only rules. Anyone can be in a fandom. A few fans feel wary of what Emily calls 'non-queer people fading in' or pretending or overly participating in queer culture that has crossed over or combined with a fandom. This, as Emily fears, leads to 'the diluting of queer culture'. But this isn't the dominant view. Tina from The Box is now nineteen and at university in Durham. She says that straight fans come into the fandom knowing Halsey is bi, so will be more educated about LGBTQ people than the average heterosexual teen. 'They know about it, they've probably even thought, "Hmm, am I actually straight?" They've maybe been through that slight questioning period, so it's welcoming for everyone.' This particular fandom is a place for questioning teens, more so than other fandoms they've come across, girls say. If you weren't questioning your sexuality before, it's considered likely you might once you've joined.

A few girls talk about their gay club at college. They say it's fine but slightly cringe-inducing at times, and not something they necessarily want to go to. 'We have pride events and GSA [Genders & Sexualities Alliance] at college but I don't really go to that, I dunno they're not really my kind of people. It's all just a bit too much sometimes,' laughs Yaz, a seventeen-year-old from Southampton. 'Music is the perfect balance of who you can be, who you are, you don't have to be over the top about your sexuality. Sometimes I feel like the Pride events are… not a bit much but sometimes it *is* a bit much, without sounding weird. Whereas music is different, you have a good time, let everything go.' Put differently: you don't need to be screaming 'I'm gay' all day, whereas sexuality is more delicately integrated into music fandom.

As the crowd pushes inside, through security, it becomes more obvious how many people have brought a bisexual flag with them. A tiny curly-haired brunette girl called Izzi is excitedly using the purple, blue and pink flag as a cape. The fourteen-year-old had come down with her older female cousin and her cousin's girlfriend. 'I picked up this flag from Pride Festival in Newcastle, not long ago. I brought the flag because I thought there'd be a lot of other bisexual people here and I could show off that I'm bi,' she says, looking around attentively. 'Then they can come and speak to me if they want – I'll speak to anyone. I haven't had anyone come up to me yet and ask questions or say hi but other people with flags, we look at each other, smile and can relate to each other there.' As someone who had only recently come out – of course, she's teeny – she is practically vibrating with the need for someone to approach and interact with her before the lights drop.

The show itself is comfortably queer. 'A couple of years ago I was dating this guy…trust me I know that was my first mistake,' Halsey says in a little ditty before a song. This prompts a titter from the audience. Even straight girls can appreciate that one. At another point, Halsey and her dancer are in leather and dancing in a fake puddle. My queer friend

Daisy turns to me and shouts into my ear, 'This is…really camp'. We snigger, feeling older and familiarly satisfied for a moment.

A handful of songs into the set, Halsey performs 'Strangers'. '*She doesn't kiss me on the mouth anymore / Cause it's more intimate, than she thinks we should get,*' she sings, as a female backing dancer with a shaved head mirrors her slinking movements from the opposite end of the stage. Behind them, the screen shows people of different genders and orientations kissing passionately.

The opening bar hasn't played out before a young woman who looks to be in her late teens scrambles to get her phone out to video call her girlfriend. From behind I can see the screen: on it her girlfriend is in bed, duvet around her, holding her hands to her neck and face self-consciously as though the grinning hurts. It could be their song. During the closing moments, Halsey and the dancer grab each other on the small of the back and pull bodies in close. Screams emanate as if outwards from the touch, anticipating it, and some girls in the crowd start kissing. 'Did you hear it?' the girl says, holding the phone lengthways to her mouth. 'Did you hear it, babe?'

A conversation between two British teen girls, aged fifteen and sixteen, about fan fiction

Notes:

Gerard and Frank – members of My Chemical Romance; ship name Frerard

A Splitting of the Mind – novel-length Frerard bandfic set in a psychiatric hospital

THROAM – short for *The Heart Rate of a Mouse*, a bandfic of epic proportions, possibly the most well-known and well loved, published in paper and hardback over several volumes

MPREG – fan fiction shorthand for the trope of male pregnancy

Kellin Quinn and Vic Fuentes – members of Sleeping With Sirens and Pierce The Veil; ship name Kellic

Get the Sheets Messed Up – Kellic bandfic in which Vic, the owner of a brothel, takes young Kellin under his wing and teaches him about sex

Summertime and *Wintertime* – paired Frerard band fics about a pair of mentally troubled young men, set about ten years apart

N: To be fair, sometimes when I'm feeling sad, I do still crack out a good fan fiction.

M: It's comforting, you know – slash. It's nostalgic.

N: *A Splitting of the Mind.*

Both: OMG YES. YES?!

M: Gerard and Frank are in mental hospitals together and Frank dies, doesn't he?

N: Yeah, Frank dies. And teenagers across the nation are in tears.

M: It's horrible. I have the most vivid memory of being twelve and I'd just finished *Splitting of the Mind* and got to the end and they're in a coffee shop or something and something happens, and what happens… oh my god, I remember. Frank goes schizophrenic. I finish it, I sit in my bed and I am in floods of tears. That was my first heartbreak, you know?

And my dad came in and was like, 'oh my god, what's wrong?' I was like, 'nothing, nothing!' I was so embarrassed. I made up this whole story about being so stressed out about school. And not that I was reading Frerard fan fiction. The thing is the fics are always like, 'oh my god, my dad hits me!' 'Me too! Let's fall in love.'

N: They all romanticise mental illness. It's like, if you have mental illness, you'll meet someone in a band!

M: Yes! I remember being like, 'damn I'm going to be depressed and someone in a band will be obsessed with me. I can't wait. Goals.' Literally.

N: It's all intertwined.

M: The kids who are writing it are like, I want that.

N: They want someone who is going to save them from their abusive whatever.

M: 'Abusive Dad' who probably just didn't let them go to a gig. Literally.

N: I bought the first two volumes of *THROAM* paperback and I literally got through the first one and had enough. It was good, it was just so stressful, the characters did all the things you don't want them to do. Oh my god, stressful MPREG fan fiction where they have to come up with some way for one of them to get pregnant. We went to the doctor's and turns out: you have a uterus!

M: Or...it's an alternative universe where men get pregnant! I feel like, who is the first person to come up with that? Who started that, because they have to have the blame. Oh my god, I was obsessed with Kellic...

N: Oh my god, yes.

M: Yes! Kellic with my life. I would look up all the edited photos of Kellin Quinn and Vic Fuentes, and stick them as my phone background. So embarrassing. Now, thinking about it, I'm humiliated. Later down the line and you start going to concerts or you meet the people. You're like, I read about you pregnant.

N: Do you remember that girl who actually deleted her account and everything because she was so embarrassed after meeting them? Took down her account, changed her name, she felt so bad for doing it.

M: Oh, yeah. Do you remember that one where Kellin was training to be a sex worker?

N: YEAH, YEAH!

M: Oh my god! I was obsessed!

N: Oh my god!

M: It had five sequels. And I read all of them. It was so good, it was so good, it was so good, it was so intense. You're thinking, 'What the fuck, who writes that, but also I want to be a sixteen-year-old and get taken in by a pimp.' It's so horrible. I literally wanted that. In my head I was like, that is the perfect relationship.

N: Genuinely. It's so fucked. There's one called *Get the Sheets Messed Up*.

M: Yes!

N: I would read that to this day.

M: Literally, a comfort blanket. Oh my god, that one, *Summertime*, where Frank gets depressed and Gerard sees a ghost, and then there's *Wintertime*. Oh my god, the memories.

N: I miss it, I miss being that person. I just realised how fucked it was.

M: Why is it *so* good? I guess it's so taboo. The taboo! All children growing up want to read that, you know? They're like, 'ooo I wanna know what happens'. I don't know.

N: I had so many visions about being older, sixteen. And now I'm here like, 'wow'. Sitting on the ground.

M: Yeah: 'I'm going to have so many amazing relationships' and here I am with my boyfriend watching nine hours of TV. Fan fiction gave me unrealistic expectations…

6

'WE ARE THE MEDIA': INSIDE THE HIVE MIND

Memory has fallen into female hands, into queer hands, into immigrant and diasporic and transnational hands, into non-white hands, into the hands of the masses.

> – Abigail De Kosnik, *Rogue Archives: Digital Cultural Memory and Media Fandom* (2016)

Bitch first of all every one of Beyoncé's albums went #1. Second of all Beyoncé has more fucking hits in a strand of her fake ass hair than Rihanna has in her entire career. Bitch if Rihanna was a track Beyoncé would sing relays around her. Bitch Beyoncé could snatch up Rihanna's entire career with one strand of her baby's hair. Bitch Beyoncé makes Rihanna sound like a dying walrus with a mic. Bitch Beyoncé could stand there and not even touch the mic and still sound better than Rihanna. Bitch don't play Queen Bey. Don't even put her on the same planet with Rihanna. Beyoncé and Rihanna is like Earth and Pluto. One is needed by every human being and the other is irrelevant. And if you just joking… I'm sorry [for] my outburst.

> – User 'Bryonce Dick', source: Facebook

The queen bee is a goddess, strictly regimented in all that she does. She will be easy to spot, as the largest in the colony, and is of course pivotal to everything that happens within a healthy group. With few exceptions, she is the only queen in a colony, a vast swarm that may number tens of thousands or more. A secreted queen pheromone sends a message to workers about her health and productivity, while chemicals influence the behaviour of others. The workers take care of the queen, feeding and grooming her – she depends heavily upon the rest of the colony, as they on her. She will lay all day to spawn the next generation of devoted bees.

Lela is driving from Connecticut to North Carolina on a road trip, music off only to talk, and once she gets talking there is no stopping her. 'I consider myself to be CEO of the Beyhive,' she says with confidence. She's in her late twenties and a star of her state (quite literally Miss Alabama in the 2016 US Universal pageant, crowned wearing a black and gold dress). She is already an army veteran with a BSc and an MA, having gone to one of the US's historically black colleges – like the one referenced by Beyoncé's 2018 Coachella headlining performance, which had every journalist and fan referring to that year's event as Beychella. 'Fierce and Fabulous' are the three words she lives by. Attending events and conferences, supporting her friends and family, coaching track and field, competing in pageants or volunteering through her sorority: time spent idle is wasted. She devotes a large portion of that time, for no money or obvious material gain, blogging about whatever Beyoncé is doing, along with happenings within the black community.

Lela grew up in Alabama, the state Beyoncé's dad is from. She lives a whole seven and a half hours from where Beyoncé herself was raised: Houston, Texas. This sort of distance is almost unquantifiable to the British mind, but in a continent as big as North America, it's a car journey. She describes Beyoncé's specific neighbourhood as 'pretty nice but if you drive a few blocks you're in the hood' – the lower-class type of neighbourhood Lela grew up in. When I ask if she could relate to Beyoncé's upbringing she says, 'Beyoncé grew up with two parents in her household, her mum was a beautician but she still was bringing in money, and her childhood house is nice, so no. She grew up middle class, I grew up poor.' Despite that difference, there was a transition that was interesting for Lela to watch as a black fan. 'When she first hit the scene, she had a hood swagger, and when I first graduated from college, I had this demeanour and the way I talked you could tell what area I was from. But as I got older I learnt how to code-switch and speak regular English, professional.' To code-switch is to alter how you express yourself based on your audience. Originally, Beyoncé's solo material was more mainstream pop, referencing blackness in a way that was palatable to a white audience. Now she's back to what Lela calls 'her roots', consistently nodding to black politics and culture. Beyoncé is a master, Lela believes, in code-switching. Lela watched the singer do it and thinks that this may have ensured that she was the member of Destiny's Child everyone would remember forever, thanks to her altering her manner of speech in interviews. Lela did the same, to ascend career ladders and be in white-majority spaces, just like other people of colour frequently have to do for social mobility or safety in the face of systemic racism. This is a connection to Beyoncé to hold close, just as she holds Beyoncé's return to her roots, as a global megastar, close: it is a tangible sign of progress.

When a fan base has become as large, unruly and faceless as the Beyhive, the individuals that make up the group get forgotten. Much of her infamous fandom – as explained to me by fans themselves and as I've found from researching the demographics online – is made up of black women in their mid-twenties to late thirties, of the African diaspora, from across America, and the continent of Africa. Many have followed her, like Lela, since Destiny's Child, though as Lela says, laughing, 'she was the leader of it'. They are well aware of the negative connotations of being involved in the Hive. When I put out calls for interviewees, it felt like their understanding of how they're perceived made them slightly more secretive: wary of me and of being documented in comparison to other fan bases. Mostly, though, minutes after posting in the Facebook fan groups, my request would be buried by other posts. Jokes about Beyoncé being better than other pop artists, collages of fans dressed up as her, conversation starters about where her latest project was at. Fans were here to get updates, not to waste their time speaking to a journalist.

'Beyoncé's fan base is the fan base that have the most smack talked about them,' Lela tells me. 'Everybody keeps the Beyhive name in their mouth. A lot of people don't even know the fan base name of other artists – like Rihanna's Navy, Gaga's Monsters, I forget what Katy Perry's fans are called. I definitely get a lot of negativity, like, "Y'all the most", "Beyoncé's fans are the worst". They say we're over the top but it's like, no, we're just passionate about the particular artist we happen to go hard for, y'all inclined to be extra negative about her.' It is no coincidence that a fandom of black women would be notorious in the mainstream for being aggressive. Though these are Lela's words, they seem to sum up a common belief across the fan base. That Beyoncé is treated with more cynicism and disrespect than she deserves, disproportionately more than other artists receive.

'There are people with double standards. You can have that worship love for a male artist but it's deemed in a negative light if you have that love for a female artist,' says Lela. 'People be calling her Beysus and I know that'd make her uncomfortable. That'd make me uncomfortable. I don't worship Beyoncé. I don't wake up and say "thank you Beyoncé for waking me up"; I say "thank you God for waking me up"… but men run the world and men wrote the Bible so who is to say God is not a woman?' And who is to say that woman is not Beyoncé Giselle Knowles-Carter?

Like God, Beyoncé has believers who write the media about her, and there are scholars who study her. Beyoncé has been a feminism starting point for many black women and women of all ethnicities. Omise'eke Tinsley is a Professor at University of Texas at Austin who started a course on Beyoncé and Rihanna. She was delighted when she greeted those at her class, students she describes in her book *Beyoncé in Formation: Remixing Black Feminism* as 'this receiving line of black women and queers in Texas looking to Beyoncé as a gilded mirror, an artistic creation with the capacity to bounce light off our own visions for next-millennium feminism'. Beyoncé was a black woman whose lessons were relatable and accessible to them. She wasn't a black feminist scholar or writer whose ideas hadn't trickled down to them yet, but she was influenced by them – she had to be – and could exist as a bridge between the average fan and those thinkers. She was never 'just' a pop star.

In her early career, Beyoncé gave interviews. In one Destiny's Child chat with Toazted in Holland in 2001, they talk about what animal they'd like to be, and Beyoncé and bandmate Kelly Rowland seem stoned, smiling dopily, laughing and slurring their words. 'I *love* whales,' she says. In another clip, she fangirls over D'Angelo with Aaliyah ('Girl! I'm with you. 'Cause you know he fine.'). Another clip sees her responding to the phrase 'You are Beyoncé' with 'thank you' – as if, like fans believe, it's the highest compliment you could possibly offer. In these interviews, she is a girl-next-door, funny and touchable, despite levels of talent that set her apart.

'These are the ground rules: Before you get to see Beyoncé, you must agree to live forever in her archive too.' This is what a *GQ* writer found in 2013 when they were allowed entry into her world, on the cusp of Beyoncé's change into image-conscious 'diva'. Here they discovered Beyoncé as documented by the media, in full: every last word, interview, photo, moment logged in physical form by her. She has an archive of every single media mention of her, ever. In addition they found Beyoncé as documented by Beyoncé: a sanctum of thousands of hours of private diary entries she had filmed onto her laptop, as well as all of the footage the 'visual director', whom she employs to document her movements, had filmed since 2005. The writer says that even the room she sits in is rigged with a camera and microphone to capture her words as well as Beyoncé's.

Beyoncé's micro-managed HBO documentary *Life Is But a Dream* was also released in 2013. Critics called it a vanity project, an act of calculated control. It was indeed calculated, slick, professional and (carefully) confessional at the same time, with Beyoncé as the director, executive producer, presenter, talking head and star. When the opening credits flash up to present 'A Beyoncé Knowles Film', it is literally so. The *Independent* humorously called it 'autohagiography at its glossiest'. The *New York Times* said, 'It is neither daring nor entirely truthful. It's an infomercial, not just about Beyoncé's talent onstage but her authenticity behind the scenes.' In it, there's a clip of her talking on a sofa, wearing a simple white shirt and no make-up, to an anonymous interviewer. 'When I first started out there was no internet, people taking pictures of you and exploiting your personal life as entertainment. People are brainwashed… When Nina Simone put out music, you loved her voice. That's what she wanted you to love. You didn't get brainwashed by her day-to-day life. That's not your business. It shouldn't influence the way you listen to the voice and the art, but it does.' It seemed in hindsight as though she were laying the groundwork for her next career move.

What came was silence. 'One day it was like we had all this information about Beyoncé, the next we didn't,' Lela says. At some point between 2013 and 2014, though it's hard to say exactly, Beyoncé stopped giving face-to-face interviews. In 2015, she was on the cover of US *Vogue* but there was no cover interview. The *New York Times* wrote about it with the online headline: 'Beyoncé is Seen but not Heard'. In the whole five years prior to this, there had been no *Vogue* cover star who did not also give an interview, and when Beyoncé was on the cover on previous occasions – in 2009 and 2013 – she had, as is standard practice, given one.

To accompany the 2015 cover, writer Margo Jefferson instead contributed a piece about her. Contacted by the *New York Times* to share her experience of writing it, Jefferson said: 'She has to be studying how effective her interviews have been so far. She may have decided that they do not contribute as dazzlingly to the portrait of Beyoncé as the other stuff. It's a perfectly reasonable decision.' By being silent, Beyoncé could mean nothing and everything; the possibility of someone or something, a concept, more than the sum of her parts. She could have award-winning writers pen essays for her. 'People made fun of how she spoke and she used to use a lot of slang and ebonics. I'm pretty sure that's one reason why she doesn't do interviews. The way she presents herself when she does speak now, it has changed,' says Lela. That Beyoncé was misinterpreted is a commonly held belief among black fans, as is the idea that the initial trigger for the shutdown was the public and press cruelty about the looks of her baby, Blue Ivy, born in 2012. To the general public and Beyoncé detractors, the move from talking person to silent concept or superstar is seen more as arrogance, but to fans it's Beyoncé taking charge of her narrative. She would later be on the US *Vogue* September cover in 2018 and writing briefly about black womanhood and her younger children, twins Sir and Rumi. It is clear her absence has reached such a point that anything she does say will be eagerly devoured, even if it only consists of a few paragraphs.

Around the same time Beyoncé went silent, the Beyhive was born. Fans had always been there since the Destiny's Child days, congregating more tightly around her when she went solo, but the specific formation was still to occur. As with most fan movements, its starting date is impossible to agree on but by May 2014 everyone knew of the Beyhive. *Saturday Night Live* aired 'The Beygency', a sketch that involved a group of friends chatting about Beyoncé. In it, one man says a Beyoncé track just 'doesn't do it' for him, and in come the Beyhive to take him out. They take others down too. Thus the reputation of the fan base was solidified within only a year of its birth: robust, angry, moving en masse against the enemy – those who do not respect and appreciate Beyoncé. Whether it was her media blackout that did it, or the strength of her music career, or most likely a combination of both, Beyoncé had spawned the most powerful and polarising fan base in the world.

She has done the exact opposite of what most musicians and celebrities in a wider context do to grow a fan base. She is not a relatable social media oversharer. Nothing she does is supposed to be hyperreal or unfiltered. Her Instagram posts are rare, highly curated, often with no text at all. Her albums come out with little or no warning, and no accompanying press interviews. She communicates like a god, dropping tablets from the skies, with no explanation. The bees will scramble, and that is simply all that needs to happen. So, between those great tablet drops – albums, rare interviews, Instagram posts – the vast majority of what we have of Beyoncé is what is documented of her by her bees.

Lela is one of hundreds of thousands of bees in various subgroups within the Beyhive who work together. She's an admin in one such group, a 'small' one of around 47,000 fans. 'There's a black woman older than me who started the group, and I'm one of the younger admins,' she explains, wind from the highway hitting the phone speaker. 'There are the bigger Beyhive groups on Facebook; I wouldn't want to be admin of those because I have a life.' Her job as an admin of her group involves organising conversation, removing excessively disruptive bees and deleting too many posts about the same thing. 'You always think you're the first one to post something on there; then you see, dang, somebody's already posted on there.'

Beyoncé's silence has endowed her fans with a sense of power, of responsibility. In bypassing the outlets she previously used, she has implicitly rejected them in favour of the Hive, who work hard every day for their queen. I ask Lela if fans follow Beyoncé news via online media, or just source it through the group. She laughs abruptly: 'We *are* the media.'

When it comes to the daily grind inside a beehive, the manual work is truly endless. Labour is enacted by powerful female bees, who outnumber males 100 to 1. Their communication method while doing so – watch them waggle and dance – tells others the location of bounty sources. Parasitic in nature, beekeepers may enter the hive and steal the food for their own consumption and distribution. They'll take the golden prize from the ones who worked so hard to mine.

As much as Beyoncé fans want more and more from her, they conversely respect that she is a private woman. They love that she is family orientated, has children, wants to keep them protected. But in the absence of anything from her, they've made their own internal structure to keep the hive going in times of absence, between album cycles.

'We act like different species of bee,' says Mouna, a teen from Morocco. 'Look, I'mma explain to you about the Beyhive right now. We got honeybees, the calm ones, they keep to themselves. Bumblebees are similar to honeybees, they might attack if someone tries to sting Queen Bey. Digger bees are hard working and find all the information about Queen Bey; they can say loads of info about her at a time, that's how they attack. Yellowjackets are fakes who just come along when she puts new stuff out. They put the jacket on. Hornets just want new stuff from her all the time, they're annoying. Killer bees: they will attack anyone, even other bees. They support Bey but all their energy is about stinging.'

Although it's the digger bees who do most of the investigative work, posting online and centring the conversation, this is something that most bees contribute to in some form or another.

'I'm checking all the time – I'd never go on Facebook if it weren't for the Beyhive,' says Tatianah, a Haitian woman in her late twenties, living in Florida. 'I don't talk to my real friends on there; all day I'm at work and checking my phone, scrolling through. Whenever I get a notification, it's from the Beyhive group.'

'I used to find things out via mainstream media but now it's from the Beyhive every time,' says Adrianna, a seventeen-year-old honeybee from

Senegal, West Africa. 'They cannot miss something about Beyoncé. We just can't, we know everything. It's all about going so deep. Every time we wake up, we're like, what is Beyoncé doing? Lurking all the time, refreshing her Instagram page, refreshing her webpage, refreshing the internet, that's what we do all the time.'

As a honeybee, Adrianna does more watching and commenting, not so much digging. But, as she tells me proudly, she was the first as far as she could tell to share the Coachella 'suck on my balls' video. It was picked up and used in news posts. She helped create a global media moment. Similarly, Lela says she's frustrated that official DVDs of recent tours haven't been released yet, but that you can find all the footage on Instagram or fan groups. That's the only place to get the visual and audio information – but rather there, in their banks, than nowhere.

Frequently in the past, before Beyoncé's projects or life events have been announced, a fan will post skeletal details in Beyhive groups and kick off discussions. The bees follow anyone online who has the remotest link to Beyoncé; they know who her publicist is, who is working on music with her, her friends from years ago, people she's come into contact with in the past twelve months. Although Beyoncé holds her team to a very high standard of secrecy, respected to an unparalleled degree within the music industry, minor slippage will always happen, and the bees are ready for it.

The Beyhive might be the fan base with literal references to bees and hives but all modern music fandoms work in this way. Fan scholar Henry Jenkins calls fans the 'early adopters of tech'. There weren't many people online in the early nineties, but a lot of them were people who were fans, and music fans at that. They were the first communities to use the internet to mobilise, by sending email chains, crowdfunding, starting social media structures, and shaping social media and the ways we use it now. They established the ways fans continue to research today. It's not unlike being a hunter-gatherer. Fans go out in search of something on a specific topic, look for clues, follow a trail, repurposing and changing direction if necessary, and publish information. They're practised in this way of life. Journalists can't even hope to keep up; they don't have skin in the game, the motivation, the direct focus that the devoted fans do.

'Gossip sites will often trawl Reddit and fandom Twitter and Facebook to bolster their stories, which is fascinating really,' says Lauren O'Neill, a music journalist at *VICE*. 'Sites interested in posting for volume and clicks will definitely just post fan footage from Twitter and Instagram. There'd be so much stuff we as journalists wouldn't know about if we didn't have the fans; they're a useful resource for anyone. Their dedication is the thing, really. As journalists, especially today, we don't have the time to trawl through everything on a particular musician; especially on a news shift. If we know fans have already been there and done that, we'll look to them.' This is the same as it's always been – fans can be relied on to bring home the gold. The prominence of fandom's contribution to reporting is just the result of online fandoms growing in number and journalists waking up to their power.

The journalistic beat has been compromised by cuts and catastrophic industry-wide job losses; in the same way you'll be stretched to find an in-house specialist for local politics or fiction books, there is no space for someone anywhere whose sole beat is Beyoncé Knowles. Even if there were – a single journalist monitoring her movements versus the Hive? There is no competition.

The music press is no longer a conduit to the famous artist. As more celebrities go the way of Beyoncé and refuse to give proper interviews, write their own small poems or captions for magazines, or even interview each other, access is ever more limited. Artists can be in touch with the public directly using their own social media accounts, or let their management communicate for them. They don't need to court the media. In her rejection of traditional mainstream media coverage and then continued silence, Beyoncé has not only avoided the possible prejudice of the media and risk of misinterpretation, but stayed, as ever, one step ahead, realising that nothing could ever beat the fans, before the fans themselves even realised.

What now can beat her own collective of investigative journalists? There are hundreds of thousands of them online all over the world, all the time, always checking, surveying, watching.

As a bee colony grows in size and seasons progress, the creatures become more protective of their stores. Particularly when there is little to forage, the group can become both possessive and aggressive. Often predators will attempt to break into the hive, and bees can be relied upon to attack. In a strong colony, individuals will defend their sisters, even die for them, and, importantly, will protect the queen at any cost.

White country singer Kid Rock had Beyoncé's name in his mouth. 'Beyoncé to me doesn't have a fucking "Purple Rain", but she's the biggest thing on Earth,' he said in a 2015 *Rolling Stone* interview. He went on to talk crassly about her body and his own sexual preferences ('skinny white chicks with big tits'). Beyoncé 'doesn't really fucking do much for me'. The Beyhive did not like this. They began to spam Kid Rock's Instagram posts with bee emojis. This did not stop. Today, when the 'American Bad Ass' singer uploads a picture to social media, you may find stray bees reminding him of his error or telling him to retire.

In 2016, Beyoncé's fifth album, *Lemonade*, was released. On 'Sorry', she sings the two infamous lines: 'He only want me when I'm not there / He better call Becky with the good hair.' There was only one question on the mind of the Beyhive: who is Becky? Had a lyric ever sparked so much buzz and intrigue? Commentators thought that Becky meant a woman (specifically not a black woman) Beyoncé's husband had cheated on her with. They had the significant reference: now the Beyhive just had to swarm.

Fans immediately thought of the elevator incident. In 2014, CCTV caught footage of Beyoncé's sister Solange attacking her brother-in-law Jay-Z in an elevator. Speculation was that the fight was over an affair, or the very least what Solange had seen as Jay's inappropriate relationship, with clothes designer Rachel Roy. 'Solange was defending Beyoncé in the elevator because Solange finds Jay's friendship with Rachel to be WAY too close for comfort and it makes Solange very uncomfortable,' a source told *Hollywood Life*. 'Beyoncé also confronted Rachel and said, "Don't talk to my sister like that," after [Rachel] confronted Solange.' Two days later, Beyoncé and Jay released a statement that revealed little. 'We've put this behind us and hope everyone else will do the same,' it concluded.

Hours after *Lemonade* premiered, Roy posted a photo of herself along with the caption: 'Good hair don't care, but we will take good lighting, for selfies, or self truths, always. live in the light #nodramaqueens.' The Beyhive found this first and fans will defend that fact. 'TMZ would say they found out but really Beyhive found it first. Ask anyone who was there, anyone in the hive. Beyhive will always have the best info,' says Lela. For hours, they were spamming Roy with bee emojis, calling her Becky. The bees are a yellow-and-black warning, the relentless volume of them says: there is one of you, there are many of us. Roy – or someone in charge of Roy's account – tried to delete these comments but couldn't keep up. By the time gossip sites and mainstream media had blogged about it, Roy's account had been made private.

On Twitter, fans were tweeting at Roy or commenting on the situation, saying things like: '@Rachel_Roy IM THROWING LEMONS AT YOU ON SIGHT BITCH YOU BETTER WATCH OUT', 'I have a Rachel Roy romper that I love but as a Beyhive member, bitch I will burn it. Do not play with me Rach [lemon emoji]', and '[bee emojis] you got stung'. Everyone came together in force to put the bee emoji under the social media posts of anyone they thought could be Becky. Some bees mistook Rachael Ray, a chef, for Roy on socials and fired bees and lemons at her. A few days later Rita Ora, who was on Jay-Z's label Roc Nation, complicated matters when she posted a picture of herself on her personal Snapchat wearing a bra adorned with two lemons and a necklace with the letter 'J'. There had also previously been rumours of the pair having an affair.

'We were all clicking: that's her, that's her. Let's go get her!' Adrianna from Senegal says. She claims she steers completely away from being hot-tempered. Her friend had been posting bees with insulting messages on Rachel Roy's Instagram page, which she saw and told her to stop, and to calm down. 'I also put some bee emojis, just to be a little more...' She pauses. 'I saw the Beyhive do it, and I was like, OK, if the Beyhive doing it, I'm going to do it too, I'm a member of the Beyhive.' Another pause. 'OK, I did it. Maybe I shouldn't but I'm not sorry. I didn't do mean comments. If Beyoncé's classy enough to not do that, I'm not.'

Bianca is a young mum who lives in Johannesburg. 'Oh, I was there, I was involved in it,' she says. 'We are her children. Let's say you are a hater, and you mention something negative about Beyoncé – we are her children and we'll come for you. That's what I like about being part of the Beyhive.' Her child makes gurgling noises in the background. 'It's good posting bees on your own – you're at home or wherever on your own and everyone goes their separate ways in their lives – but you're all together, it's nice.'

The song's main writer Diana Gordon had implied that the lyrics shouldn't be taken literally, and that there might not *be* a Becky. She said of the subsequent fan drama, 'I laughed, like this is so silly. Where are we living? I was like, what day in age from that lyric do you get all this information? Is it really telling you all that much, accusing people?' Unequivocally and irrefutably, the fans were furious, but their actions were barely comparable to the darker fringes of many fanbases. This is particularly true within stan culture – a more extreme segment of internet fan culture – where certain fans are racist or homophobic and inter-fandom wars can become extremely aggressive. It doesn't matter who the artist is, there will always be followers who sour the community for everyone. The *Lemonade* incident was the most concrete example of Beyoncé fans being supposedly 'threatening' in their approach, but most bees were simply posting bee and lemon emojis. These little pictures are iconography of a broader symbol from *Lemonade*'s message of the disrespected black woman. Considering the fact they believed rightly or wrongly that these women were flaunting an affair that had caused their leader immense pain, the posting is the Beyhive coming together to do the impossible act of seeking justice for centuries of poor behaviour from boyfriends and husbands. In doing this, they are re-centring Beyoncé in a conversation that felt in those moments – a post from Rachel Roy or Rita Ora – as though it was being taken away from her.

Beyoncé fans continue to care in the face of her silence because they tell me that she empowers them when little around them does. Her silence in fact allows her fans to defend her more forcefully. 'She keeps a clean persona,' explains Lela. 'You can't say anything negative about her because you don't know her. She writes her own narrative...she doesn't let anyone write her narrative for her. I think that, because she knows we'll defend her from anything, anywhere and her fan base is all over the world, that she low-key knows she doesn't have to say anything because we'll take anyone down.'

It's reasonable enough to assume that Beyoncé sees what the bees post for her. Professor of pop culture and Beyoncé expert Kevin Allred considers that she has to be online sometimes and therefore aware. 'I'm sure she sees some of this stuff and I wonder if it gives her a chuckle. I guess the idea is that if it made her mad enough she'd say something, like "OK stop", but I guess it'd have to be so egregious that it would make sense for her to break the media silence for her to make a statement like that, and very few things seem like they would be.' Other artists might step in and try to police the actions they see happening. It is, after all, the artists fans explode for and on behalf of. It is they the fans will listen to. Lady Gaga is a prime example of this: her fans are, to a certain extent, as avid as Beyoncé's, but over the years she has told them on social media and through open letters to stop cyberbullying, to stop sending death threats, to stop victim-shaming.

Erik Steinskog, another Beyoncé professor, who teaches a course on her at Copenhagen University, supports Allred's hypothesis. 'We know that Beyoncé has people hired whose primary purpose is to be on social media on her behalf to see what is happening, what is written about her. A colleague of mine gave a lecture in New York about Beyoncé and someone from her management was in the hall taking notes about what was said in the university lecture. I'm sure they know of my course. It's interesting to see that she, or at least her team, is also aware of everything that is going on. There are all these speculations as to whether she is part of the Beyhive groups on a fake account or something. Even if she's not, I'm sure there's someone hired by her to be a part of them.'

Is Beyoncé just sitting there at home in her Bel Air mansion, laughing at whatever the bees are orchestrating from the Hive?

A portion of the golden prize is used for the individual bees' nourishment and energy; the rest goes to the hive. After a process of working the product, small nuggets become something greater: an off-season food source to access when foraging for food would be a thankless task. Together, the bees stay sated and healthy.

Lemonade had been teased on Instagram with a trailer a week ahead of its drop and a premiere date. No one knew what the secret project was. In the trailer Beyoncé was in a fur coat, resting her head and braided hair on the hood of a car, hiding herself. Her voice asked: 'What am I gonna do, love? What am I gonna do?' The release date was 23rd April 2016.

Mouna was at school when she saw Beyoncé's first tweet in three years and burst into tears, screaming, and calling her friends over. It was simply the *Lemonade* album artwork and '#Lemonade the Visual album. BEYONCE.TIDAL.COM'. This was twelve tracks in twelve videos arranged as a full film out of the silence. Mouna bought the album and watched and listened to it there and then at school, unable to wait.

The whole Beyhive had gone into shock, despite knowing when the project would drop. Because Beyoncé might not speak to them directly – but she does through her work. Everything is for them, the black female fans, black women in general. This was the most potent proof of that. Writer Sydney Gore called *Lemonade* 'A Love Letter From Beyoncé To Black Women'. Trans activist and writer Janet Mock wrote that the visual album was testimony and that for black women 'testimony is the connective tissue that allows us to be seen and heard in a world that is intent on choking us with silence'. *Lemonade* asked very clearly: 'What is it like to be a black woman in America?' It was the story of women being cheated on, going through the stages of grief, praying for relief and an end, being vulnerable but coming through. It praised the black women who know, more than anyone else, the meaning and salvation provided by community. The videos were largely filmed on plantations in Louisiana, and used mostly black women as the actors and dancers. They showed women who were left behind and suffering, like the mothers of Eric Garner, Trayvon Martin and Michael Brown, men from a long line of black sons brutally killed by white police and security in America. One of the most memorable sections of the film quotes from Malcolm X's speech from 1962, in 'Don't Hurt Yourself': 'The most disrespected person in America is the black woman. The most unprotected person in America is the black woman.' Through this powerful work, Beyoncé saw in her black woman fans multi-faceted vulnerability: she saw fans in a way that society with its prejudices refuses to. Crucially, Professor Omise'eke Tinsley called it '(arguably) the most widely distributed black feminist text of the current moment'.

Adrianna was at home in her Senegalian bedroom listening to *Lemonade*. 'Girl, I felt so good. Back at that time, my ex-boyfriend cheated too, so I was feeling absolutely everything that she was saying. I would sit on my bed at 2am crying like crazy just because I related so much to what she was saying. That's when I got really close to Beyoncé; I was there back in those 'Single Ladies' days but *Lemonade* was just so…it was like she was talking to me, she's here to help me, she did this album for me.'

Martiese, thirty-nine, managed to wait to get loved ones over to her house in South Carolina for a Beyoncé listening party that night; they shared homemade food and sat down to watch it. 'It made me so proud to be an African-American woman, because oftentimes our attitude, the way we dress, the way we talk, our passion, it's miscommunicated or rather it's taken out of context,' Martiese said, echoing Lela's words about how Beyoncé is perceived. 'I think when she showed it in a visual way, for me it was saying, yes she's angry and mad, but there's many reasons. We know exactly where she came from, and even then she's figuring out a way to make it work. She wants to love. It really showed who we are as African-American women.'

Bianca had downloaded it sneakily on to her phone while at work. 'It gave me goosebumps. There's a lot of music about female empowerment out there but they don't get across how it is as a black woman. I came home and watched it with my younger brother, we were discussing it and goosebumps again hit me. Since Destiny's Child, she evolved, I evolved. There's always something I find of comfort in her messages.'

Lela turned the album drop into a whole viewing session with her best friends. 'She really showed that black woman struggle. With all the black women in the videos ,you knew, "OK, this is the story of a black woman." For us it showed love prevails and you can win.' She loved that it was filmed in Louisiana, not too far away, so she found the locations and took photos with her sister.

'I'm looking around trying to think of black women in our culture who are putting out music to that scale. And she's not just putting out music, she's part of the movement. The "Formation" video highlighted a lot of what we've got going on with the #BlackLivesMatter stuff in our country. People were annoyed with "Formation" but it's like, there is nothing wrong with her highlighting what is going on in her culture, in her community.' In saying this, Lela means to defend the way the 'Formation' video visually references Hurricane Katrina (some critics argued that Beyoncé was wrong to use black deaths as pop culture fodder), and perhaps also to defend her Superbowl performance, which heavily referenced the Black Panthers, irritating some right-wing commentators and viewers. 'There really isn't any other artist, I can't think of anyone else making music specifically for black women and especially music that uplifts us too. With "Independent Women", "Survivor", with the fifth album, she made a statement, she knows we've grown with her.'

In pop culture scholar and writer Bolu Babalola's paper 'Lemons into Lemonade: Black Women Re-defining and Resisting Identities Through Musical Performance', she writes that by connecting modern black women with the black women throughout American history and its oppressive past, Beyoncé is creating a 'new-world order' in *Lemonade*. 'In this marriage of time, Beyoncé brings black women from past, present and future together. This is a collective motion of resistance – black women in formation. It is not a mere question of individualistic liberty.'

What struck me early on in researching the Beyhive is that it looks nothing like a flattened reproduction in comedy sketches or a stereotype referenced in an article. Some groups are solely about positivity ('There should be space for people who stan for Beyoncé quietly,' says Lela on this topic). One prominent womxn-only (and mostly black women) Beyhive sisterhood Facebook group celebrates birthdays, posts selfies and appreciation days for other members, and has WhatsApp groups where they keep in touch. They send out thoughts and prayers when others are sick or grieving and celebrations when they move house.

Bianca talks about the WhatsApp group she has with other fans as a central, warming presence in her life. 'It's not just about us being aggressive. We are human at the end of the day. Whatever you're going through in life, we can share it. We came together because we are fans of Beyoncé but looking at the bigger picture, we are family. It's people you never met in your life, maybe you will never meet them in this life, it's a whole different experience.'

Just as in the 'Formation' video, where Beyoncé calls for black women to organise and her dancers literally fall into formation, everyone moving as one unit, her fans are a step behind, but catching up, with movements of their own; something that they – not she – have created. The sparse and minimalistic beats of the song evolve into a marching band's stomp by its close. Behind the messages in her work, she herself is a blank slate, something to project whatever they want onto. She is the template for who they could become. Black female fans spoke frequently of wanting to be the Beyoncé of their field. And so in the absence of her, Beyoncé gives her fans room to thrive.

When I next speak to Lela she apologises and says she'll have to get back to me. She was flying, actually in the air, having left her phone on during take-off. A couple of hours later, she calls me back from a car, once again the wind booming against everything in and outside the vehicle. She's on her way to Atlanta to find somewhere to live. 'It's a popping city. Martin Luther King is buried there and that's where he grew up. It's also the strip club capital of the country. When I'm car shopping or apartment shopping, I'm the type of person who picks up that day, so hopefully I'll get something I like.'

She'd just returned from welcoming some new girls into her sorority, Delta Sigma Theta. 'With us when you join, it's a lifetime commitment,' she goes on, with the cadence of a motivational speaker. Her sorority is in South Carolina, so she'll be coming back and forth from Atlanta once she's moved. 'Mine is African-American based, it was started in the 1900s because black people weren't allowed into sororities, so we made our own. We focus on informing people about voting, we do food drives, we mentor young girls in high school; there's always something to be done. It's a sisterhood I'm attached to, I like it.'

Each sorority has a different hand sign to signify honour and belonging, Lela tells me. 'It's funny because we have a hand sign and it looks like the one Beyoncé throws up, when she's throwing up the triangle? So we joke that Beyoncé needs to be made an honorary Delta because she's always throwing up our hand sign.' She laughs, because it's a nice and absurd thought, but pride shines through in her voice.

At her Coachella performance as captured in the *Homecoming* documentary, where she shows the wealth of culture from HBCUs, Beyoncé said, smiling, 'This next song is for all of my queens. Do we have any beautiful queens in the house tonight?' And she says this knowing that she does – they're in the crowd, everywhere. From this question she bounces into 'Bow Down', a demand for respect and for your crown to be observed.

For her community, rather than for a world stage, it's not that far a stretch to say that Lela is a queen.

Beyoncé fans on 'knowing' her: interviews outside the On the Run II Tour, Wembley Arena, Friday 15th June 2018

Dalila, 21

I know her brand. I can get a vibe from her that she's a family-orientated person, she's nice, she's very career focused, more so than a lot of artists, and she's someone who goes for goals. I think that's good though, nowadays people want to know more about you and I think it makes you more appealing as a celebrity to keep some stuff private, even actors and actresses. I don't want to see every part of their life, I see them as the celebrity. I know her persona. Her aura is something you'd have to get to really know her for.

Salma, 19

All the mega Beyoncé stans don't know everything about her but will still continue to support her in everything. I think it's really cool that people are respecting the fact she doesn't want to show everyone the real her. I feel like she's a figure, a public figure, everyone knows her. You know her but you don't.

Bali, 30

She's my mum. She's more of an authority figure in a way. You don't really know them *that* well but you know them in another way. You don't know your mum as a person, your mum's just a mum, she's the woman who brings home the bacon.

Rania, 20

She's a leader. I know her name, I know generally about her, I know the vague details of her. She's one of those celebrities where I love her music but I don't really care about her. Not in a bad way, but I have no interest in knowing about her. She's not a personality: she's a musician, an artist, whereas other people, they do both. You don't know if she's funny, if she's more serious, we don't know much about her in that sense.

7

HARRY'S GIRLS, LONG-DISTANCE LOVE AND GLOBAL FANGIRLING

Just stop your crying, it's a sign of the times
Welcome to the final show
Hope you're wearing your best clothes
          – Harry Styles, 'Sign of the Times'

Yukino adores fluffy pancakes with syrup and bananas, the thicker the better. Like many sixteen-year-old girls from Tokyo, she loves: posing with her friends in the *purikura* photobooths that supersize your eyes and superflush your cheeks; videos of adorable animals doing human tasks far beyond the capabilities of their species; the capital's nautical-themed Disney park, Disneysea; Chanel make-up, or at least the dream of having it once funds allow; her dance club. More than all those combined, she loves Harry Styles.

Along with between two and three hundred other girls, Yukino is standing in the otherwise barren arrivals area of Haneda airport. The girls believe Harry's flight will land at 5.55am, meaning that at some point close to the hour, he'll be curving through the doors to their left and inevitably, following common practice and expectation, stopping to engage with them on the way.

The Sunday night just hours before, Yukino was sitting online, chatting to friends and winding down for sleep when she saw that a fan had posted a photo of herself with Harry at a New Zealand airport. From the time this picture was posted – knowing that the Japanese dates of his tour, the very final shows of the entire run, were imminent – she and others were able to deduce what flight to Japan he would be getting and therefore at which airport he would land and at what time. This was confirmed to eager fans by a reply from the girl with the selfie. While each Japanese fan could've kept this delicious information to themselves, they shared the nugget, insistent that every girl possible be there. 'After I saw the photo, I told my parents I had to go and they encouraged me even though I had school,' Yukino tells me, making tiny anticipatory squeaks. 'I just didn't sleep at all. Luckily, my other friends who love Harry live in the same area, so we left the house together and got the first train.'

Some might call this stalking. Within the One Direction (and later, their individual solo career) fandoms, this word is often used. In London, 1D stalking can get very competitive, and different groups, often bound by nationality, stick together. 'Everyone is sneaky because we all want to get the information to meet them without telling other people. To the point where people lie to each other. It's mean but that's true,' says Laura, nineteen. Information will instead be shared within the group. What you'll do to get that access can be extreme and differs from fan to fan. Laura's friend Grace, nineteen, only does it in public spaces, for instance, going to a rehearsal studio. 'I wouldn't wait outside their gyms, for example, even though I know the ones they go to, because it's their personal space. It's a moralistic thing. I know a lot of people in New York who chase them in cars and call up airlines and pretend to be one of them to get their flight number.' Nothing that extreme had to happen in Tokyo.

At 6.15am, accompanied by bodyguards and airport security, Harry appears in wide-legged pink trousers. He autographs items held at stiff right angles and turns into their selfies; the mantra-like cries of 'Harry, Harry' rise in pitch as they sense his departure. It comes with a final wave. Yukino was close to the front initially but gets pushed away by others. 'I was really moved by how he took photographs with everyone and signed autographs, but at the middle I think someone pushed him and it finished abruptly. Until it ended he was polite and nice. I was too far back so I couldn't get anything signed but I did get videos of him signing…everyone else's stuff.' She starts to cry. She cries a lot. Her friends, composed despite disappointment, try to plug her tears with platitudes and condolences.

'The tears will not stop. I can't go to school,' she tweets from her phone moments after. But they do go straight into school feeling dejected. Later she'll tell me: 'I'd tweeted about it so school people knew what had happened but when I arrived I cried again and everyone was nice to me, saying things like, "It's OK, don't worry. You still *saw* him." I just wanted to welcome Harry in a warm way because he hasn't been in Japan for quite a while. That was the sentiment.' There is a respectfulness here, an acceptance that they are not close to his body, that they can never really be.

Her tone suggests what I hear over and over again in Tokyo: gratefulness that Western artists would bother to make the considerable trip over to their little island. It's why greeting an artist at the airport – an act done by many fangirls cut off from their favourites by inconvenient bodies of water – is a true event in Japan, the royal welcome a core part of fans' show of appreciation for musicians. Not that this feeling of indebtedness is qualified or necessary: Japan's music market is the second largest in the world, beaten only by enormously spacious and populated North America. The Japanese have the highest per-capita consumer spending on music: each person spends $21.54 on it per year compared to the average American, who spends $16.39. Western musicians will half-joke that they love Japan not only for the loyalty but the money. But these girls' feelings of being blessed by their favourite artist's presence in their country is familiar and relatable to anyone who identifies as a fan.

To be a serious fan is to be in a relationship with distance. Just like the act of waiting, engaging with distance is a Sisyphean task. Each act of fandom is an attempt to bridge some gap, to obliterate or quietly dissolve the space with wanting, caring, knowing. Sometimes we're content with distance, there's a respect for it and the contractual understanding between us and our object that's borne from it. Sometimes we might resent it, but we can't forget it: that's the deal. The type of closeness and distance we have depends on the artist we choose – or are compelled – to follow.

For fans of an overseas artist who rarely tours there and doesn't speak your language, there's another ocean of difference. Many Japanese fangirls choose it wholeheartedly. In his seminal text about fans *Textual Poachers: Television Fans and Participatory Culture* (1992), fan studies scholar Henry Jenkins says that fans are 'largely female, largely white, [and] largely middle class'. This is what he claims before telling us almost anything else about fans. The reality is that fandoms of Western musicians do privilege the Anglo-American experience and the English language dominates online conversations. If race is not spoken about in fandom spaces, then the general or stock fan is seen to be white, as some sort of default. 'Overseas' fans of Western artists or products are seen as additional fans to a 'core' fan base of Westerners. In the music industry, they're spoken about as another market to branch into. While the pervasive idea is that 'fangirling' itself is a predominantly Western concept, this is false; in practice it's alive globally.

Johnny's Shop has security guards outside and inside. These are real gatekeepers of a Japanese pop fandom that is simultaneously ubiquitous and secretive. It's just off the main drag in Harajuku, Japan's teen-girl fandom holy land, a place where you can find the same studded neon suspenders your idol owns, animated character pants or foam fingers branded with your favourite pop group's name. Johnny's Entertainment is the talent agency that has more or less exclusively trained and promoted the biggest boy bands in the country for decades. Johnny's is at the forefront of Japan's booming domestic music industry of genres and artists whose sound is barely heard outside the country. This particular shop is one of the only official spaces (there are three branches in other large Japanese cities, Osaka, Nagoya and Fukuoka) to buy tiny photographs of the artists belonging to Johnny's. Before coming I was warned seriously by multiple girls to avoid the weekend unless I wanted hours of waiting and a mad crush. It's mid-afternoon on a Thursday and the shop is still three-quarters or more full with the girls who love 'Johnny's boys' or just 'Johnny's', as the artists are collectively known.

These are boys and men who, regardless of age, look like timeless angels. Hairless, simpering wonders dressed like they're en route to meet your mum. They're standing on a balcony holding a rose. They're blowing you a kiss from a shining vintage car. They're together in crisp white shirts against stock backgrounds, posturing in cliché nineties boy band stances, hands through lush heads of hair, thumbs hooked into clean jeans. You can't see their chests underneath those shirts but you know you could eat off them. Here is sexuality packaged in the least threatening way, done by slotting new stars into old formulas, and making multiple iterations of the same thing.

The system here is as follows: with a pen and a form you go into the basement first, a canvas of a room with flimsy boards leading you around in a maze towards the exit. On every board there are dozens and dozens of small photographs of the artists. They look like collectable stickers or Pokémon cards. It doesn't matter if they're in popular groups Hey! Say! JUMP or Arashi, everyone on the rectangles could be mistaken for being in the same band by those outside the fandom. None of them look unlike One Direction or Western boy bands of any given decade.

Groups of girls in school uniform – not 'fangirls' but 'Johnny's Girls' or 'Johnny-ota', short for *otaku*, meaning geek – bop in front of the boards, faces only a few centimetres away. 'He's so handsome.' 'I need this, it's new.' 'Did you see his face in this one? So good looking.' 'Ahhhhh!' Just as a fan settles on one photo, she'll notice another perhaps cuter one and alert her friends to its existence. There are thousands to choose from but a limited amount of cash. One girl near me looks down at her sheet, realises it's covered in crosses, groans and prods her friend, who laughs and helps her get rid of some of the 'necessities'. Once you've picked the photos you want, you take your sheet upstairs and queue to be given your stack of physical images. Then they're yours. You can store them in photo books or frame them. Look at them, kiss them. Keep them.

'It's hard to explain why I like Johnny's,' starts nineteen-year-old Akane, 'but watching them is so enjoyable for me. They are handsome, good-looking and they make me laugh. They always dedicate all their strength.' She and the friend of the same age she's here with, Yuuka, spend much of their time talking about the boys. 'We talk about their performance on TV and at music shows. And for example when their hairstyles change, we talk about it, like "his new hairstyle is so sweet!"' Yuuka starts laughing and makes a wily grin at Akane: 'Yeah, we basically chat about their looks.'

Both decide that they spend a reasonable proportion of their yearly wages as a café waitress and a cram-school teacher on Johnny's, estimating in excess of 200,000 yen, which is around £1,335 or $1,775 per year. They've been ticking off the days leading up to The Johnny's Countdown Concert, which takes place at Tokyo Dome on New Year's Eve almost every year, and is broadcast live on TV. 'Yesterday the Johnny's Countdown Concert was announced and we'll apply for the tickets. Getting them is highly competitive, so I know it is almost impossible to go there,' says Yuuka, adding that she is still hopeful.

Like others, they've been fans of Johnny's for the majority of their lives, having first seen their favourite groups on talk shows or playing a role in a movie. Mitsuki, a nineteen-year-old student, has been a hardcore fan for nine years and became one 'without even being aware'. 'We see them everywhere, on many TV programmes and magazines. Their work is not limited to one field; they sing, act and so on, so we get to see their various activities.' These boys *are* everywhere.

Fifteen-year-old Kaho is here with her mum, who is also a big Johnny's fan. Kaho's been in love with Johnny's artists since she was only five after seeing them on TV with her brother. 'We'd just sit and watch for hours and they'd be so sparkling and such *nice guys*.' At ten she went to her first Arashi concert. I ask if she considers being a Johnny's Girl her hobby and she nods plainly. 'My hobby is everyday listening to the music of Johnny's! Thinking of them and talking about them.' All the girls I speak to, Kaho included, say that the majority of girls her age are as in love with Johnny's as she is, so there is no shortage of people to share this hobby with.

'It's expensive to have so many,' she says, showing me her crossed-out and re-marked sheet. 'I often come here but how many I buy can depend on the day. Today it's about twenty. I keep them all in a file, a collection.'

Extraordinarily, these images are available entirely on Johnny's terms. Photography in this gallery is strictly forbidden – that's why these girls are here in the first place. Security are very suspicious of me with my dictaphone out. 'Johnny's is famous for being terrified of the internet,' Tokyo-based music writer Patrick St. Michel tells me over coffee when I ask about this. If Johnny's artists are featured in a movie and the movie has a website promoting the film with a thumbnail of everybody's faces, Johnny's artists' will be blacked out. As with many of the boy bands in Japan, any fan footage of them uploaded online quickly gets removed. 'Even if you go to a book store here and look at some pop culture magazines, some of them might have silhouettes of people on the cover – those are Johnny's stars. Johnny's won't let them put their faces on the cover.' It was only in 2018 that Johnny's loosened this grip a little and allowed some of their artists' music videos on a new official Johnny's YouTube channel. Even so, this was a test with a few of the less-established bands, to see if they could carefully grow their appeal both in Japan and globally.

Despite Johnny's being everywhere in Japan, physically within the country too, it's all extremely controlled. The insularity of the industry and the one-sided contact with their idols breeds an anomalous kind of closeness – for which fans are paying a high price, because the industry knows how much it can make for that closeness.

Near the official Johnny's Store is Takeshita-Dōri, a street that looks like a gothic marshmallow nightmare and has the overwhelming smell of sugary waffles. Besides a few chain shops, it's lined with independent stores and, notably, numerous idol stores. Idol stores feel like the bandwagon version of what Johnny's Store does. They are rooms, often in the basements, covered floor to ceiling – and even over the ceiling – with photos of idols, girls and boys in pop and rock bands. Using the same system as Johnny's Store, you write down the numbers that appear on the photos you like and take them to a member of staff, who'll collect the pictures for you. Many sell raw photos, meaning someone went to the concert, took pictures of the talent and these came from the film roll. To buy these photos is to connect to their idols in a physical way. There's such an old-school, pre-internet charm to this, imbuing items considered so simple with such a talismanic power.

As this would suggest, fandom is product-driven in Japan, more so than in the West. As I'm told repeatedly, it's not about what you know, it's about what you own. 'If you like music here in a fangirl or fanboy way, you need one copy of a CD to keep on your shelf and never touch, you need one to actually listen to, one for the car, one as a spare,' says Alisa Yamasaki, a music writer and fan living in the densely populated heart of the city. 'Knowing that people will buy the physical music because they need to own something, there'll be the first-press edition, the deluxe edition, various releases with different artwork or inserts. People will buy all of them.' Often this extends to benefits of winning a concert ticket, or finding a special polaroid inside certain CDs. Sometimes buying multiple copies of the same CD – enough to mean you have to throw them away – can directly count towards voting your favourite member into a group. Importantly, the expenditure isn't unique to teen girl fans or even just music fans; across sports to TV to film, the average Japanese person spends a lot of money on their hobbies and fandoms.

However, when so much money is being spent to buy closeness, then closeness, or a near-impenetrable illusion of it, is what must be delivered. Fans don't want to buy into the band, they want to buy the band. J-Pop artists are marketed as products, and are not supposed to have boyfriends and girlfriends because they must appear available for the fans. Decades ago, pop bands under certain Western management teams were placed under similar obligations. The punishments for breaking these rules can be serious. It was global news when AKB48 member Minami Minegishi shaved her head in penance for being caught in a hotel room with a member of a boy band, and there was enormous pressure from her management and label to show public remorse. 'A big part of Japanese fangirl culture in general is that artists exist for you,' explains Alisa. 'This happens in other fan communities overseas too, which is evidenced when people are mad at Justin Bieber for saying, "Don't talk badly about this girl I'm dating, she's somebody I care about," and fans say, "You're only famous because of us, don't talk down to us." But that feeling is so strong in Japan because people think: how dare you date this girl, the only way you can take her on dates is because we support you – literally.'

When I ask Mitsuki what she finds most disappointing or difficult about being a Johnny's fan, she says, 'I feel sad when I hear about the scandal of my favourite when he gets a lover or engagement.' This is despite having her own dating life, which she does think is in some way affected by being a Johnny's-*ota* – maybe by spending too much time on Johnny's boys, not on *her* boy. 'When I feel bad, for example, when my boyfriend dumped me, I can quickly recover from that pain by thinking about Shigeoka-kun from Johnny's WEST, my favourite Johnny's boy, and that he always stands by me,' she laughs. 'It makes me strong that I have an *ikemen* [good-looking boy] in my heart, who never betrays me!'

In a district, not far from Shibuya, skyscrapers hold embassies and multi-national firms in the air. Its name, Minato, means harbour in Japanese and, certainly, this is where money comes in to dock. Avex are a renowned entertainment conglomerate in Japan known for managing some of the most famous J-Pop acts. They take up space in a beautiful glass high-rise that, when I arrived, was filled with dozens of bouquets of flowers as tall as and wider than me. Shogo, their A&R man, tells me, 'Westerners look at Japan and think teens like J-Pop, but really it's for thirty-year-olds and more.' This is the result of the nineties kids who came of age during J-Pop's biggest boom growing up, but it is a question of who has the finances. 'Fans here are collectors,' his colleague and translator Sachiko says. 'To collect you need money. In Japan, a lot of fans like to post photos online of how much merchandise they have to enjoy the reaction of other fans, and that's grown-ups doing that not just teens. Adults will follow artists from Hokkaido in the north all the way down to the south when there's a nationwide or world tour. People will use vacation days to do this.'

Shogo takes me to the top of their building so I can see the view. It's sheer glass all around and you can see the entirety of Tokyo for miles. The Tokyo Skytree, lit up in red, juts out, a piercing landmark among all the grey and black and shimmering lights. The huge billboards I noticed on my way, which show musicians selling records and face creams and phone plans and fizzy drinks, are now coloured specks.

In the night below was a city, maybe a lonely one, but also one that allowed for connection of all kinds. Small fan bases of girls put hundreds of pounds together to buy flowers to create handmade wreaths for artists, which they'll lay outside the venue their idols are playing at later; people queue in a shopping centre for a handshake event with their favourite group; mums and daughters gather together by a TV to watch their Johnny's angels on a chat show; an idol is slowly applying each layer of her make-up as people watch through a screen. Somewhere a fan was throwing out dozens of CDs, which had served their purpose, into a bin. Elsewhere a flock of women were making their way to a street where a new film poster of their artist had been erected, to take photos next to it.

'I see them as human like us,' Emma, twenty-nine, said of Johnny's boys. 'I really respect them working as an idol; someone who wants to spread love to everyone, and cheer up all the people, with a lot of sacrifice, especially sacrificing their personal life. I could never be an idol like them, but I have to at least try to live like them.' They offer an aspirational message about career and persistence: work hard and keep on trying.

This belief is repeated again and again by Johnny's fans my age. From twenty-nine-year-old Kana from Kyoto who said, 'They at least try to be a star and I love their true effort' – referring to the fact some J-Pop stars have questionable skill sets but seem 'just like you' – and twenty-five-year-old pharmacist Ly who said, 'I feel I can try hard every day when I see them shining on stage while making so much effort behind the scenes', to twenty-nine-year-old office worker Yuko: 'When we get to be a fan of somebody, we start to think of the ways to support him. Eventually, and hopefully, we get to want to be a good and beautiful person as we are a fan of a good and beautiful person.' These are people you can keep close to you your entire life. So much of fandom's proximity can be a fantasy, but fantasy is often necessary. It's not just the fantasy of closeness: sometimes we just need to believe that someone is *good*.

A phrase that Yuko said offhand stuck with me: 'There is no negative power in Johnny's world. They offer us only starry things.'

The sky in Tokyo doesn't have a single blemish. The surface looks matte and there's a heaviness to it that seems to keep excitement contained.

Roppongi is an entertainment district best known for its nightclub scene. It was formerly famed for its Yakuza (gangster) presence and now is a place where businessmen, expats and students all come together under the name of spirits. It's a popular area with a slightly dangerous reputation and, despite Tokyo being the safest city in the world, some families would rather their teenage girls didn't walk through its alternating neon and dark spaces alone at night. But the Thursday and Friday after Harry Styles landed in the city, plenty do.

The Ex Theater Roppongi is a block of black glass and concrete, indistinct enough to look like a basic new-build cinema complex, but with the design qualities of a playhouse to give the feeling that real theatre might unfold inside. Girls group together outside, nearly everyone wearing either a pink jumper with 'HARRY' embroidered over their hearts or the matching pink 'HARRY' baseball cap, or both. It's too cold to be without a coat but most have them draped over one arm or stuffed into tote bags, gleefully wanting to shake off anything that's not their involvement in the surrounding events.

On the first night, girls are handing out pink cellophane in the queue to put over your phone flashlight, with the instruction to turn it on at the beginning of a certain song to send rays of pink light to Harry. On the second, everyone has arrived with pink flowers, again to be pulled out of hiding during a predetermined number. Both of these are planned surprises for Harry that've circulated around

Japanese fan Twitter accounts. He hasn't, after all, been in Japan for years, not since 2015.

The first 'Harry Girls' I spot on Thursday are Yukino and her friend Rio in the pink jumpers, swinging bunches of pink flowers around. They had missed the surprise instructions and just brought them a day early of their own volition. 'They're for him,' laughs Rio. 'I didn't know if we could throw flowers or not but I'll take pictures. We bought them at the 100 yen store so it doesn't matter what happens with them.'

Yukino has a habit of looking between everyone as she speaks, as if we're teetering on the edge of significance. She plans to make up for missing that connection with Harry at the airport tonight. 'Because I'm standing not seated, I'm going to go to the front and not pray...but worship, almost.' Worship what, I ask. 'He's a god!' she replies, knowing the humour in the claim but meaning it all the same. 'King,' says Rio and they collapse into giggles.

What kind of girls would be into Harry in Japan? Generous girls, answers nineteen-year-old Yuika, who is here with her mum, another – albeit older – Harry Girl. 'For example, I didn't have time to get to the front to buy my merch I wanted for today, but this girl I didn't even know said, "I'll get stuff for you" because I couldn't physically get there. She didn't have to do that.'

They're funny too. Usagi and Nana, both eighteen, scarcely stop for air between teasing each other. 'I love Harry because he's so kind and he's so sweet, he is an ideal boyfriend, I love him so much,' gushes Usagi. The first piece of information she shares is that her name means rabbit in Japanese and she half-bounces in a way that reminds me of one. Nana, in glasses, is calmer, no doubt because she couldn't get a ticket.

'Usagi's going in tonight. I came along to buy merch. I'll have to wait until he plays next May and leave her behind,' Nana says, looking at a sympathetic Usagi. Without missing a beat, Nana sighs and pats Usagi's arm patronisingly. 'Harry may be Usagi's boyfriend but he's my husband, so it's fine to not see him.'

To my mind, there is something undeniably cool about these girls who choose to follow Western artists – in the same way that it was cool to like obscure music rather than the stuff in the charts when I was a teen. Most have a strong interest in British or American culture and, although some have official schooling in the language, there's an impressive degree of self-taught English through the fandom. Usagi and Nana, before speaking, say that they don't really speak good English but then continue the majority of the conversation in English. They'd used Harry interviews and singing along to Western pop songs to learn. Yuika's mum Mai said that Yuika never had to go into a cram school because she'd copied down the One Direction and Harry Styles lyrics so many times. Yuika, like others, wants to travel and live in the West in the future.

Music has a global reach, increasingly so. It's only natural then that in an effort to get closer to artists, fans want to speak their language, to speak to them online if possible, to break down any barrier that keeps them at a distance. In a large 2013 study by Kaplan International Colleges of over 1,000 people who speak English as a foreign language, more than half learned it to comprehend a celebrity, among the most common being Rihanna, Katy Perry and Beyoncé. Between Tumblr and memes, language – particularly fandom language – has become globalised in a way it wasn't before. Some of the Harry fans, for example, said they were still a 'directioner' and that they 'ship' him with women.

Lia is sixteen and has one Japanese parent and one African-American parent, so speaks good conversational English. Her upbringing had exposed her to Western music, from Elvis Presley to *NSYNC. 'From what I see, the British and American fans can speak fluent English so they know how to communicate with each other and with Harry in a way. For Japanese fans, most of us study English but aren't perfect with it, so I think in a way we have to communicate with impressions, not with words, so fandom gets different without knowing.' By impressions, she means digital and physical methods – in spending and in sharing, retweeting, favouriting, liking. Mai wishes she could speak with fans from abroad but doesn't have the skills. 'Fans from everywhere tend to unite around English. For example, at the last One Direction show, I was in the VIP section and I couldn't even communicate with the girl sitting next to me because of the language barrier.'

Nineteen-year-old Chihiro heard from other fans that apparently on the first night Harry said to the room, 'Who's been to a One Direction show before?', in order to prompt a positive reaction from the crowd. 'No one in the room said anything, so there's that disconnect in terms of communication. He said, "Never mind then." That makes me sad that no one understood what he was saying, no one was able to react to what he said.' She continues to talk of her own disconnect with Harry and his work. 'The lyrics translation from Western to Japanese is not straightforward, it's very roundabout, so to get some truth I'd rather try to read it in English rather than the translated version of Japanese. Generally, with anything to do with Harry, I can't absorb the information as quickly as people in the West.'

There is more than what's lost in translation through nuance and tiny slivers of poetry. When it comes to Western artists, there's distance in time, too. Not just the time it takes to decode information, but in the hours on the clock. These Japanese fans wake up in the mornings, immediately check online to find their idol has already spent all day doing 'things' and being reported on. Other fans get to the scene first before they were able to, making them slightly behind as well as outside of the conversation. In one sense, thanks to the internet and its time stamps, it doesn't matter, but in another their remoteness from what they care about is more palpable.

This is shown in what these Japanese fans perceive as the tangibility of Western fandom as opposed to their more emotionally abstract one: 'We think about him rather than being able to follow him in a more physical sense,' said nineteen-year-old Misaki. Obviously, no teenager is able to tag along behind a famous man who jet-sets from major city to major city, but Harry is pictured and described as jogging around Primrose Hill on many days, looking over London for inspiration, or cruising, windows down, along the 101 freeway in LA, and those are nearby places for some.

When I ask what the average Japanese Harry fan thinks Western Harry fans are like, Usagi goes up on her tip toes and starts squealing and messing up her hair. 'That's a Western fan, they're louder in the way they express their fanship. But a Japanese fan will go, "Ehhh, Harry Styles", she says in an airy voice, beating her hand lightly on her heart.

But the general consensus is, as Nana points out, that despite cultural differences, 'on the inside, every Harry fan in the whole universe is the same'.

It was heartening to find that they all felt there were no negative connotations to being a female pop fan. At Avex, Shogo had explained that, if anything, the music teen boys like is seen as uncool because that's always been the stereotype. Similarly, they believe young men like girls groups only because their members are attractive. Patrick St. Michel had said that it's embarrassing to the Japanese public that the *otaku* older men who love idols exist, so any proportion of media snark over what girls love would have to address that, too. Importantly, as Emma pointed out about Johnny's: 'We take girls-only cultures seriously because they make money.'

Not all Western artists attract fangirls and make serious money in Japan. In the last fifteen years, only Taylor Swift, Ariana Grande, Justin Bieber, Avril Lavigne, Carly Rae Jepson, Austin Mahone and One Direction have managed it. It's notably the ones who fit into the already existing models. Lori Morimoto, transcultural fan studies professor observes that, like the male musicians named above, the boy band model fits neatly into existing patterns of fandom. 'The beautiful boy aesthetic is big in Japan; they have a very strong transcultural draw to very pretty young men. This part of this person resonates with something I already know and love, so that it kind of slots in easy. People say that fandom is predicated on being both different and familiar. With One Direction, for example, it had been more or less the same but there's a special flavour to it.'

In addition to being somehow familiar, musicians who have cracked Japan understand – or have teams who understand – how fandom works there. For decades, Johnny's and idol culture has been an integral part of shaping what people need to do to be successful in Japan, and what fans expect from the artists. A key part of this is having an official fan club.

Lauren Kocher at Sony Music Japan played a crucial role in launching One Direction in Japan. Not only did she know that the group should be seen on TV and commercials, like Japanese artists, she helped begin their official fan club – the only one in the world. Members paid just under 5,000 yen (about £33) to get fan-only merchandise, access to a website featuring messages from the group and more. 'For Japanese fans this feels like the most legitimate way to connect personally with the artist, even more so than maybe the album or going to shows.'

According to her, the main reason Japanese fans will always join a fan club is because they want to support the artist and to know that they are an *official* fan supporting them *officially*. It's not a casual affair. Secondly, fans want access to priority ticketing; most fan clubs will make the first round of presales and best seats accessible to fans, and sometimes tickets are even only available through the fan club. The third important consideration is that they want fan club-exclusive merchandise and that often includes the fan club ID. 'They will have their name on it with "official member of the official fan club" and a numbering system, so the earlier you've joined the lower your number. If you're someone who came on board really early, you'll be fan 600 and someone who likes them a year later is 10,000, allowing you to impress by showing you're one of the originals.' And so, even after One Direction broke up, though fans know they won't achieve the same 'closeness' as they do with Japanese artists, and don't expect to, Japanese fans feel a strong connection to Harry.

Inside the theatre, the show is about to begin. A single security guard walks out along the pit in front of the girls. Suddenly the entire venue of girls brandish phones and push forward; they look like a sub-water creature. 'Harr-eee,' they call over and over insistently but politely. Everything goes black and 'Okaeri!' begins – *welcome home!* – and their lights seem to guide the way, gravitating towards the middle of the stage. A spotlight comes on through the floral brush strokes of the Japanese-style pink screen and there he – or his shadow – swaggers forward holding a guitar. Every time another bar of the song is teased for a second or two, a burst of screams for 'Harr-eee' rise before stopping for the next signal. The silkscreen falls and he is physically there.

Between songs he attempts basic Japanese phrases, which the audience delight in. After one of these he passes the microphone over to his Japanese keyboardist and vocalist, who tells the girls a story about Harry's kind heart and good nature in Japanese. When Harry initially arrived in the country, he chatted to all the team, didn't act like an arrogant rock star, his mum came along too and they all met them. Everyone was humbled. This was the unassuming man that they know and love and it was perfect.

After the encore, when he appears like a vision on the audience's right side up on a balcony in another spotlight, the reaction is bold. All seem to notice at the exact same time and scream. Holding an acoustic guitar, he says 'shhh' a few times and the crowd go quiet enough to hear a camera wink. For thirty seconds all you pick up is the exhalation of lungs, no one moving a muscle, barely shifting their weight. In Japan you can't legally take a photograph on your phone without a shutter sound, so every five to ten seconds, a rogue noise will go off; a display of self-control rarely seen anymore. After the final 'shhh', Harry starts strumming and sings his cover of Little Big Town's 'Girl Crush' without a mic. *I want to taste her lips, yeah, 'cause they taste like you / I wanna drown myself in a bottle of her perfume.* Everyone listens silently. There were nearly 1,750 people there but it was one of the most intimate shows I've ever been to. He was practically kissing the words at us. *I want her long blonde hair, I want her magic touch / Yeah 'cause maybe then, you'd want me just as much.* Various videos of this became instantaneously legendary for Harry fans worldwide, this event a key part of his story. One of the most famous men alive was serenading these girls, by extension a gift for all fans. *I got a girl crush. I got a girl crush.*

This was only possible in Japan, and nowhere else on this tour. When The Beatles played their first (admittedly heavily policed) show in Japan at the Nippon Budokan auditorium in 1966, it was reportedly so quiet that, for the first time in all the years of fans' intense, loud and persistent screaming and wailing, The Beatles could hear themselves play. It's something that's since been noted by artists and the press repeatedly. Just as screaming and elation create the exhilaration of a live show and had, moments before, accompanied Harry strutting around full of sexuality and adventure, this precious quiet, the antithesis of the hysterical stereotype of pop crowds, allowed for a rare creation. The most magical moment seeing one of the biggest pop stars in the world play a song that feels like it's just for you, something only made possible through a team effort.

Harry tells the crowd that he purposely finished his tour here because he loves Japan so much and, in Japanese, says that he wants to live in Japan and doesn't want to go home. The girls of course love this and the show climaxes with 'Sign of the Times', a ballad that promises that everything will be alright, that we can 'meet again somewhere'. This song, Styles told *Rolling Stone*, was about the maddening obstruction to equality: 'Equal rights. For everyone, all races, sexes, everything... This isn't the first time we've been in a hard time, and it's not going to be the last time.' Every person in the auditorium seems to hold up a physical last sign of gratitude: a pink A4 printed-off piece of paper that reads 'THANK YOU FOR THE AMAZING FINAL SHOW'.

Inside the corridor of the venue, identikit pink jumpers, caps and smiling faces flow out in waves. They look like backing dancers exiting the set of a musical. I'm eyed curiously. A few girls see me holding Harry's record, which I'd got signed by girls I'd spoken to outside the venue both nights. I'm white, in my mid-twenties, one of the only people in the building not wearing merch, alone and hanging back strangely. 'Are you Harry's girlfriend?' one pink girl asks me. To which I can say sadly I am not. Just as any Harry Styles fan anywhere in the world might ask, she continues, 'Do you know Harry?' Again, I don't, but I tell her they can sign this record if they'd like. 'Are you giving it to him?' says one. 'Will he touch it?' adds another. I don't want to lie to them but I also don't want to deflate their hopes. I tell them he'll know whatever they want him to and hand the first girl to come over the marker pen. She says, scribbling away, 'I want him to know he has made every girl in Japan happy tonight and please, *please*, come to see us soon. Harry girls will wait for him.'

'They're Gone, Get Over It': A Roundtable on Uncertain Endings and Boy Band Break-ups

Amanda, Bros fan, South Wales
Barbara, Backstreet Boys fan, Italy
Grace, One Direction fan, London
Karah, New Kids on the Block and Backstreet Boys fan, US
Melanie, Bros fan, Essex

Did you believe that your respective bands would under no circumstances cease to exist?

Karah: There was never that feeling that they'd break up, not like *NSYNC or Take That or practically every other boy band. They made a point of making sure the fans were reassured that they weren't.

Melanie: For me the anticipation of the grief helped. Because I had a feeling it was all going to wind down, it wasn't a massive shock. They were getting more negative press, then there was that 'Is This The End For Bros?' article and part of you goes, 'No!' But another part goes, 'Well, you know what, the death knell is coming'.

For all of you, there was the news of a member leaving. Did that prompt feelings of abandonment?

Barbara: Kevin leaving Backstreet Boys upset all of us. It was still early for being online, so the only thing I could look up was the odd article. We needed answers to all our questions: Why did he leave? How could he make this decision? We needed more info that we couldn't get at this time. We needed a reason, basically. We didn't have the tools to understand. Emotional tools or literal ones – these days I could just tweet Nick Carter and ask him. Maybe he would answer. We were even insulted: How could he dare leave us? It was similar to gossip at school because we felt we knew them, and everyone was talking about it. Kevin wasn't my favourite boy; if it was Nick, I would've screamed. In this group, a fan of all five guys is very rare. We are Kevin Girls, and Nick Girls and so on.

Karah: When I saw them perform without Kevin it was really weird because he had a specific presence: he was the older one, the mysterious one. A lot of fans, especially the Kevin Girls, refer to that as the Dark Period or the Dark Years. I wasn't that shocked when he left because it felt like he was getting annoyed with a lot of stuff. Turns out it was his record label, he wanted to start a family, he'd been married six years.

Grace: Up until recently Zayn leaving the band was the worst moment of my life, ever. I would've been sixteen. It was more that I wasn't sure the band could go on without him. But I thought they'd come back after Zayn going because they kept saying, 'yeah, we're taking a break, we'll be back'.

With one member down, how difficult was the uncertainty to contend with? With 1D, there was no confirmed and final end to the group.

Grace: It was only a matter of time between one of them leaving and the group completely breaking up. I feel like we should've accepted it. But we just didn't want them to; it was: we didn't want them to, so they won't. A denial stage for the first year. Upset, then denial, then being upset at them for saying that they would continue when they wouldn't. A lot of people would rather they just didn't talk about it at all, when they had actually no intention of coming back. But it's easier for them to say 'sometime in the future, definitely' than 'no, we're done'. If 1D tell you something, you're going to believe them. It was just promises they broke. I think everyone deserves an ending with an actual ending. An official 'we all decided to go our separate ways'. But I don't think we'll ever get that.

Does that post-One Direction experience sound different from the finality of a real split?

Melanie: Yes and no. When Bros broke up, I wrote in my diary: 'I feel so bad, I don't know what to do with my time now'. It was like a void. I didn't take down my pictures for a long time, until I was about seventeen, until I was a bit too cool for school. Those years were hard. You still had the loyalty, but a lot of people didn't say they were Bros fans and fans pretended they weren't. The bubble had burst. It was: 'you don't like them still, do you?'

How did you deal with the loss? Are there certain rituals for processing that?

Barbara: I suppose me and my best friend did grieve in a conventional sense: we spent a lot of time looking over video clips and listening to their music, watching old programmes they were on, and trying to relive it. Until you go through your own fan grief, whatever it's for, I don't think you realise how strong that sense of being a fan is.

Grace: For us, there was only defence. People outside of the fandom would tell us '1D broke up' and we'd defend them and ourselves, saying 'no, they're just on a break'. It took a while to come to terms with it. When you fully invest yourself into something and then it disappears, it's hard to live on without it… That sounds so dramatic, but it is, especially when you're at an age where everything's changing, and it's this one constant thing, and then that changes too.

Barbara: At some point you have to understand that it's their lives and not yours. You have to understand they're not your friends. It's two different worlds; it's your world and their world.

How deep does the grief for a band breaking up go?

Karah: Honestly, I feel like if Backstreet Boys broke up, it would be almost like grieving a death. A grandmother or a friend dying. Nick might be my favourite person on this earth, if something were to happen to him – god, I don't even want to think about it – I would cry. There's not a day when I don't talk about something to do with Backstreet Boys. Whether it's to my mother, to my friends I've made because of them, or even to *them* because it's possible on Twitter. If, god forbid, they broke up or something awful happened to them, I'd definitely have a panic attack. I don't even think I'm joking.

I told Nick after a show about how I dropped out of college and he literally talked me into going back. Now I have a good job in marketing, and get to leave town, and it's all because of them. My mum almost died two years ago, she was in ICU, and Nick saw on Twitter because he'd followed me for a few years and sent me a message saying he hoped I was doing okay. It's little things like that, they explain why I might be so hardcore about it. You can even never meet someone and feel like you have a strong and meaningful relationship with them.

Grace: When Zayn left I was such a mess. My mum said, 'you didn't cry this much when your grandfather died' and it was like they – people who don't like 1D – associate it with the same grief. It's more dis-attached. A group are the soundtrack to that part of your life, all good memories went with it. You know you're never going to experience the same kind of thing ever again. You have this hole in yourself that you have to refill, especially when you spend time dedicated to this one thing.

Amanda: It's horrible having to move on and talk about the band in the past tense.

Grace: It's hard for non-fans to understand it when they've not experienced it. You have this fake relationship that you don't want to admit you have. Because you don't want to say you feel you're friends with a celebrity you don't know. You rely on this person and they have no idea who you are. If you asked me all this stuff a few years ago, when I was sixteen, and had never experienced being a fan outside of social media my answer would be completely different. You realise there are other things in your life that are so much more important. Obviously they're still a huge part of my life – I followed Harry on tour – but I know how to prioritise now, I have a dog and uni.

Karah: We all understood where the 1D girls were coming from. I get why they would be upset. Thankfully I never really had to face that with Backstreet Boys, but if Backstreet Boys did break up I'd probably take the day or week off work and cry myself to sleep.

Barbara: I always try to become friends with some of the slightly younger fans and help them, because there are hard times as a teen girl and as a fan.

What advice would you give to a fan whose favourite band just broke up?

Amanda: You can continue to show your support when they're not there anymore. And with social media, you're still in the fandom, sharing and keeping in touch with other fans. Life does go on, definitely. Also, don't give up hope: because as Bros have proved, boy bands do have reunions. We all got to have this moment of saying to people, "I told you I'd always be a fan. I haven't gone anywhere for all these years."

Grace: Very few bands can last forever, because there's only so long they can be iconic. There's a lifecycle of a boy band: fizzle out, finish, members go solo or do whatever they want. All boy bands have ended at some point but they do come back. I guess 1D could come back in ten years, for a reunion tour or whatever.

Amanda: Even if there was no more Bros, there are their solo careers, the acting career. Bros, before, to all of us, came as one. Yes, we want them together, and I hope it all goes on for longer. When I was younger I saw them as perfect, you put them on a pedestal, but now, you recognise them as flawed people, and as individuals.

What happens during that time where outside life goes on?

Amanda: Quiet, nothing, a black period, really. Bros fans had a good twenty years of that. You had no idea what they were doing. The boys had autobiographies come out but that said nothing about what they were doing there and then. The lull was punctuated by little glimpses of the boys but then they'd be gone again. You'd see one article on one of them and then nothing again for a year. Then social media got big and being a fan now is like being a teenager again, but you can handle yourself better.

Karah: In a way I'm glad that if Backstreet Boys break up, it'd be now, because I could still follow all their lives on social media.

Most fans never had social media as a tool for processing boy band break-ups. Do you think those platforms are a help or hindrance?

Karah: We have this understanding in the Backstreet Army. There are some people in the fandom who don't like me and I don't care for, but when something big happens, like one of our parents dies for example, we all come together for them. If Backstreet Boys broke up tomorrow, I know I'd have them to grieve with and beyond, even the ones who I don't see regularly.

Barbara: Yeah, when Kevin left the band, I had maybe four or five girls at school who knew what I was going through. They weren't big fans but it was better than nothing. Fandom was more of a private thing. Now, you have people who understand what you're really feeling, no judgement. I saw, watching with celeb break-ups and deaths, especially with the 1D break-up, fans now get over it faster.

Grace: With 1D it was different. 1D created 'Fan Twitter', everything was more intense. Before it'd be all about seeing bands play or meeting them, but with 1D you had constant 24-hour tech contact. Even if you just went on social media, because of your feed, you'd always be seeing pics of them or videos or this and that, and all of a sudden there wasn't anything new. Old content, all from the past, things we'd already seen. As a band they used to be in such contact with their fans too, but now Harry doesn't even use social media, really. Stan Twitter has kept going even when 1D didn't. Fans of other artists were sympathetic about the 1D break-up at first because they knew it would suck so bad. But after a while it either became a joke or a comeback, like '1D's gone, get over it'.

Grace, do you want the band back?

Grace: We can joke about them not coming back now. There are a few people who think they're actually going to. We all want them to and we say we miss them, but if they came back now I don't even know if it'd be better or worse because we know they'd go again. It might be better for that chapter to be over forever.

8

DANGEROUS WOMEN AND POLITICAL FUN

In slow motion / Can't seem to get where we're going / But the hard times are golden / 'Cause they all lead to better days
            – Ariana Grande, 'Be Alright'

When Caitlin and Erin came down in their pyjamas to the fire-lit lounge, on Christmas morning of 2016, they were given their two main presents. Santa had picked calendars for the coming year: an Ariana Grande calendar for fourteen-year-old Caitlin and a Little Mix calendar for eleven-year-old Erin. Each had a post-it note on the front that said: 'Flip to May'. They scrambled with the pages quickly, understanding the game, and there was another note in their mum's handwriting with hearts around the words 'Ariana Grande concert, Manchester, May 22nd'. They screamed, and shouted, Erin the most excitable of the pair. Of all her presents, that was the one Caitlin put on her Snapchat story for her friends to see. It would be her first pop concert – a huge deal. Elsewhere in the north of England girls opened similar presents with that date settling in their minds as the night that would provide the longed-for object of delayed gratification.

There's a routine to pop concert preparation when you're a tween or teenage girl fan. The lead-up to the concert that would become known as the Manchester Arena Attack was no different.

There's the countdown for months: Erin's class had to answer the register at school with *good morning, I'm excited for....* 'I'd always go "I'm feeling excited for Ariana!"' There's talking about it constantly with friends, as she was: 'I think they got a bit annoyed with me'. Like Caitlin, you blast the artist's tracks out 'in the car, in the house, everywhere'. Like seventeen-year-old Carys and her younger friend Lucy who had tickets, you start an official countdown on a calendar or a phone app to knock off each day. Importantly, you plan your look in advance – in the case of seventeen-year-old Millie, you start as soon as you know you're going (pink-berry-coloured eye-shadow with her hair down and curled).

On the day of the concert, the morning of which Erin could finally tell her class that she was 'really, really, really excited!', the final part of the ritual could begin. No one has told you this happens but somehow you know what to do. You put the artist's music on while you're getting ready with your friends. Paint on each flourish of glitter carefully, tuck your top into your skirt just so, practise walking lines in heels, imagine the costume changes you're going to see there. You take some selfies and think about the official photos that will be taken – pictures that fans who didn't get to go will see, and so will you, later, to relive it. You will be one of the glamorous fans, perhaps zoomed in on, to represent everyone else. Or, if you're Caitlin, you unfortunately run out of time after school, rush back home, throw on a bit of make-up and a 'random' outfit that 'wasn't even nice: now I look back on it and I'm like, "wow"'.

Many of the girls at Manchester Arena that night were at their very first pop show, or the first with no parental supervision. Carys's parents hugged her and Ella goodbye in the car park before going to the cinema and for dinner nearby, a meeting point confirmed. Inside that auditorium, Carys looked around and thought about how the thousands of people in the room were there for the same reason as them: 'It makes you feel like you're in another world.' Erin couldn't believe she was breathing the same air as Ariana, while Caitlin looked at everything with wide eyes. She'd never been in a dream world like this before: 'It was the best feeling I've ever had in my life and I know that's really dramatic or seems exaggerated but I walk in and because we were late, it was a full arena and Ariana was about to come on in half an hour and everyone's dressed and everyone's cheering. I can't even describe the feeling. Ten minutes before Ariana came on, there was a little countdown. 9-8-7-6-5-4-3-2-1. It was one minute, then the veil dropped and she came on...'.

Ariana blew a final kiss to the audience and moments later the bomber detonated his weapon. A visceral silence you could taste settled in the building. When it eventually broke, Carys remembers 'girls, everywhere, screaming and crying'.

One of the first girls to exit to the foyer, Millie was close to the bomber. 'Me and Lucy were linking arms but when the bomb went off it was obviously really powerful so it pushed us apart. I remember being thrown up into the air and brought back down. It was really hot on my face and I thought someone had thrown acid, so I covered my face and curled up in a ball. You know when you jump in a pool and water goes all in your ears? It sounded like that. When I opened my eyes I knew it wasn't acid. I knew it could only have been a bomb.' Her phone had been blown out of her hand and she hadn't realised yet but three of her fingers had been partially removed and were hanging off.

Shock can produce entirely different responses in people. Carys wanted to stay and help but Ella pulled her away to run. Sprinting over and around bodies, Carys tried to ring her mum three times and each call went straight to answerphone. Immediately, she thought her mum had decided to meet her in the foyer instead of where they'd agreed, back in the car park. 'Everything goes through your head. "Did I say 'I love you' when she said she loved me?" I got through the fourth time I rang her and I remember telling her there'd been a bomb scare and she said to me, "I know sweetheart, I know. I'm on my way."'

Caitlin, Erin, their mum Annette and their friends were initially together. 'You're either fight, flight or fright. I didn't look back for Mum and Erin but my main priority was just to get out,' Caitlin remembers. She sped ahead with Gemma and Ellie, the friends they'd been with, and got on the phone and told her mum to meet them by the Cathedral near the Arena. Caitlin stood on a bench next to it to get a better view. 'I was panicking because I didn't know if there was anything else coming, a shooter or anything, so for me not to see my mum, knowing I'd just been on the phone a minute ago, I was like, "What's happened?"' She caught sight of them in the frantic crowd. 'Erin's eyes were so red, she'd been crying so hard and Mum had proper tight hold of her. Mum was about to go in the wrong direction, so I screamed 'Mum!' She turned around really fast and we screamed, "We're over here, over here."'

Erin saw more than any eleven-year-old should ever see, and more than Annette and Caitlin had. As Annette and Erin had been running, something inside of Annette had told her not to look left under any circumstances, which was where 'everything' was. 'I wish I'd have said that to Erin,' she says. 'Unfortunately, it was just the way I was holding Erin's hand, caught up between other people, we were all sort of tangled up. She was looking back.'

Together, Caitlin and the others returned to the car park, got back into their car and didn't speak. They absorbed the sounds of the sirens, and watched the ambulances, police vans and media vehicles jerk about. People from Caitlin's school started to reply to her Snapchat story of Ariana's performance. Some said things like 'Wow, she looks amazing' and Caitlin just replied, saying 'Look at the news'.

The Manchester Arena attack in 2017 killed 22 people and injured 800; it was the deadliest UK terrorist attack since the 7/7 London bombings in 2005. ISIS – the jihadist militant organisation known for their treatment of women and girls that includes rape, torture and imprisonment –claimed responsibility for the atrocity. Most of the violence committed by ISIS-style groups is against Muslim women, girls and children, and being broadly anti-iconography, they've targeted and obliterated art, architecture, and whole histories in Iraq and Syria. When the Manchester attack happened, the 2015 ISIS attack at an Eagles of Death Metal concert in Paris was fresh in people's recent memories. When ISIS claimed responsibility for the Paris attack, they called the gig a 'party of perversity' – their point being anything deemed 'perverse' under the Islamic State must go. Of those killed in the Manchester Arena attack, two were gay men, who often make up a proportion of a pop fan base. The vast majority were girls and their parents, either with them or waiting to collect their daughters in the foyer.

Georgina Callander, eighteen, who had met Ariana Grande backstage two years previously, was the first young person to be confirmed dead. Her happy meet-and-greet photo became synonymous with the attack through its use in the media coverage. The day before the concert she tweeted her idol 'SO EXCITED TO SEE YOU TOMORROW' in ecstatic caps. Having dreamed her whole life of looking after children, she'd just won a place at university to study paediatrics. Olivia Campbell-Hardy, fifteen, always sang and wanted to be a singing or dance teacher. Eilidh MacLeod, fourteen, played bagpipes with her local piping group and loved going down to the beaches on the tiny Scottish island where she lived. Sorrell Leczkowski, fourteen, wanted to become an architect so she could build her mum a house. Kelly Brewster, thirty-two, died trying to shield her eleven-year-old niece. She was a long-time pop fan who had once travelled to Las Vegas to see Jennifer Lopez perform. Saffie Rose Roussos, only eight years old, was the youngest Ariana fan taken victim that night.

Almost no one wanted to call it what it was: an attack on girls and young women. Theresa May made a statement about violence against 'children and young people'. Mainstream press followed suit, focusing on the age and innocence of the victims. The response to the attack differed from recent collective acknowledgements around terrorist violence: that the Charlie Hebdo shooting was certainly an attempt to stamp out free speech, or that the attack on the Pulse nightclub in Orlando was a crime against the LGBTQ community. Some liberal male commentators and writers opined that 'it could've been my daughter', giving their pieces a personal slant, but stopped short of making the larger, and more political, point: that this was an attack on women and girls. Instead, it was left to mostly online opinion pieces by adult women, often with an earnest pro-fangirl slant, to correctly point out that pop concerts were spaces – formerly safe spaces – for girls. And when some publications – mostly online – did point to the misogyny of the attack, this infuriated other commenters, who said they were 'playing the feminism card'.

This resistance was strange. At the time, I watched, confused and angry, blessed as ever to be in the safety of my own home, as the updates from Manchester came in. No other terrorist attack in memory had affected me – revealing of my own positionality – to such a degree. I thought, as other women did, of my own first pop concert at eleven: Birmingham NEC to see S Club 7. The car journey up on the motorway screaming their songs, my mum nervously joining in with us, and my friend's mum probably wondering what she'd let herself in for; the scale of the building as we pulled up, thousands of tiny cars in the car park for the same reason as us; the cavernous insides; a night that was infinitely better but not dissimilar to a school disco where I'd made myself sick on cheap fizzy drinks. There's a photo from that night of my friend E and me with our arms heavy over each other's shoulders like men at a pub. CDs, it became apparent, were only there to tide you over until the next time *this* could happen. Those early pop shows are about production values, sheen, performance but more about you and the other fans, all on the edge of the glory of young adulthood. You all know *it's coming*, looking around you at the fans like you but different, maybe older, cooler.

One man had come to the unwavering conclusion that the Manchester bombing was an attack specifically aimed at women and girls. His name was Nazir Afzal. The former Chief Crown Prosecutor for north-west England, he was responsible for prosecuting the Rochdale grooming gang in 2012 and has spent a quarter of a century specialising in understanding why men commit atrocities against women.

I contacted Afzal months after the attack to clarify his position.
He remained as firm in his view, and described how he came to this
decision – or rather didn't have to. 'It was obvious to me. I looked at
the death toll and how many girls there were out of the twenty-two,
and I work with the organisation that provides support for victims and
they told me that the vast majority of people who were injured were
women and girls. I asked myself, "Why that particular event of the arena
schedule for the month?" He could have chosen KISS, who were playing
a concert a couple of days before, or a wrestling event in the same week
– two male audiences – instead he went for an event that would've had
teenage girls and some LGBT people as well because that's her fan base.'
It was a comfort to him that a few journalists and members of the public
who agreed with him got in touch to show solidarity with his views; but
they were in a minority. Many did not.

Ariana Grande began her career the way many American pop princesses
do: as a heart-faced Nickelodeon sweetheart. Except, as the usual
narrative goes, those sweet babies come of age, good girls go bad.

Dangerous Woman, the album she was touring at that time, is a
collection of fifteen songs basically about sex. When sung in Ariana's
breathy four-octave voice, *I'm so into you / I can barely breathe* is surely
one of the sexiest lines committed to record. She might've once said,
'I don't see myself ever becoming a sex symbol,' but here she was, on
her third album, with her famously long ponytail, tiny mini-skirts and
absolutely having (reportedly very good) sex before marriage.

Even worse to a misogynist than a woman singing about 'bad decisions'
in cat ears, Ariana has conviction. She shows her anger at bad interviewers
who ask her about her dating life instead of her music. Where other
pop stars shy away from being overtly political in order not to alienate
right-wing American fans, Grande is pro-gun reform, has aligned herself
with Black Lives Matter and had been anti-Trump since well before
the election. She's consciously made efforts to be viewed as someone
here to empower all fans, especially young women. In late 2016, Ariana
complained that a man approached her and the late singer Mac Miller to
congratulate him on 'scoring' her. 'Ariana is sexy as hell, man,' he said. 'I

see you, I see you hitting that!' In response, she said online that she was 'not a piece of meat that a man gets to utilize for his pleasure'. Many of her devoted fans are, and certainly were at the time of the attack, tweens and teen girls who had followed her since her days on a children's programme on Nickelodeon; they had seen her as a cool older sister, and growing up just ahead of them. To go against what she was originally marketed as, and push sex positivity to very young women, even to girls who are only beginning to have an understanding of her message, is provocative. To do that and become one of the world's biggest pop stars, hugely successful, with one of the most loyal and vocal fan bases, is not insignificant.

At the Manchester show, as at every show on that tour, a video played clips of Ariana posing seductively with messages stamped over them. 'Wild' was one, 'free' another, 'soulful', 'wilful' and pointedly, politically, 'not asking for it'. All markers of womanhood, as Ariana sees it. ISIS aside, this sexual freedom has been seen as something toxic by the right-wing press: after the Manchester attack, one prominent journalist asked of the fans and their parents: 'Should they have been there? Was it appropriate?' This was not a space for them, a concert of a 'woman singing about sex and little else'.

As Nazir Afzal says, to ISIS, all of this would be beyond unacceptable; to them, even the idea of female musicians is a disgrace, when famously one of the first things ISIS did was to outlaw music entirely. 'Ariana is very outspoken in the lifestyle that she wants to lead and wants other women and girls to have', Azfal told me. 'These people who want to harm girls are against it; they don't want it with the women in their own families but they certainly don't want it in the wider community either. It's always very much a message on their part.' It's why Afzal calls the attack gender terrorism – terrorism reinforcing gender stereotypes and aimed at keeping women in their place. 'His target wasn't any of those individual women and girls that he killed, but he wanted to send a message out to the wider community of women and girls in this country.'

Afzal was Chief Executive of the Association of Police and Crime Commissioners in 2017. He pushed to have the Manchester attack acknowledged and described as gender terrorism. His board rejected this suggestion. He resigned because he wasn't allowed to speak out to the press properly on the broader issues related to the attack, and has since articulated how he feels about its gendered nature on social media.

A year on, we knew more – it was confirmed that the vast majority of the 14,000 there that night were girls and very young women aged between eight and twenty years old, and that many were there at their long-awaited first or second pop concert. Yet to say that it was an attack on them remains controversial. Even with this information, only one writer, Anna Leszkiewicz for the *New Statesman*, outlined it in an anniversary piece, and though the proliferation of online outlets means they usually copy each other for quick clicks, it did not happen with her feature. Twitter users were not discussing it. Afzal was the only other voice, in the same publication, echoing what he'd said a year before. 'Extremism is not confined to so-called caliphates,' he wrote in a *New Statesman* column on the 23rd May 2018. 'It is found everywhere and anywhere you look. Gender terrorism pervades every society – although men never call it that, because it would then need a national and international response.'

This acknowledgement is unquestionably owed to the injured and the survivors, many of whom believe that this act of violence was the result of such regressive misogynistic beliefs. 'It was an attack on teenage girls and women for expressing love for music and who they were and their femininity,' said Carys. 'They were expressing anger at how women have become something over the years, and how we can celebrate that through music. When you come to an Ariana concert to celebrate her music, she shows that women are strong.' When Millie came out of hospital, she and her mum discussed how people like the bomber don't want girls like her to be free, but rather to be scared. 'Mum said to me that there was a concert the night before and it was Take That and it was probably busier at Take That than Ariana but they chose her and us. They wanted to turn the night into a horrible thing that happened, something they'd want to stop.'

'We live in a patriarchal society,' Afzal said when I asked why he thought people had been reluctant to support his views. 'You know that, I know that. We're always trying to minimise the impact on women. We want to suggest that there is a bigger picture here, which means, of course, an attack on all men and all society.' One comment I saw online, criticising a feminist publication for considering the gendered aspects of what had happened, summarised this: *This isn't a gender-biased crime. It's an atrocity against humanity crime.* Afzal tweeted, 'In the aftermath of Manchester Terror Attack, I was approached by many wealthy individuals saying they wanted to do something. Few weeks later when I went back to them with proposals for youth and women engagement, it no longer fits their business plans! Should I Name & Shame them?'

To many living comparatively comfortably in Britain, even those who are not extremist or outwardly misogynistic in their views, Ariana and her fans are tiny, dangerous girls. How do dangerous girls respond to such an incident? They don't sit in silence that settles.

Millie was saved from the building that night. Four paramedics came and carried her friend Lucy off, while she was left with Lucy's phone. She tried to unlock it so she could tell her mum not to come near in case there was another bomb. She wondered why she couldn't unlock the phone and realised it was because of her fingers. Charged with adrenaline, she touched the visible bone. 'Why doesn't it hurt?' she asked herself. Her hair was burnt, and there were shrapnel injuries on her face and leg.

'I remember saying "Please don't let me lose my fingers" to the paramedic bandaging up my hand. A girl called Stacey called my mum with Lucy's phone and she guided my mum through the crowd and was telling Mum what she was wearing so she could find us.' Millie's mum had to flick pieces of other people's bodies off her: it was determined soon afterwards that Millie had been only six feet away from the bomber. She would be diagnosed with PTSD and referred to specialist trauma therapy, and had to drop out of college owing to the frequency of her hospital and counselling appointments.

Six weeks later and finally out of the wheelchair, Millie is standing in front of her mirror at her mum's house in Wigan, hair up in a messy bun, doing her make-up. When she rubs moisturiser into her skin she sometimes finds pieces of shrapnel in her face. Even months later, tiny flecks of metal rise to the surface. That night is the first thing she sees when she looks at her reflection.

When the world hurts you like this, what does it look like when you continue to be a fan? When the world is hurtful, you have to be a fan still – or can you?

Initially, for some girls, there was an aversion to noise. Carys, for weeks afterwards, struggled to listen to music at all. 'Dangerous Woman' was the final song Ariana had played before it happened. She still can't listen to it because it takes her back to that moment. 'I just didn't want to hear anything. I'd never put music on and if it came on in the car, I'd turn it off; if it was playing at school, I'd just walk away. It seemed wrong when twenty-two people lost their lives loving music. I was guilty that they could never do that again. Music was so beautiful and it understood you more than anyone ever could, but they could never have that.' Naturally, with all the coverage and public interest in the news story, Ariana's song 'One Last Time' became popular in the UK after the attack; it was played a lot on the radio, and Annette and Erin were deeply upset when they had to hear the opening bars.

The previous year a particular conversation about fandom had started in academic and online fan circles. In the US, Donald Trump was elected, a president whose ideas about women and policies with regards to minority groups caused outrage, and, in the UK, Brexit and the Conservative government's persistence with austerity were deeply divisive. Separatism, suspicion and a sense of alienation were global themes – and yet fandom had become mainstream. Across all cultural media – film, comics, music and more – it was on trend and more than acceptable to be open about what you love. There seems to have been a blurring in the clear distinction that previously existed between fans and non-fans. Commentators put this down to a number of factors: Twitter; the new participatory nature of our media consumption and the conversations around them; the binge model of TV and documentary through streaming services; the increased presence of fans, and therefore an increased visibility of fan language and practices, which have dispersed and become normalised. The idea of the modern, loyal consumer is reflected in revivals, remakes, reunions of artists and bands, and an overflow of fannish experience. Everyone, it seems, is a fan of something.

How could those two realities – the divisive, almost apocalyptic state of the world and the positive enthusiasm and consumption of fandom – sit, however uncomfortably, alongside each other? Fan academic Elizabeth Minkel wrote in 2017, 'As 2016 came to a close…I speculated that fandom would diminish somewhat in the new year. "Maybe it's my own distraction," I said, sort of meandering around the point. "The conversation will be less loud and less focused on cultural products and more focused on politics. Not the politics of our cultural products, but capital P Politics."' In other words, what right did people have to spend time doing what they loved? Shouldn't we be politically active in all our endeavours? The idea arose for some consumers of popular culture that it felt wrong or perverse even to enjoy something for its own sake.

It's in these times, however, that you need to feel camaraderie and some hope. It can be a dark world and it is important (probably crucial) to have the things we enjoy, however frivolous or escapist they may seem to some, and perhaps even especially if they are frivolous. Many of the girls I spoke to refused to consciously think of the concert on the night of the Manchester attack in negative terms. Caitlin said immediately afterwards and when I spoke with her that she couldn't have asked for a better first concert. It still gives her the good kind of goosebumps thinking about it.

Caitlin's story is similar to others'. She returned straight away to her school in Preston. On that first day she had a drama class and instead of doing exercises, students and teacher sat in a big circle and talked about what had happened that night. Most of the questions were what was her favourite song? What was the choreography like? She challenged others: why are you asking about what happened afterwards? Why not talk about the gig? After a more difficult evening, she stayed home on the third school day after the attack, and went for a dog-walk with her friend Ella. They spoke about how thrilling and positively life-changing the concert had been, while listening to Ariana's album from a phone, and singing along. 'Just having it on as a background noise, it made me remember the best bits of the concert and that's always what I've thought of her. When people say, "Oh, you were at Ariana Grande", I want to say "Yeah, she was amazing" not "I didn't get hurt".' Caitlin was determined they shouldn't let the incident stop them from being music fans.

Immediately after the attack, Ariana flew home to her loved ones. Conservative commentators said she was variously selfish or weak for leaving and going home briefly. In policing how Ariana was dealing with the grief and the situation, they were doing the same to the girls who were there: Ariana was one of them. 'You have to run to your life,' says Carys of Ariana leaving. 'After something like that you need to be with your family and friends. Piers Morgan having a go at Ariana for going home: how can you even say that when you haven't been in that situation? People who haven't experienced it saying what they'd do – you don't know. You can't know.'

Within hours of arriving home Ariana knew she had to return to Manchester and be brave. This was an unusual situation in which fans and artist were dealing with the same trauma alongside each other. In the tween and teenhood of the girls, it's easy to overlook Ariana's age. Only twenty-three at the time of the attack, she was not immune to PTSD through fame; she was not only there that night but the reason they were there. She had to deal with the burden of feeling responsible; as Caitlin and Erin's mother Annette did. Ariana's own mum was as concerned as these mums: Joan, fifty, was there that night it happened. She'd had to sprint to find Ariana, and then find an exit for them. 'Not to be overly dramatic – I struggle with this every day – but I didn't know what I would find when I got to her,' she told *Elle* US. 'I sympathize with every parent who was waiting for a child. Those minutes when you don't know what's happening...there are no words.'

Back in Manchester Ariana spent time with those injured in hospital and organised One Love, a big charity concert held in the city only weeks after, to raise money for the victims and their families. When the One Love concert was announced, Caitlin convinced Annette and Erin to go with her.

Taking the steps to confirm and later follow through with a concert after what had happened: I cannot imagine doing it myself. When the Bataclan attack happened in Paris, I was supposed to go to a rock show in north London but I couldn't. It wouldn't happen again but, fearfully, in my mind, I kept replaying the clips of the attack I'd seen. It made sense to not go because worry would've ruined the show anyway; attending would've been pointless. Terrorism expects to create a fear that prevents people going about their lives. It could stop people wanting to listen to Ariana and certainly stop girls from wanting to go to other concerts. Those behind terror want people to rethink what was once routine to them – saving for a concert ticket or listening to music they love – and second guess everything they do. To demoralise and restrict the activities of women and girls is what ISIS wants.

What an extraordinary thing, then, to continue as before. To pick oneself back up from a terrifying and potentially traumatising experience. It wasn't coming simply from a youthful resilience, the ability to brush aside fear. It came, according to the girls, from being a fan. Ariana was a sterling example, leading with her strength. The Arianators far from Manchester were more vocal than ever in their support of her on Twitter ('we love you Ari, we are a family and we stay together until the end') and to the fans in Manchester ('we'll get through this together', 'Arianators, we got you'). They told those going to One Love to enjoy the concert, to live again as they had for Ari's previous show. In Frankfurt, fans held their own big remembrance meet-up to spend time together as a community, where they ate and drank, brought helium balloons and sourced gifts and donations for those affected. Manchester, too, was supporting them – a northern city so resolute and earthily pragmatic. Local Muslim communities, who faced increased instances of Islamophobia post-attack, showed love not just by helping save victims on the night but later by raising thousands of pounds for them and their families and taking part in a peace march from a mosque to the site of the bombing. An immense part of the strength displayed came from the survivors themselves and their love of the music.

'Caitlin from the outset was just adamant that this awful thing was not going to affect her and actually she went the other way,' said Annette. 'Erin very nearly didn't go and dug deep. But she said to me, "Both you and Caitlin were there and if you both do it, so can I." If I'm honest, if I didn't have such a feisty fourteen, now fifteen-year-old, I would've said, "Whatever, concerts aren't my thing," but we do love them. Caitlin won't realise this but her strength and resilience absolutely rubs off on both me and Erin.'

It snowballed from there. 'She said, "This will not stop me doing what we're doing and Mum, you're going to book us loads of concerts."' They booked many concerts for that year when they'd only planned two. Now they've seen Sam Smith, Zara Larson, Steps, Vengaboys, Katy Perry, and the list goes on.

'I have to show that I can go out and it's not going to define me, it's not going to stop what I do now,' said Caitlin. 'If anything, it's going to make me go out and do more things.'

Caitlin has genuinely helped her sister. 'I have a lot more sympathy for Erin just because of how young she is and I know there were loads of young people her age as well. No one's going to be normal afterwards but with the younger girls you can see the changes it's had on them, especially Erin; she doesn't want to go and do more things. She's kind of the opposite of me, she's been a little snail, she's gone back in her shell. She doesn't think she's as good at things anymore, and that's just really hard to see. I hate how it's defined and shaped her as a person. It's made her more scared of the world.'

Eventually, Erin began to speak about what she saw that night; speaking about it helped, as did being brave enough to go back to Manchester Arena many times during the year with her family for pop concerts. 'I didn't want to say anything. It got easier when it went along, it got easier to talk to the therapist about what happened that night. I wasn't feeling as sad and wasn't crying as much anymore, and having therapy and speaking to someone really helped.'

It's a similar story across the rest of the fandom. Millie has been going to pop concerts almost once a month – ten in the space of just under a year when we spoke. 'Music's always been a big part of my life. But after that happened it's become an even bigger part of my life. Since I was going in for my operation on my hand and my fingers, I was always determined not to let it ruin me experiencing life.'

Her mum was also diagnosed with PTSD from the trauma of seeing her daughter covered in blood and in the state she was in, and was reluctant to let her do anything at all. Millie was about to turn eighteen and so should've been ready for going out clubbing with her friends. But despite that, she celebrated out in her garden, with her friends, listening to Ariana. 'It's not Ariana's fault and I didn't want to bottle it up or blame. That's why I listened to her; it's not her fault or our fault it happened. Obviously, it reminds me of that night but I also think that before the bomb went off I was having such a nice time with my friend that I don't need to think about that, I just need to think of the good time I was having at the concert.'

Ariana was watching all this unfold too. In an interview for the July 2018 issue of British *Vogue*, she told the interviewer, 'Harry Styles had a concert coming up in Manchester and I know some of my fans were going, and it was their first time going to a concert in that venue since mine. I was so proud of how they were interacting with one another and caring for one another...'

Pop music does resist aloneness by its nature and, in every element of it, you feel others there enjoying it. You hear it in the earbuds of the man next to you on public transport with it turned up too loud, girls play it off their phone in their pinafores and matching socks, in nightclubs you slur the words in a joyous and dumb state, you see it being danced to through windows, hear it played on a stereo as someone potters around and gets ready for bed. There's the feeling of presence, that we're all listening together, and somewhere in this destructive world with all our differences, these reference points exist. In the simple words you can memorise, in the auto-tuned vocals and the familiar beats, pop music is not a solitary experience.

The girls knew they were all together then, listening to the music in one space. They are still listening to it now. It's non-negotiable, that's their bond. Ariana, treading the same path, 'knew' she had to sing again, and got to work on a new album, and did magazine interviews, sharing her experience of anxiety and healing, which was powerful, too. To those who hate women, just to be one of these teenage girls enjoying life is a rebellious act of sorts. Being involved in the attack galvanised these girls in a community sense; it meant their fandom and their 'political' way of existing in the world couldn't be so easily separated.

'Theresa May or whatever, I wouldn't have a clue,' Caitlin tells me, 'but definitely I'm political as in I'm up to date with what's going on. I'm more tuned in now to all the disasters – the stabbings in London, Grenfell fire, London Bridge attack – because I know what people go through now. Before it felt like a news story, but it's not just a story; it genuinely will affect people for a long time.'

Millie agrees that she feels more political, and has made it a pastime to care for others involved in terrorist attacks. She and her mum are in a group for survivors of global disasters, a chat group where you can speak to others. 'I've made friends with people in America who were in the Boston bombings. We're all part of a club that we don't want to be part of.' She plans to do the Boston Marathon with some of those survivors.

This camaraderie doubles back to fandom – Millie has made friends with people who were at the gig. 'I've never met them but we talk to each other on Snapchat every single day. If I see a post on Facebook or Twitter, we always comment saying "So proud of you".' When Ariana returns to Manchester, Millie and all the girls who were there that night who speak in a group chat – who have never met – are going to go to the concert together.

Carys now volunteers locally and helped to set up a platform for victims of terror, mostly made up of Manchester victims and those who lost people in the bombing. 'There are lots of parents putting up videos of their children onstage or singing again or listening to music again, and it suddenly dawned on me that music was what started all this and it's going to be with us for the rest of our journey, so why not make something from it that makes us stronger, braver and more united?' She sings in a Manchester attack choir that has raised large amounts of money for charity and Carys credits it with her recovery.

For Carys, every day something reminds her of that night. 'The number 22 always gets me: there were twenty-two victims, it was on the 22nd of May and it was at 22.31. I always wear things with bees on and that makes me feel safe, but when you go to train stations or if you see blood on the floor or if you hear sirens, even if it doesn't panic you, you still have those five seconds of wondering in your head or hearing the silence again from that night.'

In 2018, Ariana Grande released an album, *Sweetener*, which is near-impossible not to read as life 'post-Ariana', as Caitlin would say; about how the singer rebuilt herself, about the severe anxiety she suffered. Like her fans, she turned darkness into light, silence into sound. The album's first single is 'No Tears Left to Cry', a softly powerful anthem, dancing around an individual's grief and collective catharsis. The second single 'God is a Woman' is about womanly sexual liberation and ultimately, domination. It harnesses the same sexual prowess of *Dangerous Woman* – when all is said and done in the bedroom, her lover will believe God is no man – and affirms with obvious conviction what a woman can be. It's about all those types of womanhood she gathered for her *Dangerous Woman* tour.

The video for 'God is a Woman' has her placed into re-workings of famous works of art in a bid to write women into history, art and philosophy, if just for the space of a short video. Ariana is The Thinker, Rodin's musing intellectual, now a woman in calm contemplation while men throw insults at her (*And I can be all the things you told me not to be / When you try to come for me I keep on flourishing*). Ariana is in a re-imagining of Michelangelo's 'Creation of Adam' as a female God reaching out to (wo)man because God created her in Her own image. Ariana is Cerberus, the three-headed dog that prevents the dead from leaving the underworld, so strong and fearsome that very few got past (music and sweet treats could soften it). Ariana is the maternal she-wolf that raised twins Romulus and Remus, the mythical founders of Rome; Ariana wears a helmet with animal ears and wields a hammer inside the Pantheon, the temple of the gods of Rome. She lip-syncs the Samuel L. Jackson *Pulp Fiction* version of the Bible verse 25:17 from the Book of Ezekiel, but it's gender-flipped and spoken by one of Ariana's idols – and the woman who brought sexual liberation to pop decades previously – Madonna.

'And I will strike down upon thee with great vengeance and furious anger those who would attempt to poison and destroy my sisters. And you will know my name is the Lord when I lay my vengeance upon you.'

Attempts were made to poison and destroy the lives of sisters; the revenge exists in every pop concert the girls returned to, every second spent listening to Ariana. It's best served lived.

A year on from the attack I tell Caitlin I'm glad her mum and sister had someone kind like her to keep them buoyant and lead the way, but that it seems very much in her pragmatic nature. She walks around her garden as we chat. Annette has popped out once to check on her; it's getting dark outside. Caitlin slows in her pacing to consider this for a second and says, 'I've never really thought of it like that, like it's "in my nature", but I think it might be, you know. If someone's nasty to me, I'll just fire something back.

'I've never been one of them people who is just told something and then shuts up. You can't target something that I've been to and expect me to not go again because I'll just show you that I won't listen to what you say.'

Jan, 65, New York, an Elvis fan, on proximity, pilgrimage and loss

I have pictures of my grandmother outside Graceland when Elvis had just bought it and the driveway was only dirt. My whole family loved Elvis, *especially* the women. Memphis was so small back then. My aunt's housekeeper who came once a week was his part-time cook. My ex-mother-in-law went to school with him. My best friend's aunt was his private nurse. I have, my entire life, been on the outside of the circle of people around Elvis.

Have you been to Graceland? Out front there is a parking area, really for the fans' cars, so they could get out, stand outside and talk and take pictures and hope that he'd come down and sign autographs if he was home. When the gates open there's a little guardhouse right there and that's where Harold worked. Harold was Elvis's cousin. When I was younger I'd be there with my family. I remember one time, my older sister and myself drove up to Graceland to the house. She was taking pictures, and Elvis drove up in his pink Cadillac. I was young, so I was more interested in looking at the house, and peeping through the windows, but the other women, they were losing their minds, just totally lost it. When I was in my twenties, I'd go with friends of mine – or by myself sometimes – for hours to chat with Harold. He'd tell us funny stories and he'd love to play games. The phone would ring and everybody would hold their breath as he answered, thinking it would be Elvis's voice to say he was coming home. I'd always try to sneak up the driveway, then Harold would go, 'Get back here, girl, before I have to call the cops.' Then I'd have to go back.

People, fans, would be there twenty-four hours a day, seven days a week. That was the norm for Graceland even then. The joy was in talking to other fans there who understood why you were there and to see how expansive his popularity was, his reach: Germany, England, Australia, or within the United States – their holiday destination was to come to Memphis. To know, whether he was home or not, that you're there at his home, even though you're not inside, it was something special. But not many people at all were allowed to get inside those gates, like me and my friends were. It was about those relationships with cousin Harold or Elvis's Uncle Vester, who was always there during the daytime, that meant whether or not you were allowed inside. I was just out there so much that I got to know Harold, others got to know Uncle Vester.

Eventually, I moved away to New York. I've been back to Graceland many times but never August 16th, not on the date of his death. I *couldn't*, you see.

The day Elvis died, I was not feeling well. A girlfriend of mine woke me up around 12.30pm, and said: Elvis is dead. Well, what came out of my mouth wasn't nice. I turned on the TV to see and I took off and spent the rest of the day and all night at Graceland. It was like family had died. I had lost family. I cried hysterically for days. The day of Elvis's funeral – and this was how intense this was for me – I told my boss I was taking the day off and he said no and I said, 'well I'm going to go, I'll quit my job but I'm walking out of here at 12 o'clock. That's the way it's going and I don't care.' He just looked at me and he knew I was a huge Elvis fan, everyone did. So right there and then he shut down the entire office and let us all go to the funeral. Everything stopped. I was standing right across from the entrance to Forest Hill Cemetery, where Elvis was buried, when the funeral procession came out.

The last time I got to see Elvis, I was hanging out with Harold, and Elvis had come home from the last concert he did. Harold didn't kick me out of the guardhouse. The phone rang and he said, 'OK, Elvis is coming in', and I thought 'Harold's joking', and the next thing I knew the gates opened. And in came his car and it was Elvis. I was so grateful to Harold for not kicking us out of there, and for letting us be there, because that was the last time I ever saw him. He was about two feet away and I got as close as I could without getting hit by that car.

The grieving process took quite a while. For three months I listened to his music constantly; it was four months before I could go back up to Graceland. I couldn't go back. Eventually, I went with a couple of friends; we all sort of sat there with Harold, deep in our own thoughts.

I went back to Graceland one night, by myself, I don't remember the time frame. Harold let me in. There had been so many rumours flying by that point about how Elvis had died and what happened, and how he was found, and I asked him, 'please tell me what happened'. He drove me up to the house and showed me from outside the windows where Elvis was found, and told me he had a massive heart attack. I guess knowing specifically from him what happened helped, rather than having the rumours. It took quite a while to get to the point where I could go out there and deal with it; I still felt the overwhelming sadness. But Elvis loved being at Graceland, it was his escape from being him and from the business he was in, and I could go to Graceland and be with other fans who loved him, and we could talk and laugh and share memories. That was a big part of the process, of living through that.

I went back to Graceland when they opened it up for tours and it's so totally different and commercialised now. Back then it was very personal. Even though I'm not in Memphis, out here in New York I'm meeting new Elvis fans. I'll talk to people who say 'oh, my mother was a huge Elvis fan' or 'my mother went to his concert' and I'd tell them the date of the concert before they'd even finished with it coming out of their mouth, because I kept track of everything! I've helped plenty of strangers who are planning trips out to Graceland, and so I still have some of that connection to Elvis here.

Growing up in Memphis and although it was the outskirts of his circle, to have the access to that circle, it was a huge gift and I've always known that. It didn't happen to many people. I'm so appreciative of that, I really am.

9

OUR TEARS DRY ON THEIR OWN: AMY, GRIEF AND BRITISH FEMALE FANS

Q: What's the difference between February and Amy Winehouse?
A: February makes it to 28!
> – Jokes4Us.com

Over futile odds / And laughed at by the gods / And now the final frame /
Love is a losing game
> – Amy Winehouse, 'Love Is a Losing Game'

A beautiful blonde jewellery designer in her thirties is bouncing a child on her hip and touching the window slats with a free hand. Through each clear rectangle, you can see out onto the road. Down there one night, the woman, Tiffany, had been walking the family dog, Bowie, when a next-door neighbour approached for a chat. He told her he used to pull a ladder up to the house, climb up, remove the slats, slither – unbelievably – through the window and go down to the front door and let a previous tenant in. Amy Winehouse, he told her, used to lock herself out all the time.

'I told the guy, like, "Greeeeat, just please don't do that while we're living here."' Tiffany looks at me in disbelief. The kid in her arms wriggles with joy as if in on the joke and takes to the floor.

From the shearling wool rugs to polished wooden ceiling, the house is the Scandi dream you'd expect of a trendy couple – Tiffany's husband, Sion, is a creative director at a fashion magazine. The pair found it through a rental ad on the internet; a perfect joint space, especially for a freelancing mother who works from home. There's something about the feel of it, they realised walking around it for the first time – the air, the acoustics, the shapes – that suggests special things could be made here. At the bottom of the ad there had been a caveat telling, or perhaps warning, prospective renters that it used to be Amy Winehouse's house. In February 2008, a month during which she won numerous Grammy awards and performed at the Brit Awards, all while a special deluxe edition of *Back to Black* was about to top the UK album chart, Amy moved into the house with a view to work on new music. It looked very different when she was there. She is believed to have slept upstairs in the open loft, which she'd painted pink. She loved the fifties, so all the furniture was retro; she had a jukebox set up in the hall and a Slush Puppy machine on the kitchen counter. There was a drum set and all her music gear in the living room. One photo of her living inside the house exists on the internet: in the image she's playing the keyboard in her bra, and behind her, under the stairs, you can see photos of her and her husband Blake Fielder-Civil embracing.

Tiffany says that a few times a week, a guy with an iPad (now known to the family as a local, cash-in-hand tour guide) and a group of between four and fifteen tourists come by. The first time it was a shock. 'I was putting him to bed one evening,' she gestures at the child, now wiping a runny nose, 'and he sleeps at the room at the front of the house onto the road, and he's not a great sleeper. I heard people talking so went down and looked out and there's a massive group of them at 8pm. It's a strange feeling. But we're used to it now.' Sometimes Tiffany and Sion might be about to go to bed, or are in the middle of an argument, which they have to pause. 'It's part and parcel of being on this little pilgrimage.' Perhaps it's not as prominent or obvious a stop as The Hawley Arms, the pub where Winehouse used to drink regularly, or Camden Market, or even the house where she died, which is a ten-minute walk away – but this house is a cultural spot to hunt down if you've done a little research all the same.

'We've taken the piss with each other saying, "Should we just charge people five quid to come in?" but obviously we wouldn't do that,' she laughs, looking at Sion. The couple have done enough cultural tourism of their own to understand why people would be interested in coming to their house. They've taken a trip to Jim Morrison's grave and the bar in New York where Dylan Thomas drank just before he died. This is different though, a personal space of Amy's. Tiffany wonders if there'd be any point in allowing entry. 'People might have a romantic idea of what it's like inside – walk in and might not ever want to find out that it looks like somebody else's house, not see all those instruments there.'

In the kitchen, Tiffany tells me she spends a lot of time by this window because she has a passion for people watching. 'Usually in the evenings when we're cooking or washing up or just sitting here having a chat, they all get together on this little corner and get embarrassed because they want to take a picture but they see us here and walk by. Then they do this thing where they get nervous and walk back that way, then I see them walk up to the pavement here' – she laughs, gesturing below us, by the front door, tight to the house – 'to get away from the window to do it'.

From this vantage point, I see a couple of young women self-consciously shuffle like pigeons on the far pavement. They take it in turns to have their back to the flat and pose while the other takes a photograph on their phone, and then group together again to look at what they've captured.

Ten years previously, at the same house, two Liverpudlian teen girls, Megan and Hannah, managed to force their way through the paparazzi semi-permanently stationed outside the front door. Megan pressed the intercom button. It had Winnie The Pooh stickers all over it. 'Is this Amy?' brunette Megan asked through the speaker. They wait. Both wore the mid-to-late noughties, British white girl uniform – flappy woollen hats that sag around the back of the neck, lipgloss over thick concealer-covered lips and heavy bronzer. Amy answered. She loved Liverpool and told them so. Her voice sounded knackered, each sentence deflating in the middle. But she took care to check the spelling of their names: M-E-G-A-N and H-A-N-N-A-with an H. 'I've got some photos up here so I thought I'd sign them.'

Megan was elated. 'Amy, you're so nice,' she told her. 'I'm really not that nice,' replied Amy. 'You are! You are!' they called. 'Nah, that's why I don't go out because I'm not that nice and I've just learnt that. Only joking.' The fans, as well as Amy and the photographers, knew she did go out. If Amy was not hidden away inside, she was out boozing in Camden. If she wanted to go further afield to Liverpool, she was welcome ('You can come and stay at mine any time,' offered Megan).

The paparazzi – as much a part of the street furniture as the lamps and post box – started asking for signed photos too. Amy was saucy with one of them called Ben, and told him he wasn't getting a photo. She temporarily hung up the intercom, and blonde Hannah turned around to Ben and the rest of the photographers and moaned, 'Oh, no, you've ruined it.'

Moments later Amy was back on again, getting ready to go out shopping. 'Listen, I'm gonna sign those girls all over their beautiful... limbs!' She was too busy to come down and take a picture at that time, as per their next request, but that didn't stop her chatting away. 'Don't you worry 'bout nothin' girls. You're good girls.'

Megan said, 'Amy, is your dad a taxi driver? So is my dad.' She replied: 'Aw, is he? Tell him I said hello...' 'I will' '...and tell that prick Ben to get a proper job.' Everyone outside her door laughed together. Satisfied that photos were coming, the girls bounced away, and Amy shouted from an open window, 'Get a proper job!' Sure enough, Megan and Hannah were soon in the street smiling broadly and holding their signed Amy photos.

Amy Winehouse loved women. 'Women don't try to use me,' she told *Rolling Stone* for a feature during which a reporter spent hours in her home in the period she was abusing drugs. 'Her trust is remarkable,' the copy reads. 'At one point, she even discusses her night's outfit with two female fans over her door-bell intercom.' The same intercom, two different fans. This was very normal – thanks to the paparazzi, the houses she lived in during her life in Camden were well publicised. When approaching her, girls would treat her as if she were a friend, and not just one of the country's greatest living performers. Amy would treat them similarly.

No one in Britain has been hounded by the press like Amy Winehouse, neither before nor since. As her alcoholism, drug addiction and eating disorder grasped her tighter, her power over performances weakened. At the Isle of Wight Festival in 2007, I watched her, a formidable vision in tiny denim hotpants, adored by a crowd of people holding cider and wearing daisy chains. By the following summer, performing at Bestival down the road, she was a different person. Late to the stage, she walked on like a puppet with cut strings. I remember sensing that islanders had been expecting a repeat performance of the year before. She was booed, the crowd tumultuous.

The media were fascinated by every detail of her addictions as they naturally made profit selling each chapter to the public. There was no real progress of narrative: each development could be summarised as 'She's still a mess'. It wasn't just right-wing press and tabloids that stripped her slowly of humanity. She was the regular butt of jokes on BBC talk shows, and the Dave award for Funniest Joke at 2008's Edinburgh Fringe Festival was one about the singer self-harming. *Observer* columnist Barbara Ellen wrote, 'How sick I am of seeing pictures of Winehouse shambling about like a stick insect in a dusty Liberace wig. The pictures last year of her wandering the streets...then, one could feel sorry for her, wish this wonderfully talented young female could get herself well. Several months on, she's still shambling about and patience is wearing thin.' The piece ends with a condemnation that manages to be cruel in various ways: '*Back to Black* was written by a gutsy, heartbroken young woman; the next one, unless things change, will be written by a drugged-up skank.' Whether that view influenced the public mind or reflected it, it was shared: a laugh at her expense down the pub, portraying her in a quick hammed-up Halloween costume.

'The press basically became aggressive fangirls of her, while the real fangirls had a certain understanding with her that she was going through shit,' thirty-year-old fan Emily told me. 'I do believe all of us instinctively didn't want to add to what she went through. It was the days before social media, so that would've made a difference, but we weren't the type of fan base to scream down the street at her.'

The goading was near-matched from across the Atlantic, too. Lyndsey Parker was a music journalist who watched Amy Winehouse's downfall from the States. Back then she remembers internet sites had a different tone, comparable to that of current social media. It was the voice of Perez Hilton, Defamer or the early days of VICE and, in Lyndsey's words, 'bloggy and mean-spirited a lot of the time'. She remembers Amy's last concert in Belgrade. It was the opposite of a triumphant comeback. She was being propped up, seemed drugged or drunk or, as Parker thought at the time, had the air of being forced to perform. 'It gave me flashbacks of when Britney Spears tried to stage a quote unquote comeback at the MTV Video awards and was clearly medicated and not in a condition to perform. Reports were just making fun of it. No "someone please help her" or "this is disturbing" or "this is sad". Whether it was the tabloids or the mainstream media or even the full-on music media, it'd become an international pastime to gawk at her antics.'

Each indication that Amy was in trouble – the clear abuse of substances, the fights with her husband, the emphysema from the drugs and smoking – was another blown-up aspect of the sketch. A troupe tailed Amy's every move around the city, creating photos that were evidence for the public to see how awful her condition was. Writer and thinker Susan Sontag said that a single photo acknowledges suffering, while an endless parade of them deadens response to it. With every update, we continued to gape and lose the bleak reality of Amy Winehouse's situation.

When she died on the 23rd July 2011, it still felt like a surprise. Even though, in this case, we'd watched her die a hundred times. Every splash on the front of a tabloid said: 'Not yet'. For her fans it was uniquely devastating because, while the public watched on with perverse curiosity and an insatiable lust for the violence of those images, they, the fans, were willing her to get better, daily.

'In an industry where women were coming out on a conveyor belt and everyone looked the same way and no one had any opinions, she did, she had it all,' said Emily. 'For someone who was that famous she was normal despite the caricature tabloids portrayed. She'd become an idea, not a person. Press should've looked at her with humanity and gone, "We seriously need to help this person". There was no compassion for addicts or understanding of how addiction works. We as fans just wanted that bright, funny, brash, crass person back.'

When some fans looked for news updates on Amy Winehouse, they scanned for hints of recovery, of rehabilitation. Here, at least, it looked like she'd eaten a meal. Here, she seemed coherent, or with a female friend. Something about the way in which the press covered her, and left the images to speak for her, meant her fans weren't a typical fanbase who met up with other fans or always tuned into that media coverage – they were more engaged in an individual relationship with her. A couple of fans I spoke to stopped looking at press about her entirely. There were other factors that kept fans isolated in their fandom, of course – social media was not fully fledged and while she was on the peripheries of the indie scene, she stood apart with her soulful music, so different from what anyone else was creating. Echoing others, Ruth from Newcastle told me, 'I had collective fandoms – I was into rock music and worked at a metal bar, the only one in Newcastle. I'd do photographs to get into shows with mates – but with Amy it was a one-on-one relationship.'

Sarah from London was on a train when she found out about Amy's death. The event eclipsed any other details of that day and, in the way that grief disorientates you, she doesn't remember where she was coming from or going to. She received a text from a friend she'd not spoken to in a long time. It said: 'you were the first person I thought of'. Other texts started appearing. 'I had total denial, that no, this is not how this ends. My phone was really slow and it took ten minutes to load a page on the train. I saw it confirmed and I was just in pieces. I always imagined her with a family, she talked a lot about wanting kids, and that's how I imagined her. Living in north London and going through it and coming through it. I almost felt like the persona had won. I missed her, I missed her so much.'

Liv came back from a shift at a petrol station in Cheshire. The tills were quiet, barely a car rolling through, so she was sent off early. She walked the two minutes home, went in, and put her dead phone on charge and thought about texting her friends to ask if they wanted to go to the pub that evening. All of a sudden, her phone came to life and friends reached her first. 'All these texts were coming through. I had about twenty people, like: are you alright?' Tears streamed down her face as she watched the TV giving updates of the circumstances of Winehouse's death. Unnerved by the state he found his sister in when he arrived home from work, her brother tried to get out of her what had happened. 'Honestly, he didn't know what to do because he'd never been a fan of anything like I was of Amy.'

I was working at a bar at home on the island that summer. I was nearly twenty, a couple of years older than Liv. I had thick eyeliner like Amy and back-combed my hair into a bouffant, which I pinned into a ponytail. Sometimes I'd do back-to-back night shifts at a bar across the road. Most days we'd play *Back to Black* – we all liked it. Half the people who worked there wanted to be musicians themselves or were in love with someone who was, and it was classic soulful music acceptable for yachtie locals and older tourists. When we heard she'd died while on our shift, customers were quick to comment: it'd been a long time coming, that's what you get for partying that hard. One of the staff immediately put *Back to Black* on. I scuffed around in my ballet pumps holding plated-up meals, and eventually told my manager, please, to turn it off. For the rest of the summer everyone had to hear it wherever we went: a funeral march. Every opening bar felt like a taunt.

From outside a fandom, grief for a celebrity was thought of as pathetic, if not fraudulent and self-indulgent. This changed somewhat during and after 2016, a year David Bowie, Prince, George Michael and other notables died, and male fans joined in what had been previously perceived as a feminine and overly emotional online response to loss. These were some of the same men who had been vocal in condemning or joking about the hysterically disproportionate displays of girls dealing with the loss of One Direction breaking up just months before. There have been so many band break-ups and artist deaths since, and we know what is expected of us when partaking in online grieving and have grown into the rhythms of that.

When Amy Winehouse died, grief for a drug addict – and a female drug addict – was denied validation. The public response to any girl and young woman mourning her was to brush it off. RIP Facebook statuses were met with sneering and eye rolls, even anger. *She had it coming to her. She was a druggy wasn't she. This day was always going to happen. Surprised she lasted as long as she did at that rate.*

However, the press now began to tell a different story. Before, there'd been pictures of her looking gaunt and ravaged, with tabloid taunts and op-eds posing the question: when will she die? Now there were tributes. Wasn't she talented? Wasn't she a star, a blessed angel, someone who shone too brightly, and simply, sadly, had to leave us all? The same columnists, the same papers. How quickly everyone forgot what they'd made of her just months, weeks, days ago. The 'drugged-up skank' had become the 'singer of a generation'. *Rolling Stone,* which had done the profile at her home in 2008 – as she became more reclusive and troubled – talking about her 'emaciated' figure and the 'little scabs that raid her face', detailing that she had a photo on her camera with a dick (presumably her husband's) in her mouth, later published vast numbers of tributes to her after her death. As Sady Doyle writes of Amy and other 'difficult' women, dead after being mistreated by the press, in *Trainwreck,* 'The outpouring of love and grief that these women receive, in the wake of their deaths, tends to wipe their records clean.' In essence, it is easier for journalists and publications to erase what they'd done and rapidly begin with the work of memorialising a victim. It all, as Doyle notes, sells copies.

This hypocrisy was furiously rejected by British female fans. The twisted nature of the betrayal made it hard to take what was being said about the loss of Amy. It was gutting. Impossible to take after the years of cruel one-liners and flash photography on the streets of Camden. For many, even the sight of the papers made them feel physically sick. The fans had to forge their own ways to grieve.

The first thing that Sarah did when she got home from her train journey was write a letter to Amy. 'It absolutely flowed out, it just kept coming. I thanked her and I think I apologised because of getting angry with her.

It was a compulsion in my body. This is really daft but I remember I put it in an envelope, put a picture of her and I on the front, and wrote "You should be stronger than me" because that was one of her big songs for me.'

Despite the fact that Amy never had a solid fandom community as such – rather, lots of individuals who felt they had personal relationships with her – for a brief moment after her death many fans felt the strong desire for connection with each other. Sarah says she just needed to see other fans, 'to see their outpouring'. The fact that none of them wanted to believe she was dead linked them; they shared that. So, she travelled to Amy's house, where she knew others would be. 'That for me was therapeutic. I didn't really connect with anyone up there...maybe I didn't really want to, maybe I was giving off the vibe that I just wanted to go and come away.'

Sarah placed the letter in a memorial area with everyone else's little offerings. 'It was just really sad, the whole thing, it wasn't even dramatic, it was just sad. I didn't stay long. It felt a little bit voyeuristic. I felt that I'd done what I needed to do for my personal relationship with her. I'd written to her and I'd taken it to her house and that felt like the right thing to do.'

Liv, sadly, was too young and poor to go alone across the country into the capital, but it was all she wanted to do. Having seen people camp outside the house for days on the TV, she told her mum she'd go on the day of the funeral. No one around her understood the feelings she was having and she felt like she 'had to *be* with people who felt that way and I felt I had to go to where she was from because that's where it all started. And I've seen her house in photos with all the paparazzi outside it, hassling her, all the time, and I felt like I had to be there and see it in my own context, rather than it used with her being slated in the papers and it being a photo of her outside her house in a moment of looking shit. That was the feeling behind that. It didn't pan out, of course.'

The press and public call her 'Amy Winehouse' – the two names work together well for their purposes. A girl-next-door but also something that referenced the booze she needed and was buried by. British female fans call her Amy, like she was a mate. She was brash and sharp and crude and kind and local enough to feel like one of them. She would suffer no fools: this was the Amy they knew first. Calling her by just those two syllables felt intimate to them, as if after her death they were holding someone dear, and her suffering, close to them.

Neneh has the happy gait of someone who knows her way around; a walk that makes you follow like a puppy, even if you're familiar with your surroundings. Everything in Camden is held in a golden beam, and our skin looks bronzed. The character of the area itself is so well established that despite everything seeming to be under construction or dug up – bollards, pub exteriors, paving slabs, shop fronts – it's a place that could upend its roots and walk off and anyone would recognise it. We reach a bridge over the Lock, and cars slowly tumble over it behind us. As we lean on the warm bridge, we let it take our weight, gazing out, to help Neneh search her memory. Men work on the canals, their Cockney accents echoing against the walls of the canal, the sounds of the strong vowels circling back on themselves.

On this lock ledge, Neneh used to lie out. She and all the other emo kids of Camden would be here every Saturday in term time and every day that they could during the summer holidays of 2007, 'playing music, underage drinking, doing all the bad things and claiming this dock for our own'. One day a beehive bobbed across the bridge. Neneh sat bolt upright and pointed, calling to her friend. She had a digital camera with her, so grabbed her friend and they sprinted after the beehive, which bounced away from them. She realised it must have gone into Sainsbury's and the two girls ran up and down every aisle. After a good twenty minutes looking and thinking they'd missed her or made a mistake, they caught a glimpse of her, over by the ready-meals aisle.

'We were so nervous, we were huge fans and I thought she was about to say she wouldn't take a photo with us. But she was there with her shopping basket, doing something as mundane as her weekly shop, being so polite and nice to us, just a couple of excited fifteen-year-old fans. She put her arms around us, and spoke to us properly.' This was during a time when Amy was terribly thin and unwell, but a rare hour without a string of press following her.

Inside Sainsbury's again as an adult, standing next to me with the chill of the fridges and beep of the checkouts, Neneh says, 'This is a bit triggering, to be honest. Literally every time I come here, I always think of the day I met her, this aisle. It'll forever be in my memories.'

Forever memories mean fans don't need the official memorialisation. And with Amy the memorialisation was extensive. The Jewish Museum worked with a graffiti artist agency to cover Camden in images of her, some rather gaudy. Camden Council allowed a statue of her to be erected in Camden Market, a decision agreed with Mitch Winehouse, her father, intended to be a positive way to remember Amy (whether it looks quite like her is frankly debatable). None of the fans particularly like those – 'it's all meaningless,' says Liv – although they understand why they should exist. Neither do they think there is much merit in the walking tours or visiting her old house, some describing them as 'creepy' or 'invasive'. Why would you want to go to her house now? Somewhere she was trapped in by paparazzi, where she died – and so recently. It feels raw, so dehumanising. Or as fan Ruth says: 'I understand when fans would go to other artists' houses, but the press probably didn't hound those artists to death there?'

Mostly it's generalised music fans or casual overseas Amy fans who do the visit to her old flat. Something about all of it reeks of how she was treated, people trying to get closer to the body that was pried on, its deterioration monitored with sick fascination. The interest is both comparable to getting a photo by a cartoon house at Disneyland and trekking out to a cult murder site.

Liv might've wanted to go to the house just after Amy's death but this is a different time. You won't see Liv or any of the others going to a hologram tour, or circling around Tiffany and Sion's home to take a photo outside. 'Everyone memorialises people in their own way, but people visit the Amy Winehouse house on a paid-for walking tour as a tourist thing, and someone profits from that, or you do it to say you've "done" something.' That doesn't generally sit very well with her. Liv finds it disingenuous. 'It's hard to explain but I don't think visiting the house is a genuine thing to do anymore. It's grief tourism. There's something about the organised-ness of it.'

Having knowledge of and a feeling for what happened in those places does not make fans necessarily want to associate them with her, posthumously. For those fans who live overseas or who enjoy music and have an interest in Amy, the literal modes of pilgrimage make sense. Without the same cultural touchstones and personal relationship as the British fans, they want to feel as though they're actively getting closer to her. Henry Hate, Amy Winehouse's tattoo artist, sees about eight people a month at his London studio who have come to him specifically to have a piece of Amy, somehow, on their body: an Amy-themed tattoo. 'I think if someone gets a tattoo here and walks away with a sense of wholeness, my job is done in that respect. But,' he adds, 'I am not the lightning rod to Amy.' Some of them ask him for replicas of her statement tattoos, the pin-up girls, the singing bird, which he declines. It's tacky, far too close to the bone.

When he holds needle to flesh, he considers that they're all looking for something. 'Everyone wants their own insight into this myth because that it essentially what art does, it draws you in to make your own conclusion based on your experience. Like Jim Morrison: they have cornered his grave off now, which has just heightened it even more. The more you block something off, the more ravenous people get because there is a barricade, a detachment.' With Amy it's that she is now dead, the physical her is completely unattainable. He adds, without a hint of mockery: 'I honestly believe that, especially now with celebrity culture and the diminishing of organised faith, people are looking for a form of identity or closeness and because right now things seem so uncertain they want an affiliation which will make them feel good about themselves.'

After my visit to Tiffany and Sion, and much digging on the internet, I found a blog belonging to Nico, the owner of the house, the one that Amy briefly lived in. On it, there are photos of the house and his words: 'My greatest regret about Amy's time in my house is that she wasn't inspired or motivated or capable of continuing a music career while she lived there. Perhaps it was the last place that she should be but it was where she wanted to be. She's gone now and we look back and realise what we had and perhaps what we stopped her from being.' She was restless at Nico's house, just as she was restless in her body. Where she should've spent her days writing the best songs of her life, she was in turmoil. The place where she was most content, or at least truest to herself, was in that music.

At the forefront of the ways the fans memorialise Amy is the music, which they still listen to, sometimes multiple times a week. Although Sarah lives up the road from the statue, she won't make the trip to see it. 'I sometimes wonder if I did move to north London because of Amy, whether she influenced me. She was gone by the time I moved but I think of Camden fondly because of her mainly.' Instead she goes to the local pubs and has a quiet drink and might remember her then. But she mostly wants to highlight to me that it's singing the lyrics that feel like a little prayer to her friend.

Liv wore liquid eyeliner for the first time in her life the day after Amy died. She went into work with two thick black lines she'd soon learn to draw more carefully. 'My boss said it was a bit much and I had to take it off, and because I was going to uni soon, I said, "No, Amy died yesterday, you can sack me if you want me to take it off."' One of the cleaners continued to make digs about how Amy wasn't that great and that Liv didn't even look like Amy. Now everyday she puts her eyeliner on and does it thinking of Amy. 'It's just become a part of the way I look. If I've got somewhere to go, I'll put Amy on and think, alright, I can do my eyeliner now,' she laughs.

Often fans centre themselves in a time before Amy's heavy drug and alcohol use, when she wasn't hounded by paparazzi. Sarah listens to her first album *Frank* more than *Back to Black*, to keep those early years of falling in love with Amy at the forefront of her mind, but also because of how well Amy seemed then. 'I remember her as when I met her before she was properly famous, in Brecon; as that girl who was a bit like me but a lot cooler. That's how I remember Amy; I don't think of her with a beehive, with tattoos or swigging on whatever at the festivals. And I don't remember those tabloid photos, that's not Amy to me. That's the cartoon character to me.'

Sitting in Granary Square, in the borough of Camden, a walk away from Camden Town, I meet Emily. We sit overlooking fountains and I notice on her arm is a tattoo of Amy, golden in the end-of-the-summer light. It's a stylised portrait, black and white but realistic. 'I don't like to think of her in the way a lot of people recognise her.' She wouldn't do something like go to Henry Hate – that wouldn't get her closer to Amy, she thinks it a fake fan thing to do. When she went to get her tribute tattoo done, she looked through lots of photos of Amy. 'The alternative to this one was her on the *Rolling Stone* cover in denim shorts and her hands are slightly in her shorts and she's got her bra on and her big beehive and that would be a pin-up style. But I thought, that's not the aspect of her that I particularly liked. Her personality was phenomenal. I wanted her at her best. Because that's how she should be remembered, instead of as their tortured junky.' People have got this image in their head of this tiny skeletal Cockney lass with two teeth and a needle in her arm, she says. That's scraping the surface, you just need to *really* listen to one of her songs. 'It doesn't take too much to connect with the real her and what she was trying to say but I don't think people even got that far.'

Public memory has settled on an Amy Winehouse that exists somewhere between the original press and public treatment of her and the memorialising of her as a British pop legend. It has written her as part of The 27 Club, the group of rockstars who died at that age. With time, the fact she never made it to twenty-eight will reduce her further. But if fans continue to reject what is being pulled together in the collective consciousness as her lasting image and legacy, what is the one that they co-create for themselves? From their memory maps – across London, from her early shows, from meeting her, isolated moments listening to the music – they have an old Amy, one based on intimate connection and personal recollection. It's still a factual image, rooted in old interviews of her, and an extensive knowledge base. In their rejection of the repeated paparazzi photos of her, and the silence of her death, fans have the closest thing to a real idea of who she was. At the very least, the most honest one. Documentaries, opinion pieces and retrospectives will all continue to ask the question: Who was Amy Winehouse? A valuable option will be to defer to the authority of the fans.

'Amy managed to speak what I felt and made me not feel the shame,' Ruth told me of when she initially bonded with Amy's music while at university. 'I've done stuff I'm not proud of at all, things I wouldn't want done to me, but she made me feel like I wasn't the devil, like I was human and there were reasons for it.' More recently, Ruth was lied to by her then-boyfriend of seven years, who she lived with in London. 'He was on a secret holiday with a girl we'd been fighting about for months and months. He told me I was crazy for thinking it.' She had the sort of year that tears you down and leaves you in the rubble, blinking, wondering how you can start again. Each time Ruth goes into the corner shop near her new place in the city, the shopkeeper seems to have Amy playing. 'No matter if it's 2am or after work, he's got "Tears Dry On Their Own" on. I know it's my imagination but it feels like she's trying to give me a message or a kick up the arse, or just be a friend.'

Through the pints and the pool and the standing barefoot at the bar and singing at local music festivals and fan photographs and lyrics scribbled in pub toilet stalls, there is a specific Amy, and it's exactly the same Amy that fans I spoke to all feel they know and remember. Others, even new fans, don't walk up to their local Sainsbury's and remember a tiny girl with a shopping basket grinning and letting them take a photo with her. They don't remember a very specific affinity with her, based in locality and sensibility, in going to the pub and getting pissed and falling in love and being a ladette, the opposite of what you were supposed to aspire to be, according to the British pop charts in the noughties. It's an Amy that can only be distilled if you were one of these people, living in this specific time, in this specific place.

'There's a difference,' says Emily, rubbing the singer's image on her skin in the sun. The lines have further penetrated and dulled with the years. 'Someone will see my arm and go "Valerie! Amy Winehouse!", referencing her cover of the Zutons' song that was a massive hit. Or they'd say "Amy" and there'll be a different sort of understanding there. You know they're a girl like you who felt as deeply as you. And as deeply as Amy did in the first place.'

Ex-Courtney Love fan, Zara, thirty, New York, on new connections

I don't really look up to Courtney anymore. I'm at a stage in my life now where I don't really go to shows or concerts. Even a year or two ago I probably went to a show every week. I just don't feel the same way. I drive a lot, so I really like listening to music then. I grew up in New Zealand and Courtney Love was there briefly as a child. Inside the *Live Through This* album cover there's a picture of her when she's probably about ten years old, a child, wearing a plaid shirt and jeans on her farm in New Zealand, and that was me when I got into her. I played drums all the way through nine or ten to about twenty and I wanted to be in a girl rock band. When I moved to New York I learnt bass. When you look through the history of women in rock 'n' roll, Courtney Love came out and she was just fucked up and wrong. She didn't have the Disney upbringing and an amazingly trained voice. She gave me hope that I could be a musician. If you tried to act like her, you probably could.

I had to go to Portland a couple weeks ago for a job and I couldn't take my assistant, so they hired people there for me. I hate travelling alone, so I'm quite shy and nervous about going. I'll usually stay in my hotel room or go out for dinner by myself. I arrived on my first day and I had two really cute assistants. I was like: thank god. Anyway, I'd had 'Live Through This' tattooed on my arm when I was a teenager and one day on set an assistant, Ada, saw and knew what it was instantly. Some people who don't know what it is just assume it's some cheesy life motto: 'live, laugh, love', that kind of thing. She saw that, and her and the other assistant ended up taking me out every single night in Portland, out for dinner, to the clubs; we got on really well.

On the last night Ada said, 'Can I give you a ride to the airport?' and I was like, 'Oh no, you don't have to'. I actually felt like getting an Uber and sleeping on the plane, but she'd spent so much time looking after me. So she picks me up. She pulls up in an eighties sports car, so small my suitcase would barely fit in there, one where the doors go up on the side like a Batmobile. Inside her car she'd brought a Hole cassette tape – *Live Through This*. 'Hey... I bought this for the drive.' She planned the whole thing. So she puts it on and I had the most unprofessional time with her, where we drove to the airport on the freeway with the music so loud and both of us screaming every single word to every single song. Essentially, I was her boss. It was really weird, and amazing… I don't have that any more with Hole. Once every couple of years I'll have a moment like that. You know, when you listen to certain songs or you have certain smells that can take you exactly back to one period of time in your life? That drive to the airport that night was so crazy for me; it took me back *exactly* to being an angry, emo teenager. It's amazing how one fucked-up musician could have such an influence on little girls all around the world, and how her music could bond two strangers intimately together for a few minutes of their life.

Courtney Love fan, Ada, twenty-eight, Portland, on serendipity

I was born in 1990 in Portland right around when grunge was happening. I used to work at this store where my boss knew Courtney Love when she was a teenager. He would talk about kicking her out of the store for shoplifting and maybe ten years later she was walking around the shop in her underwear, trying things on. When I was a teenager I probably would've been stealing clothes there too if I hadn't have been working at the same shop. I've always been intrigued by her from a young age with that little connection. It was this taboo thing to like Courtney Love, almost. It was one of those things I kept secret; I was almost embarrassed. Maybe because grunge is so commonplace and deep-seated in the community in the Northwest that people are like 'oh, whatever, that's passé' to really respond to her and think that it's cool.

I remember one day my friend Jack gave me my treasured Hole tape and said, 'I know how much you love this; this is for when you want to get in touch with your angst.' I ended up buying this car because it had a cassette player and I wanted a place I could play my cassettes. So, when I met Zara it was such a special experience to be able to share that.

I'm an assistant stylist for random people all the time. I just remember being at work and seeing her tattoo. My friend was also assisting and the three of us totally clicked, but me and Zara connected on a real musical level. She asked about going to record stores, and I found out she was a big Dead Moon fan, so I took her to see Andrew Loomis's grave, in an ancient cemetery, which is just a couple of blocks from my house. I think we made piña coladas and had them on our little patio that overlooks the street beforehand. The next couple of days we worked in the day and hung out in the night; it was so effortless, her company was amazing.

On her last day, I went home to grab my car so I could pick her up from her hotel downtown. I thought to myself, 'I have to bring my Hole tape, otherwise it's a lost opportunity.' It was this sisterly feeling, like I knew she'd love it but I was almost a little nervous. I also thought: might she think this is weird? I definitely felt like I was putting myself out there. But decided, 'OK, I'm taking a chance on this because I never get to share this album with anyone but myself.'

It was about 6 or 7pm, the sun was starting to set and it was golden hour when I got to her hotel. From that moment of putting that music on, I was singing so loud, Zara was too. I was shoving my hands on the steering wheel, full of energy, just so exhilarated by that experience. I was also sad because I didn't want it to stop. It's so hard to find someone you respect in multiple ways and you feel are kindred too. It was this beautiful blessing from the universe that I got to connect with her. I don't think I've ever had before. It was straight out of a movie; there was some sort of blur to the corners of that experience. It didn't feel too real, almost like a dream.

10

WITCHES ALWAYS *LIVE THROUGH THIS*: COURTNEY LOVE'S OLDER FANGIRLS

I'm nobody's daughter. I'm nobody's widow. I'm somebody's mother. Other than that, I don't identify with these other female roles I'm supposed to have.
　　– Courtney Love

One of Courtney's vintage cami dresses was for sale when I was unemployed, so I sold my boyfriend's car for scrap metal. It's me and her, even to the point where I want to put her camisole dress in my coffin with me. Unless I could find an absolute diehard fan in my life to leave it to. It either goes in the ground with me or in the fire with me.
　　– Sam, thirty-eight, Australia

The Basilica Hudson is a renovated industrial factory, magnificent and incongruent on the brown and green banks of the Hudson River, a body of water that goes all the way to the Atlantic Ocean from the Adirondacks in Upstate New York. Fairy lights billow from the Basilica's ceiling, like droplets on spider webs, too pretty for the building's weathered textures. The river is so still. The stagnancy is unnerving a few nights before Halloween. An explosion of hellfire rain would begin at 2am as if a spell had been cast and continue on throughout the night and all the next day and following night. It'd pass through the town at a perfect 45-degree angle.

Jennifer and her dirty-blonde friend Tracy had picked me up in Hudson city in a huge, polluting, all-American silver car, its lights and number plate arranged in a severe expression. Jennifer was standing in front of it, on Warren Street with its many antique shops. The number of them surprised me when I came into town: how could one community need so much old stuff? 'Ha-nnah!' forty-three-year-old Jennifer called, elongating the first 'a', as Tracy nodded at me from behind the wheel. Once you've been told that Jennifer is a Courtney Love fan, you see a resemblance between the two. Her everyday dress code is casual but elegant, her cat-like features are striking and framed by golden hair always styled. Her eyes look like Courtney's. A contrast to Love's trademark throat of gravel chips, everything Jennifer says in her dainty Boston accent sounds like she's reading a recipe for apple pie. That night she wore tight black leggings and a black fitted puffa jacket and her hair smoothed back in a helmet shape. She reminded me of a celebrity mom from an American reality TV show.

'I can't believe it! You're *you*,' she said. 'You're right here, a real person!' looking at me with outstretched arms, and then pulling me into a tight hug. We'd spoken many times after connecting in the Courtney Love Facebook fan group, Broken Dolls. I discovered Courtney on the internet as a pre-teen. There was no one around me who knew who the Hole frontwoman was let alone loved her like me. Mine was the kind of love you base your identity on, the singular idolisation you never forget. I'm not sure I'd be exactly me without having had her. And so I've been in iterations of those fan groups ever since, chatting with people on comment sections, sharing writing about her and gossiping about her latest social media posts, but had never physically met another fan from those groups. 'Get in, now,' Jennifer said, turning to business. 'We've got a mission on our hands.'

In the car she turned from the front seat and sprinkled pink flyers for the event the following night into my lap. 'Some for us, some for the group' – by which she meant the Broken Dolls group – 'don't worry, I've already posted a photo in there.' As we pull into the Basilica car park, Tracy turned her lights off. 'God, it's beautiful,' Jennifer whispered.

'This is naughty,' I told Jennifer, doubt creeping in. She knew it too and started whispering 'Oh god, oh god' under her breath.

We walk up, crunching over the grey gravel as lightly as possible. An Amtrak train wails past – as they periodically do through the night – and makes me jump. The building looks abandoned and Jennifer wonders out loud if the lights have been left on for show. Then we hear some people singing 'Miss World' by Hole.

Suck me under / Maybe forever, my friend

One old window, partially covered with greenery, provides an opportunity. Inside, a band of teen girls are performing to an empty room. Jennifer pulls out her iPhone and I notice the smeared beauty queen on the cover of *Live Through This*, Hole's second album, on the case. Jennifer takes as many photos and videos as she can manage while Tracy keeps watch behind us. 'Is that Courtney?' Tracy says out of nowhere, twiddling her glasses. I edge around the building to another piece of glass, and it is her, in a fur coat, watching from along the side of the wall.

'Oh my god, I've got chills,' Jennifer mouths. 'Even after all these years.' In my pocket, my phone vibrates with notifications flying in from the Facebook group. Jennifer has been updating the global fans who couldn't be in Hudson tomorrow, when the big event is happening. I feel high from the access, a behind-the-scenes look that I've always dreamed of. Whenever something like this happens, it's always me watching the group and missing out on some Courtney event, often happening in the US. I feel almost superior, but that's too simple. It's as though this is kismet, gifted to me; a logical conclusion for the years of loyalty.

Jennifer gets as close to the glass as she humanly can, her black matte acrylics casting squares on her iPhone screen to pull Courtney closer.

'My heart is beating so fast.' The female vocalist – a teenage girl – starts going for it, pushing her voice half as loud again. Courtney head-bangs to her own music.

'It's just a wall between us. Only a wall between us,' Jennifer says between narrating everything Courtney does ('Oh, she's sitting now. Look at this. She's going over to the seats.'). Tracy stands amused, back from us, watching out for security, with her hands held clasped in front of her. She's a Courtney fan, but not on the level of Jennifer or me, preferring other rock acts. In the cold, my ears burn with the knowledge that we shouldn't be doing what we're doing. Between our jostling – coats brushing against each other for room – we miss the moment Hole bassist Melissa Auf der Maur appears to join her. The pair embrace. 'Look, they're friends. Look at that! The contact! You can't argue with that,' Jennifer says. There is always a delicate monitoring going on between fans of how close or feuding Courtney is with certain contemporaries, especially with the other members of what was Hole.

Every now and then we draw our eyes away from the windows to look at each other. We're visibly stressed, Jennifer the most, Tracy least. 'It's like, I don't wanna be that person but I want to be that person,' says Jennifer. A translation: she doesn't want to cause stress for Courtney or be an embarrassing fan stalking her, but there is no question in her mind, we *have* to be here. Despite the stress, I agree. They'd only wanted proximity to something special. Now we were here, and she was too, there was a new possibility: her noticing us. This wasn't what I wanted. It'd been too built up; on some level, it meant too much to even bother, on another, my adoration had almost transcended any need to meet her. Mostly, I knew that if her face showed boredom or irritation as bluntly as I knew it would with her, I'd be devastated. I had to protect everything that she had been for me.

Tracy squints from behind her glasses and mutters, 'Come *on*. Just come out and say "Hey, bitches!"' Then a noise from behind us. Instead of Courtney, we'd summoned an Australasian woman, who burst out of the doors with back-up. 'What do you want? Who are you? Do not take photos and please leave.' Tracy asks to use the bathroom. I cringe at this and the woman looks back at her as if to say 'Nice try' and tells us forcefully to leave and goes back inside. OK, I tell them both. We really need to go now. This is going to get us into big trouble.

Jennifer, with her huge blue eyes, acts as though it never happened, and creeps around the building to find a more opportune spot. Tracy moves like a chess piece backwards into the shadows. I curse. Jennifer is still videoing as Courtney and Melissa start playing 'Miss World' with the girls. I start videoing too, up at the window, watching it through my phone. Suddenly a man consumes the frame and I scream. Bursting through the doors are the previous woman and other staff, rightfully fuming now. I start running back across the gravel – 'Come on,' I yell to them. I hear something about leaking to the internet. Tracy is laughing and Jennifer is somewhere behind me. I feel as if I have an exoskeleton, in the mix of the cold and the tension and thrill. As soon as the car opens, we throw ourselves into it. Jennifer, last, hops in neatly.

'You're our good luck charm,' Jennifer tells me solemnly in the car, and Tracy agrees, smiling and shaking her head in disbelief. 'I kind of love that we got told off, even if it doesn't matter,' I say, thinking: actually, it does matter, I could get into huge problems with the team that have allowed me access the following night. But being something of a professional fan means you frequently miss out on the bizarre situations you can get into with other fans. 'I know,' Jennifer giggles. From the leather seats our phones vibrate with notifications from the Broken Dolls.

'Pffft,' says Tracy, swinging the car out of the drive, up past Hudson station. 'If they were concerned about fans, they should've had more security.'

Jennifer turns back around and stares out of the car window, lights from the street lamps blown out through the raindrops. 'It reminded me of when I used to do ballet as a little girl, before you go up to perform and you're standing there on the floorboards in the wing,' she says. 'You're sick. Your heart is fluttering, you can hear it, but god, you're so excited. You know what's coming. Or maybe it's that you don't know anything at all.'

The following day was Basilica Hudson's career retrospective for Courtney: 'A Tribute: Celebrating the Magic and The Power of Courtney Love'. Courtney herself would be there, as would her daughter, her only child with Kurt Cobain, Frances Bean Cobain. It would be a series of feminist and queer performances, drag, spoken word, and a conversation between Courtney and Melissa in honour of her and to reframe her as a legendary feminist figure, celebrating her cultural relevance over the years. From across the US, various fans would be coming in that day, some travelling hundreds and thousands of miles. They are her core fan base, women in their late thirties to fifties as well as gay men, and all have been hardcore followers since their teenage years or twenties – for over a quarter of a century of her career. 'Look, honey,' as one such fan from Boston, Carrie, would tell me on the night when we were seated waiting for the performance to start. 'Events like this, shows or what have you, only come around every year or two. When Courtney calls, you answer.'

Courtney Love wanted to be famous enough for an event like this. Fame: it was that simple. In her mind, she would be a star and then everything in life would be fair. The trajectory was inspiring to me: a troubled teen with supposed mental health issues, she was shuttled around family members, sent to juvenile detention for shoplifting then to foster care, and worked as an erotic dancer. She decided to be a musician and soon after, an actor, despite having no particular skills. The result was the creation of one of the greatest rock albums of all time, numerous high-profile acting awards for her performance in *The People vs. Larry Flynt,* and becoming a rock and feminist icon. Her late husband, who considered himself a feminist, once said, 'I like the comfort in knowing that women are the only future in rock and roll,' but sadly didn't live to see her grab the genre by its horns. She never ever sat around and waited for anything to come to her. There's an aggression, sometimes coded as masculine, that, doubled up with her loud and communicative personality and sharp mind, made her notorious and reviled by many. She did everything to attain those levels of success and the obviousness with which she did it was hated.

The world came down on her for this hunger. Although Kurt Cobain was an addict while Courtney was pregnant and after Frances was born, the difference in their treatment by press and public was remarkable. They called her a bad mother, a whore, a junkie, a bitch, a witch. References to these evil female archetypes were threaded through her music from the start. She has been the subject of conspiracy theories since Cobain's death in 1994. To this day you can find accounts that claim she killed him by arranging a hitman to stage his suicide, and that completely ignore the fact that she was tragically widowed. When I get my daily Google alert email with every new mention of 'Courtney Love', I'll frequently find references to those accusations. Over the last twenty years, she's had comebacks, a film career, relapses with drugs, frequent attacks on her character in low-quality articles, documentaries and a film featuring the Kurt conspiracy theories – a content drive which continues – and had her daughter taken away from her. Yet ultimately, nothing blocks her from doing what she wants to do. In 1995 she said, 'The American public really does have a death wish for me. They want me to die. I'm not going to die.' She wouldn't allow it.

Courtney Love operates on her own terms. She's the witch that has been set on trial, drowned, burned, but whose image rises for another round. And she's always had fans alongside her who have believed in her unique powers and her real strength, when other people dismiss her entirely or prefer the darkest and most cynical version of her myth.

Early one morning in a muggy workout studio in Massachusetts, Hole's 'Celebrity Skin' was blaring out of the speaker system. Courtney Love snarled '*Make me over / I'm all I wanna be / A walking study / In Demonology*' to women who were spinning on their exercise bikes in hopes of transforming their bodies cell by cell. It was three months prior to the Courtney event, and at the front of the room, you'd have found Jennifer in a pink vest top and black spandex with blonde hair scraped back, instructing the class to whip up their legs quicker. 'I try not to play any Hole songs in my class that are too vulgar; not that Hole is *vulgar* but we know Courtney drops the f-bomb a lot,' she told me, with a wink.

She has two daughters and a husband. Hours of her daily life tally up to caring for them ('I like to be a very hands-on parent'), driving them to wherever they need to be (dance classes, school, friends' houses), volunteering at her youngest daughter's school, going to fitness classes for herself, date nights with her husband, and attacking the housework, as well as her part-time hours at the gym.

'If you're stranded on a desert island, which album do you bring with you? No brainer: *Live Through This*,' she told me once, chores for the day done. 'No matter what I'm doing if I need some music on in the background, it's Hole. To give you an example, I mowed my lawn yesterday – so glamorous, right? I listened to *Live Through This*. I never get sick of it. I listen to it when I'm happy, I listen to it when I'm sad, and thankfully I haven't really had that much to be sad about in recent years. I hope I don't ever have to revisit that pain I felt back when I was eighteen years old.' That was coincidentally the age she found Courtney, and a similar age to when other fans did.

Hole's classic album *Live Through This* was released in 1994. That's a long time to be infatuated with a dozen songs – hours of joy, weeks of sorrow, years of growth – and a long time to be fascinated by one woman. 'She's magnetic, that one,' said Jennifer. 'You're just drawn to her. I'm hardcore, I'm with her 'til the end. I will stand by her 'til the day I die.'

When Courtney sang '*Like a liar at a witch trial / You look good for your age*', she wasn't talking about ageism in music fandom, but she could've been. Adult female fans like Jennifer are invisible to the eye of cultural relevance. Girls are the ones who 'should' be presenting publicly with such passions. Out of teenage years and women are surely mimicking the interests and practices of those much younger than them. It's difficult to generate an image of middle-aged and older female music fans when the 'adult music fan' is a construct based on age, gender, class, sexuality, ethnicity and other factors. When I hear those words, I see a Radiohead-listening, vinyl-loving, t-shirt wearing nerdy man, probably white.

The persistent idea of an older woman pop fan is the frustrated housewife, apathetic or twitching until a reunion tour pops up. Then out they go, with any other unlovable female friends who can get their husband or ex to look after the kids for the night. Tied to a romanticised past, they long pathetically for something that could stir up the excitement of youth, freedom and crushes. Their nostalgia is unsettling. Similarly dominant is the idea of the ageing female rock fan as white heterosexual wife of wizened rocker, really the partner to the fan, still engaged in the subculture by virtue of said partner. She supports the scene along with him, silently backing everything he does, never questioning the dynamics within it, and never claiming it for her own.

This latter woman doesn't exist as a fan, and the opposite is true of

Courtney's fan base. They stuck with her through all that was thrown at her, and, to a minor degree, would be directly or indirectly thrown at them for being women who would align themselves with someone like her. It's a statement to say you're a Courtney Love fan: it's co-signing a difficult figure, a feminist, someone with very few cisgender heterosexual male fans. To other rock fans, it's saying you're a problem like her.

Research on the topic of older female music fans is almost non-existent. In a much-cited study on punk rock in older generations, academic Andy Bennett said he struggled to find women to interview and the ones he did find declined or had moved on from punk. In research on older female fans of Kate Bush back in 2004, Laura Vroomen found that with age fandom became very insular and personal: women listened alone and at home. Rhian E. Jones, a politics and music academic and writer, was concerned with this when she put together her book *Under My Thumb,* a collection of women aged in their twenties to fifties writing about 'problematic' music they loved. She told me: 'I know not all male fans of the same artist think the same and I know that because they're very vocal and their responses to music are well covered. In terms of what women think of the same music, how do we know? Maybe blogging or the comments section. No one asks them.'

Be a fully signed-up member of a fandom and you'll discover that these women very obviously exist – all around you. None of them have left wish-fulfilment behind. No passion has died, far from it. And their horizons stretch way beyond the outdated womanhood signifiers of 'marriage' and 'family-making'.

There are differences, of course. It would be naive to think otherwise. When you're younger there's a formal similarity to being a fan: now, online fandom is dominant, you tweet about the artist, go to shows, listen to new music, you're all doing similar things, you want to fit it all in. As a teenager your experience tends to be very like others of your age; your time is spent in a homogenous way, and you don't have many demands or responsibilities. Not only does this lend itself to a communal experience of fandom but it *supports* the fans. As an adult, time thunders away with you. You're no longer on teen hours; the responsibilities swarm in even if you haven't planned a straightforward heterosexual American Dream of an existence. As an older fan, you have to make time to be one: it becomes an even more active process. Some very much choose not to engage with other fans or be 'online' in any sense. Some find enjoyment purely through playing Hole songs on their guitars or listening to the CDs or records a lot. Some Courtney fans have notifications on Facebook, some 'fall down the rabbit hole' in the evening after putting kids to bed, some have just been quiet but avid observers of what everyone else is saying in the fan groups – it is less time-consuming than commenting, and they're still there. It's a case of purposefully doing it or else letting it die, and the latter isn't an option. This became obvious in the way I was communicating with them: I was speaking to people in their teens and early twenties in the day or at flexible times at the weekend, whereas with the Courtney fans it was often late at night.

Sometimes responsibilities pull women away, but the loyal ones come back. Music and fandom can be the first to drop off, like any other ardour that's purely selfish – pleasure for you and no one else. One woman said she became addicted to drugs again and her Courtney fandom fell off for years, along with anything else that gave her an ounce of joy. For others, it was divorce, death or bankruptcy. There was much talk of their fandom being 'on the back burner' or 'cooling off' or fans 'dipping out' when Courtney is between small projects, as she has seemed to be recently. Despite all the hiatuses and minor projects, the fans are still active; they all say if Courtney came back with a show, they'd be there: any time, any place, any amount of money.

The disparate experiences of older fans – and the sad fact that love for music can get forgotten – means they often struggled to find anyone in their present lives who was as into music as they were. This is a primary reason for fans becoming less visible. 'I've been thinking I need to put an ad in a paper to find a gig partner,' Sam from Sydney tells me. 'When I go to gigs, there are always older single men standing around on their own but never older single women. I'm nearing forty and this is what I'm thinking about and dealing with right now.' She talks about a show coming up soon that she wants to go to and she had thought a friend would definitely be keen to go. 'I was really surprised she wasn't making the time for it. I guess people do grow older and have different priorities...'

If you're in a pair like Jennifer and Tracy, you're more supported. Jennifer was best friends with Tracy's sister just after college. In the last ten years she and Tracy became very close through a desire to see music live. 'My sister and I have the same taste in music too, but I was a little more committed,' said Tracy. 'We're hardcore rock fans. We love grunge. It all began after we went to a Courtney show together, the *Nobody's Daughter* show. We suddenly started going to all sorts together, going out on our own little rock tours.' Jennifer added: 'If she's interested in something and I'm not that into it, I'll still go with her because I know it's important to her, and vice versa.' 'You know, like Foo Fighters,' Tracy laughed. 'Oh, I love Foo Fighters. If I didn't have her to go to these shows with, I guess I'd just have to go alone. Or not go,' said Jennifer.

Carrie, another fan at the Courtney event, has a very different life that had enabled her to be a fan for decades. She is a high-powered lawyer with her own law firm. 'I'm lucky because I've never had a husband, I don't have kids, I have a cat. I'm my own boss. It's great because business is over the top right now but I think that's the confidence that Courtney gives me, if she has done it with everything she's been up against. I make sure I've done everything I have to do and when I have I'm like, "Okay, I can go away for three days and see these shows". This weekend, I was like: this is *Courtney Love*, this is for her.'

If Courtney is a witch, her fans are a coven. The majority of them are women, all of whom repeatedly, when I spoke to them, boiled a fascination with Love down to her being a 'survivor'. Courtney should feasibly be dead. The same could be said for many of the women who follow her.

A high number of them did or continue to battle with alcoholism or drug addiction. When I spoke to ex-addict Tisha, thirty-three, from Iowa, she was tapping away at her computer, distracted, constantly keeping busy, because busy is good, just like loud is good. 'I've been clean seven years and her sobriety is half the reason I stay sober,' she told me. 'Regardless of what I went through, if Courtney Love can survive her shit, I can survive mine.' Maybe, like Stephanie, forty-seven, from California, they had a brother who was an addict and died of an overdose when he was twenty-seven, the same age Kurt killed himself. 'I know the loss she feels for Kurt, and

I've never known my dad either. I've related to her in that certain things have led to the decisions that she's made.' Some fans had been young single mothers or left abusive relationships. Some have chronic mental illnesses. There's an understanding within the fandom that to be a Courtney fan, some fucked-up things have happened. And, of course, you're still here.

As they intuitively understand each other, they defend her. 'I can't think of anyone in music who is so hated. If you mention her name, people will say "Ugh, how can you like *her*", said Sharee, in her late thirties, from Sydney. 'I get really protective of her, it's a tribal thing. You get it in the comment sections about her on certain articles about certain people' – she means Kurt Cobain – 'and it's hard, I just want to fight them. The lack of understanding, it makes me sick'. She sighed. 'People are shit.' This has continued over the course of many years. Occasionally, fake fans – often those of Kurt Cobain – will break into the Facebook fan groups, adding themselves in order to spew hatred about Courtney.

What's so precious about a lifelong fandom is that the musician, their work and way of being (fashion, strength, vulnerability) ages with you. They are morphing, evolving, going through terrifying changes, being thrust into new eras just like you. Courtney's made efforts to age in her own way, and the fans found that spellbinding to follow. I often think what is scary about ageing is not having older people around you who are both aspirational and you can feasibly see yourself in.

Rather than having a fixed love or view on Courtney and her work, for many of the fans, collecting experience through their life led to their renegotiating how they felt about the music and the lyrics. 'You know it's good poetry when you're fourteen but, what she had to say, there was something I didn't understand,' Tisha told me. You already know the female rage as a teenager but don't understand the subjects and what colours them. 'When you're twenty-four or forty or whatever, you get it. You're at the age she was when she was writing it. It doesn't matter what generation you're in because as you age as an adult, the emotions are all the same. I must have listened to "Malibu" a hundred times after my first adult break-up because it made so much sense suddenly. When I was getting sober, *Nobody's Daughter* never left my car; that was my sobriety album.'

The more fans I spoke to the more a split became apparent. In terms of temperament, women either saw themselves as similar to Courtney or they were like Sarah, thirty-seven, from Philadelphia who saw Courtney as someone who 'represented everything I thought I didn't have inside of me' and who 'didn't have anybody like that in my life, someone who really stood up for themselves'.

Who sticks up for you? Courtney does, and then you do. You have to.

From the stage of the Basilica, Melissa Auf der Maur reads a love letter she'd written to Courtney, with Courtney down below, Frances Bean next to her. Courtney had, inexplicably, altered Melissa's path forever, she said, by inviting her into Hole and hanging out with her every day, but it was the female fans whose worlds she had transformed on the grandest scale.

'The lives you really changed were those in the front row, at home in their bedrooms, holding on to every word and every scream. The people at rock festivals around the world, the ones you pulled up on stage to play your guitar. You were singing for them, you made a safe place for them to be angry, to be beautiful, to be heard and to be understood.'

I take a look over my shoulder and see Jennifer and Tracy feeling like me, and to my left and behind is Carrie, the lawyer, who is straining her neck to look at Melissa, with tears in her eyes too.

I think about stories of the women in the group, delicate scraps worth more than any of us could've individually collected over the years. Fandoms are a sphere where contribution increases with age, the more stories the better, the more access, the more information, the more gossip, the longer loving. On the *Celebrity Skin* tour, Joann rushed the stage ('I stood directly behind Courtney. I just studied everything about her. She had silver booty shorts on and a white tank top and she was barefoot. I remember every tiny second, the living it, the crowd.'). Tisha sat playing *Live Through This* on repeat for nine months to the foetus inside her swollen stomach; now she has a six-year-old boy with blue hair who plays Courtney's songs on the guitar. ('Classical music!? I wanted a little punk rock kid.') Waiting outside the Fonda Theatre in LA, Stephanie was asked by Courtney if she could have the old Hole hair barrette she was wearing, one from Stephanie's merchandise collection, a piece Courtney had obviously lost over the years. Stephanie traded it for a set list and some merch. One day soon after, she got a phone-call from her friend, another fan, telling her that Courtney was wearing her very barrette during a live performance. Nikki lives a matter of streets away from where Courtney temporarily lived in her early years in Liverpool and collects stories from people who knew her, every walk she takes around the city imprinted with that knowledge. Chris spotted Courtney at LAX airport and sprinted over to her; since Chris was travelling with her guitar, she asked Courtney to sign it. Her fifteen-year-old baby niece got that guitar handed down to her and now plays it. Allie will never forget that Courtney recognised her – her face – in the crowd at an Australian date on her 2014 tour. At that time Courtney was in one of the fan Facebook groups that Allie was in and, in front of a live audience hanging on Courtney's every word, they chatted about the group. I think about how tonight would be one of my Courtney stories.

There in the crowd, I could see all the different versions of myself in some sort of union. Not in a linear progression or through line but as though they all existed simultaneously. I was carrying them all inside me like a Russian doll, and I felt quite invested in taking them all forward in me – especially the first one. The one who had discovered Courtney, who went out and bought bleach from the chemist for her hair, who saved money all summer for a new guitar, even though she was terrible at playing, who was obsessed with this other person's narrative as she became invested in her own. There was also the one who survived that time, the next time, and all the other times. When I tell people, as these women do, that I will always be a Hole fan, this is how I know. Being a fan means you don't have to be the person you are in this moment, restricted by time, space and circumstance, rather you can be strengthened by and exist through all the others you've been. I felt alive right there listening to Melissa because every old and present me was activated and in communication; it was some special kind of magic.

After the event had finished, Joann, who had been one of those girls pulled up onto the stage, raced to the front of the Basilica stage and all the Broken Dolls present that night joined her. 'We've got to find her, meet her once more, I'm sure she'll come out,' Joann told everyone. Together we dowsed to call Courtney in – there was this door she went into, there's that man she had on her arm earlier, you go around the back of the building to scout for signs, someone else to try to get into the VIP area.

After half an hour of staying put with some others, a middle-aged woman in a Hole t-shirt ran over to tell us: 'She's gone, she's gone!' A couple of women holding hands looked so heartbroken they dropped them. 'She left around the back straight away in a car with Frances.'

'Oh, no, darn it!' Joann said. 'I thought this might happen.' She started to pack her merch away back into bags. 'It's OK though, we all got to meet, some of us for the first time, and that's pretty phenomenal.' Another fan suggested taking a group photo, so we did. I tried to recall the last time I socialised with women of different ages, rather than just my own generation and couldn't. We all lined up with our backs against the stage and smiled holding every bag of merch we had. 'Well, it might not have Courtney in it but look at us go,' said Joann warmly, looking at the photo.

'That's not true,' a woman called Meaghan said, 'we have quite a few Courtneys between us.' She was right: everyone was wearing t-shirts or jumpers or holding bags with Courtney's image on it.

'You got to meet her anyway, Joann, at least,' someone said. I'd been at the venue hours before it had opened to the public, and Courtney had been inaccessible throughout the night. I could not work out how Joann had conjured that scenario under our noses. 'Oh, yeah, I met her earlier,' she said in an offhand manner but with eyes twinkling. 'After all these years, you learn a thing or two.'

AFTERWORD

When I said my dad wasn't a music fan, that wasn't strictly true. On the day before my first birthday, he was at his football team's home ground, praying for a win. Alongside him was the lead singer of an old British pop group that he liked, doing exactly the same. My dad told the singer that his only daughter had made it some twelve months around the sun, and the singer bought him a bottle of expensive champagne to celebrate it. When I was small he would tell me the story at any opportunity, singing, off-key: 'Love grows where my Rosemary goes / And nobody knows like me'. I was disappointed the first time I heard the single and every time after that. The sole notable product of one-hit wonders Edison Lighthouse, it's a cloying seventies love song with a grating chorus that makes me think of pageboy hair and bad teeth. A man croons about his manic pixie dream girl, a woman unspectacular, strange even, to look at but able to cast a certain magic in the right light. My middle name was Rose, so that was destiny enough, although I didn't appreciate any parallels that could be drawn between us. Still, it's a fun story. And I always enjoyed the idea of a stranger celebrating my birth in the appropriate style. Music had begun to weave itself through my life without me registering it.

Whenever Dad would drive to pick me and my sister up from school there'd be the radio on, crackling away like an audio migraine. It picked up static noise as much as the songs of the sixties, seventies and eighties that the station purported to play. Dad's hearing isn't especially sharp, so it'd be loud enough to hear outside the shell of the car as it turned into the car park. The car was first a dirty old people carrier and later a fish and seafood delivery van with an enormous cod painted on the side. Either me or my sister would dive into the vehicle and turn the volume dial down in one movement. 'Don't play this, it's so embarrassing.' 'Don't have it up so loud, for fuck's sake, Dad.'

The station's playlist was fairly limited, so I remember most of the songs clearly. 'Stop! In The Name Of Love' – The Supremes, 'Ride A White Swan' – T Rex, 'Band Of Gold' – Freda Payne, 'What Becomes Of The Brokenhearted' – Jimmy Ruffin, 'Love Really Hurts Without You' – Billy Ocean, 'Everlasting Love' – Love Affair, 'Waterloo Sunset' – The Kinks. Each one has a sadness now: nostalgia for a time when I never existed but Dad did, a by-product of growing old enough to realize your parents had lives they left behind to have you, as well as exhilarating memories of my own – driving along with him, greens and yellows of fields and woodlands, blurred wheat and marshes over the downs. The blue always on the horizon, a 360-degree moat. Him forever shuttling us around the island, taking us to whatever we were doing that day. No one sees the sacrifices their parents make to facilitate their life. I had always assumed he was lukewarm about music and now neither him nor I would be able to decipher for certain if it was one of many pleasures that got put aside partly because of me.

During the final days of editing this book I asked him whether my recollection of him not being a music fan was correct. He said it was, but added, 'I was working six days a week, I would never have had the time.' On the seventh day, rest came only after pacing about the garden, unearthing weeds, feeding animals or knocking around the house doing DIY. The only music, he says, was, as I recalled, in the car going between jobs and sometimes from a huge radio he'd lug around the garden, as it picked up and dropped frequencies. When we'd lived in London previously, his job was more stressful with only brief snatches of free time but clients had taken them to regular football matches, which he loved and was disproportionately upset to leave behind. Watching matches on our TV was his one hobby, something he had to make room for, for himself.

In late adulthood, his life has slowed down, and no one would doubt that he is a music fan. He plays songs every day from his iPod or a virtual assistant and each wall in his house presents both football and band memorabilia he's accumulated. Whenever I visit him, there will be a moment I catch him sat at the family desktop watching filmed live performances on the internet: The Who, The Rolling Stones, The Beatles, with marginally better audio quality than he could get on the radio. I like to imagine the music is heavy with the job of transmitting all the memories it has collected through the decades.

We all prefer to centre ourselves in our own self-making but it'd be disingenuous to say all this didn't contribute from the behind the scenes. My cruel adolescent embarrassment meant that I swerved my family's attempts, however minor, to shape my tastes or connect with me through theirs. I'm sure in some small way it put me on a path without my realising. But what makes a person into a fan and why evades clear definition.

When I wanted to look back through the external documentation of my teenage fan life – the photos, the fan fiction, the videos and playlists of music I loved – I couldn't. It was all uploaded and saved on sites that had lost files during a server migration or had folded altogether. I had never thought to save it anywhere else, or revisit it in the meantime, and now it is gone. This is important in the context of what this book, in some small way, has done. So much of fan histories are lost. As fandoms rely increasingly on online platforms and often change where they congregate on social media, we need to find new ways of documenting and protecting those goings-on. Social media platforms want to profit from our cultures and memory-making but have shown no desire to archive and care for them. As fans, we have to ensure that what we've made isn't just data to be dropped into the online ether. Because what we do matters. We make cultural history. There is a wealth of narratives from gay male pop fans, fans outside Western English-language speaking countries, fans of smaller artists and overlooked music scenes all over the internet currently, on sites from Twitter to Soundcloud. There are so many stories on and offline that are deserving of preservation, of celebration, of being there when fans want to rediscover them in the years to come.

Because, regardless of how the music industry changes, fans will always exist. There'll always be a new next big artist to take the last one's place; the cultural pleasure-points and anxieties that their personality, style and songs tap into will differ but the roles they fill for people are unlikely to. The media and music industries will still ask: how far are the fans going to take them? Another fan base who dress like the artist, call themselves by a special name and want to be a part of something greater than themselves.

When editing this book, I thought a lot about the regeneration of fans. While I scrolled through my social media feeds, girls I had no relationship with other than having interviewed or met them for the book appeared between my friends, family, colleagues, musicians or writers, venues and publications. Some of them, I realised, have unfollowed me – and fair enough – the need or desire for that connection no longer apparent. But I had become used to them being there, and knew I'd miss having a reason to stay up to date with them. I'd become invested in them and the minutiae of their lives, in the way they were with musicians.

Like chameleons adjusting to their surroundings, teenage girls use social media to (co-create and) adopt the latest memes, expressions, looks. It's as natural as breathing. The clothes they wear, the flavour of selfies they take, the way they perform themselves to others drastically alter over days, weeks or months. Some of them have fallen in and out of love, others have broken up with friends and made new ones, moved schools or across countries. All of them, I am quietly pleased to see, remain dedicated to the same handful of artists they'd liked when I'd met them, and their appetites for new music are still insatiable. Some anonymous fan accounts have revealed their owner and continued as a user account with a face and name, wanting to keep the valuable followers but be a real individual in the world.

All were going through a reinvention before starting college or going away to university, that second stage in your late teens and early twenties of becoming yourself, the one I remember feeling like a second puberty, and more traumatic than the first. They cared about more than just music, and that was clearer now. They organised their profiles into compartmentalised interests, like activism, friends, concerts, support for crowdfunding and future careers. Many of them went to the student climate change protest in London in March 2019 without their parents. Of every post from every fan, one stood out. I felt compelled to return to it multiple times to see if any revisions had been made to its caption. It was an old photo from around the time I'd first met her, showing her and a friend, one I had also interviewed, outside a venue. The caption asked if anyone continued to camp early to go to shows, and remarked isn't it sad that we don't do that anymore. Other girls commented underneath that they occasionally would or that they wanted to but no one else did. I flicked between the profiles of the two girls to see if they were still close, but couldn't tell.

Some of these fans I know will move on somewhat from music but many would be like the Beyoncé or Courtney or boy band fans: for life. I self-indulgently tried to guess which fans would read the book and think I got it all wrong and didn't understand them. I wondered which would laugh with recognition.

One by one, I started to unfollow the girls, to let them get on with it. Making the break didn't feel as odd as I thought it would; not quite a goodbye, something more like a show of encouragement. The next generation was already waiting to grow up and do fandom their own way. The girls I had studied had left a template – if the new ones wanted it. Now all they would need was an obsession.

BEYOND 'FANGIRLS: SCENES FROM MODERN MUSIC CULTURE'

The following works were essential to the creation of this book.

Beatlemania: A sexually defiant consumer subculture – Barbara Ehrenreich, Elizabeth Hess and Gloria Jacobs (1992)

Gender, Metal and the Media: Women Fans and the Gendered Experience of Music – Rosemary Lucy Hill (2016) (Palgrave Macmillan)

Good Ol' Freda; dir. Ryan White (2013)

Hole's Live Through This (33⅓) – Anwen Crawford (2014) (Bloomsbury)

Nothing Feels Good: Punk Rock, Teenagers and Emo – Andy Greenwald (2003) (St. Martin's Griffin)

Rock She Wrote: Women Write About Rock, Pop and Rap – Edited by Evelyn McDonnell and Ann Powers (1995) (Plexus Publishing Ltd)

Rookie Mag online archive

Sign(ifier) of the Times: On Pop Stars, Populism, and the Harry Styles Fandom – Allyson Gross (2018)

The Punk Singer; dir. Sini Anderson (2013)

Trainwreck: The Women We Love to Hate, Mock, and Fear…and Why – Sady Doyle (2016) (Melville House)

'The Stories of the 22 Manchester Victims' – Helen Pidd and Frances Perraudin (2018) (*Guardian*)

ACKNOWLEDGEMENTS

Every day I thank my Grandma for teaching me to read and telling me I'd be a journalist. Thank you to my Dad, for always taking an interest, for giving me sixties and seventies music and a sense of humour.

I'm grateful to Kate Loftus-O'Brien, Susannah Otter, Rebecca Carter and Hellie Ogden at Janklow & Nesbit, as well as Bethany Rose Lamont, Lauren O'Neill, Mitch Stevens, Tara Joshi, Daisy Jones and Emma Garland.

Finally – to every single fan who spoke to me for this. You were the most hilarious and thoughtful people to connect with, and I won't forget you. To all the fans who bought this book: I hope you recognised yourselves in these pages.